Digital Computer Structure and Design

Second Edition

R. TOWNSEND MSc(Eng), BSc(Eng), FIEE, SMIEEE

Butterworth Scientific
London Boston Durban Singapore Sydney Toronto Wellington

First published 1975
Second Edition 1982

British Library Cataloguing in Publication Data

Townsend, R.
Digital computer structure and design
1. Electronic digital computers
I. Title
621.3819'58 TK7888.3

ISBN 0-408-01158-0
ISBN 0-408-01155-6 Pbk

Typeset by Scribe Design, Gillingham, Kent
Printed in England by Redwood Burn Ltd., Trowbridge, Wilts

Preface to Second Edition

In the six years since this book was written there have been two major developments, which have radically changed the outlook of computer designers and users. These are the development of large semiconductor memories and microprocessors on a single chip. Both of these have emerged from the spectacular progress in the design of microcircuits.

Minicomputers have been largely eclipsed by the appearance of powerful microprocessors at astonishingly low prices. The small computers now in use are usually based on an internal microprocessor with input-output and peripheral devices.

Visual Display Units, which for some time had been regarded as the ideal general purpose input-output device, have at last reached the threshold of economic take-off, and are in common use. The more advanced examples of these also incorporate microprocessors.

The general use of the all conquering microprocessor does not absolve users from having some knowledge of the principles of what is happening inside, even though they may never need to design one. An understanding of the internal operations is also a help to programming. The organisation of a microprocessor is not very much different to that of the minicomputer. To a great extent, the microprocessor evolved from the minicomputer, by shrinking the whole circuit on to one silicon chip. Reduction of the word size to 8 bits leads to some changes, but the newer 16 bit microprocessors are getting back to the equivalent of a 16 bit minicomputer.

For this reason the organisation of a 16 bit minicomputer is still relevant to the present situation. In writing a book on computer design one either has to invent an architecture, or base it on an existing one, as has been done here, using the NOVA mincomputer as an example. The NOVA has a sound architecture and still provides a good basis on which to discuss the principles of computer design.

Chapter 1 has been revised to eliminate out-of-date material, and comments on the latest developments have been added.

In logic design the emphasis has moved from the design of actual processors to peripheral circuits, and special purpose logic into which microprocessors are embedded. This type of circuit is often unclocked, and requires the interfacing of synchronous and asynchronous systems. I have therefore added a section on asynchronous sequential circuits, as well as bringing Chapter 3 up-to-date in other respects.

Chapter 7 on computer memories has been entirely rewritten to provide an introduction to the various types of semiconductor memories. Their overwhelming success has rendered ferrite core memories almost completely obsolete.

Material has been added to Chapter 9 regarding large scale integrated arithmetic processors. The reference lists at the end of each Chapter have been completely revised.

I wish to give special thanks to Martin Gibson who carefully read the first edition and made invaluable comments for the revised edition.

Contents

Chapter 1

Introduction

In the light of the present day it may seem almost antediluvian to discuss the ancestry of the modern computer. However it may be of some interest to mention briefly how we arrived where we are now. Machines evolve like the natural world, and the present day microprocessor is descended from very different ancestors.

It used to be easy to distinguish calculators from computers, essentially the latter could be programmed and the former were keyboard machines, but now many calculators incorporate simple programming. Simple mechanical calculators were constructed by Pascal and others and culminated in complicated electromechanical machines in the 1940s.

Another line of descent can be found in the punched card machines, which can trace the idea of controlling a machine by holes in a card, or similar device, back to automatically controlled looms. These machines originated in the requirements for sorting and counting in the United States census. Later the concepts of the calculating machines were combined with the use of punched cards and evolved to produce a range of different machines which made possible elaborate automatic accounting systems and other applications.

The decisive step which seems to have resulted in the appearance on the scene of the digital computer as we now know it, was the introduction on the one hand of electronic counting and pulse handling techniques and on the other of the concept of the stored program. Both of these ideas were inherent in earlier work, but their tremendous potential had not been appreciated and they had not been clearly stated. Professor Babbage with the invention of his Analytical Engine in the 19th century had foreseen the possibilities and attempted to realise them mechanically, but his ideas were too far ahead of the technology of the time and he failed to complete the mechanical equivalent of a simple computer.

The technology of the first electronic digital computers was based on the vacuum tube and derived mainly from circuits developed in World War II in radar research and atomic energy work. Although these machines were made to work successfully there were severe limitations, particularly in size, heat dissipation and device reliability. The invention of the transistor occurred at an opportune time, and after a period of teething troubles, the first transistorised discrete circuit computers appeared in the late 1950s, due to demand for reduction in power consumption and size. Further need for reduction in size, heat dissipation, and reliability, stimulated by requirements of the armed services, has led to the evolution of microcircuit technology.

These advances have made possible the development of the giant 'number crunchers' having millions of individual circuits, each having a high enough reliability for the total aggregation to run for long periods, without failure, and having small enough power requirements that they can be reasonably housed without need of the elaborate cooling and air conditioning systems of the early computers.

At the other extreme the microprocessor has now appeared, having the capabilities and processing power in the latest devices of a medium size computer of several years ago. And all this in a device one can hold in the palm of the hand and costing only a few pounds.

Although the first effects of microcircuit technology have been felt at the smaller end of the computer range, their influence is now being felt in the design of large computers. Bit slice devices can be assembled to create processors with larger word sizes. Array processors have been designed using standard microprocessors, but it seems likely that special types may be designed to be used as elements of very large machines.

In parallel with developments in the design of processors, there has been much activity in memory design. Semiconductor memories have now superseded ferrite cores for the main computer memories, being used for both random access memories and read only memories.

The momentum of the computer industry has led to refinements and advances in many other technologies associated with computer engineering. The pace continues and there is the possibility in the future of the introduction into the computer art of new technologies such as Josephson junctions.

In distinction to the steady technological advance, the idea of a stored program, and in particular the storage of both numbers and instructions in the same memory in coded form, appeared as a strikingly new concept from which has developed the whole discipline of programming and software. Once the initial step had been taken the concepts of programming leading to assemblers, compilers and high level languages developed rapidly, although the realisation of these concepts in practical programming systems has proved a far more complex problem than was imagined.

Physical Description

A block diagram of the major components of a computer's system is shown in Figure 1.1. The Central Processing Unit (CPU) contains the main memory, the arithmetic unit and arithmetic registers, the control unit with its associated registers, and other control logic associated with the input-output bussing system. The CPU, usually housed in a somewhat undramatic series of cabinets, containing rows of cards with printed circuits, and transistors or integrated circuits, forms the hub of the system, and a large part of this book will be concerned with the organisation and design of the CPU.

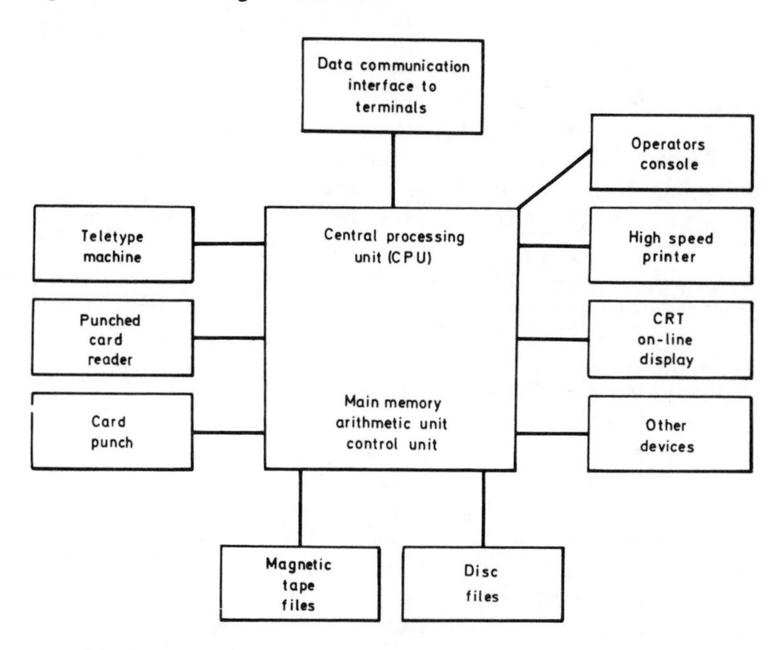

Figure 1.1 Block diagram of the major components of a computer system

Large machines may have, in addition to the CPU, one or many input-output processing units, which are dedicated to handling the many low level chores associated with input-output devices and release the CPU to devote the major part of its time to higher level calculations for which it is specialised.

Disposed around the central processor there will be a variety of peripheral devices. The operator's console usually now consists of a typewriter type keyboard and a visual display unit with a T.V. type tube. For service and debugging purposes, lights are sometimes provided to enable the display of the contents of various registers in the CPU, and switches allow the processor to be put into different operating modes such as Run, Single Operation, Single Step, as well as Manual Halt and Start. Because computers have now become very reliable, this maintenance console may be a separate portable device plugged in by a service man, and no longer ordinarily used by the operator.

A computer system may have some only of those shown in Figure 1.1, or possibly other input-output devices not shown attached to it including the following:

(a) *Visual Display Units* (VDU) are now the common means of communication by the operator even on small machines. Both graphical and alphanumeric data can be displayed. In larger systems there may be a number of VDUs in various parts of a building or remotely joined by a data communication system.

(b) A *Teletype Machine* enables one to type data and instructions to the computer via a typewriter keyboard, and the computer can also print information at a moderate rate to communicate with the operator. In addition it is possible to enter pre-punched data on punched paper tape, and also to receive data to be punched on paper tape for permanent retention.

(c) A *Punched Card Reader* for reading data into the computer from punched cards. Cards are a convenient medium for entering programs or data because it is easy to modify a few statements without having to repunch the whole program.

(d) In some cases a *Card Punch* is used, so that data can be punched in a form which can be read in conveniently at a later date. The tendency is to use these machines less as they are expensive, and programs can be stored now on disc files for short periods, or dumped on to magnetic tapes for longer term storage.

(e) Most larger installations have a *High Speed Printer* which allows data to be printed out rapidly in suitable format. This is especially important in commercial applications where large numbers of bills, invoices, pay slips, and cheques etc. must be printed.

(f) *CRT Displays* are used in more advanced systems for on-line operation with which there can be immediate man-machine interaction. Both graphical and alphanumeric data can be displayed. These will probably be used more in the future, when on-line communication with computers becomes more common.

(g) Mass storage is most commonly used in the form of magnetic tape or magnetic disc files at the present time. *Disc Files* have a large but limited capacity and have the advantage that any piece of data can be accessed fairly rapidly within a fraction of a second.

Magnetic Tape having its data stored in a linear arrangement on the tape, can be much slower in finding a particular piece of information, since the tape must be wound to that point. Since the reels of tape are removable it has the great advantage of unlimited storage capacity in reasonable volume, and is used for many semipermanent records.

(h) *Data Communications.* Some of the largest machines, for example the London University Control Data 7600 have systems for data communications, so that they can receive and transmit data to many remote terminals, and possibly other computers. This leads to the concept of a computer utility in which one can plug in to computing power in much the same way as one would plug into electric power or the telephone.

(i) The number of other devices which can be connected to a computer is almost unlimited and new uses are constantly arising.

Minicomputers

The overwhelming success of microprocessors has largely invaded the territory until recently assigned to machines that were styled minicomputers, although there has been a proliferation of smaller machines both for business and scientific purposes, but also for the computer hobbyist. They usually contain a microprocessor, plus extra semiconductor memory, and input output circuitry with a keyboard and some display device. The small size of these machines should not delude one as to their capability. The latest 16 bit microporcessors have a computing power which would have been considered respectable for a medium sized computer, not many years ago.

Special Purpose Computers

Because of the low cost of microprocessors, special purpose processors now tend to be designed with microprocessors embedded in specially designed pre-processing logic and linear circuits. The program, which is fixed, is stored in PROM s (Programmable Read Only Memories) and a small RAM (Random Access Memory) serves for data manipulation.

Computer Applications

Scientific Calculation The first computers were designed by laboratories and universities to enable them to attack mathematical problems, which would have been too laborious to solve manually due to the sheer calculating effort required. The original stimulus that led to the development of ENIAC and later UNIVAC was the need to calculate ballistic tables during World War II. Scientific enterprises generated the need for the solution of simultaneous equations, and differential and algebraic equations.

Statistical Studies The evaluation of statistical studies on the many aspects of our complex life in today's industrial society requires the processing of vast amounts of data obtained from sampling, which would not have been possible without modern computers.

Simulation It is possible to write a program to make a mathematical model of either a physical system, or an operational problem. For example it is possible to design a mathematical model of the arrival, unloading and loading and departure of ships in port. By varying parameters in the model, the operation of the existing installation may be optimised to maximise the traffic or minimise the cost. The same computer might be used to study a tidal model of the estuary to find the best way to channel the river and tidal flow to remove the hazards of sandbanks. Alternatively, the motion of a ship in the water can be modelled and the shape of the hull changed to find the best compromise in design to optimise the ship's performance under the expected conditions.

A notable improvement in the performance of lenses has been achieved due to the ability to model the lens on a computer and by the use of ray tracing optimise the lens design. In all these cases it is possible to discover the effects of changes in the environment or the design without the necessity of actually making the changes, or building many experimental designs.

Accounting The largest application of computers at present is in handling the vast load of accounting work generated in modern industrial organisations. Typical examples are the calculation of the payroll, invoicing, billing and interdepartmental transactions. Banks use computers to lighten the load of the increased flow of money throughout the nation and internationally. Automatic sorting and handling of cheques has become possible by the invention of machines which can directly read branch numbers and account numbers printed on the cheques in special characters.

Reservation Systems The world's airlines use giant computers with world-wide on-line communications to keep track of the reservations and available seats on planes removing the need for flying planes with unnecessary empty seats or the confusion of overbooking.

Controllers It would be difficult to enumerate the diverse variety of control applications in which computers can be applied. They are being used in London and Toronto to control and optimise the flow of road traffic throughout the city. Input sensors at various points continuously monitor vehicles, and taking the overall situation into account, they can modify and divert the traffic to maintain smooth flow and reduce jams.

Oil refineries and petrochemical plants need the continual monitoring and control of variables throughout the plant to maintain them in a safe and stable operation and to optimise the final products. Computers are used to continuously compute the optimum conditions, control variables, issue warnings and even take emergency action if necessary.

On a small scale the minicomputer is entering into everyday use in applications such as instrument control and processing of data, and apparently trivial occupations such as controlling of lighting in large factories, control of lifts in large buildings etc.

Communications It could be argued that the automatic telephone exchange was one of the first computers. Telephone exchanges are now becoming electronic and provide a good example of a special purpose computer designed for the specific application of remembering and routing telephone calls in the optimum way. They require less power and maintenance and are more reliable than the older electromechanical systems.

Computer Aided Design When a design procedure is well understood, whether it be the design of a building structure or bridge, or an electronic circuit, a program can be devised to obviate much of the labour associated. On large projects it also allows the possibility of many trial designs and the choice of the best by varying the parameters based on known factors.

Data Retrieval Computers can be provided with batteries of mass storage devices which make it possible to store and retrieve data at short notice, for example all known chemical compounds and their properties, for all National Health patients, and their health records, or the history of traffic offenders.

Computer technology has placed a powerful instrument in the hands of society, and it is up to us all to control its use for maximum benefit to the world.

The arrival of the low cost microprocessor has resulted in innumerable applications, which would not have been envisaged until recently. Many instruments now incorporate microprocessors as part of the circuitry, and they are becoming popular in T.V. games, and such things as controllers for sewing machines, washing machines and even toys.

REFERENCES

1. HAMACHER, V.C., *Computer Organization* McGraw-Hill (1978)
2. TOCCI RONALD J., *Digital Systems : Principles and Applications.* Prentice-Hall (1977)
3. MALVINO, A.P., *Digital Computer Electronics,* McGraw-Hill (1977)

Chapter 2

Switching Theory

Logic Elements

The basic element from which the control system and arithmetic unit of a computer are built is the gate. By interconnecting various types of gates the required binary logical functions needed for computation and control of the computer can be obtained.

The study of the properties of interconnected networks of gates is called switching theory. Switching theory, unlike circuit theory, does not have its basis in the laws of physics, but is purely mathematical in concept. The theory deals with binary functions that are assumed to have two values representing 1 and 0, and to change instantaneously from one to the other without intermediate values. Also information is assumed to travel instantaneously from the input to the output of the gate.

In practice voltages and currents cannot change suddenly, and there are intermediate values during transition, and also internal delays occur in gate circuits. These problems remain in the province of circuit theory whereas switching theory deals with the relations between the binary functions at the input and output of logic networks.

Some of the basic gate elements used in logic design are listed in Table 2.1 with the Boolean algebra expressions and diagrammatic symbols.

The NAND and NOR elements are of particular interest since they are now more widely used–particularly the NAND element–than others in modern computer logic. Logically these are important because they are universal elements, since all other functions can be realised from either. It is thus possible to build the logic of a computer from NAND or NOR elements only. An added reason is that they can be realised with the simplest electronic circuits.

The examples have been shown for two inputs, but in practice gates are made with many inputs. The limitation on the number of inputs is

Table 2.1

Descriptive Term	*Boolean Symbol*	*Diagram Symbol*
AND	$A \cdot B, (AB)$	A, B → [&] → AB
OR (inclusive OR)	$A+B$	A, B → [1] → A + B
NOT (inverter)	$\overline{A}$	A → [1]o → $\overline{A}$
NAND (NOT AND)	$\overline{AB}$	A, B → [&]o → $\overline{AB}$
NOR (NOT OR)	$\overline{A+B}$	A, B → [1]o → $\overline{A+B}$
exclusive OR	$A \oplus B = A\overline{B}+\overline{A}B$	A, B → [=1] → $A \oplus B$

due to circuit design considerations, and the convenient number of pins which can be placed on an integrated circuit package.

The diagrammatic symbols used throughout this book are those now in general use, though certain computer companies and countries have standards of their own (see Appendix). Similarly the symbols for Boolean operations are those generally used by computer designers although mathematicians often have a different notation.

Switching Algebra (Boolean Algebra)

The mathematics used in the design and minimisation of logic circuits is called Switching Algebra or Boolean Algebra, and the basic postulates are as follows:

$$\overline{0} = 1$$
$$\overline{1} = 0$$
$$0 + 0 = 0$$
$$0 + 1 = 1$$
$$1 + 0 = 1$$
$$1 + 1 = 1$$
$$0 \cdot 0 = 0$$
$$1 \cdot 0 = 0$$
$$0 \cdot 1 = 0$$
$$1 \cdot 1 = 1$$

These rules can be applied to the development of relations for manipulating expressions in switching algebra. Some relations for 2 varaibles are given below:

$0 + A = A$ $0 \cdot A = 0$ $1 + A = 1$ $1 \cdot A = A$	Zero and Unit rules
$A + A = A$ $A \cdot A = A$	Idempotence laws
$A + \bar{A} = 1$ $A \cdot \bar{A} = 0$ $\bar{\bar{A}} = A$	Complementarity
$A + B = B + A$ $AB = BA$	Commutativity
$A(BC) = (AB)C$ $(A + B) + C = A + (B + C)$	Associativity
$A(B + C) = AB + AC$ $A + BC = (A + B)(A + C)$	Distributive laws
$A + AB = A$ $A(A + B) = A$	Laws of Absorption
$A + \bar{A}B = A + B$	
$\overline{A + B} = \bar{A} \cdot \bar{B}$	NOR — De Morgan's Theorems
$\overline{A \cdot B} = \bar{A} + \bar{B}$	NAND — De Morgan's Theorems

These relations can be extended to any number of variables, but these have not been listed as they become unwieldy. De Morgan's theorems are important when using NAND and NOR gates, and when extended to N variables become:

$$\overline{A + B + C \text{-----} N} = \bar{A} \cdot \bar{B} \cdot \bar{C} \text{-----} \bar{N}$$

$$\overline{A \cdot B \cdot C \text{-----} N} = \bar{A} + \bar{B} + \bar{C} \text{-----} + \bar{N}$$

Truth Tables

Any Boolean function may be expressed in the form of a truth table. Frequently this is the starting point in designing a logical network, and it defines all the conditions of the network. A truth table shows every possible combination of the variables, and often arises from design considerations for some portion of a computer. The truth table may also be used to check the validity of the algebra. For example the truth table for the functions:

$$F_1 = \bar{A}B\bar{C} + \bar{A}BC + ABC \text{ and } F_2 = B(\bar{A} + C)$$

are shown to be equivalent (Table 2.2).

Table 2.2

A	B	C	$\bar{A}B\bar{C}$	$\bar{A}BC$	ABC	F_1	B	$\bar{A}+C$	F_2
0	0	0	0	0	0	0	0	1	0
0	0	1	0	0	0	0	0	1	0
0	1	0	1	0	0	1	1	1	1
0	1	1	0	1	0	1	1	1	1
1	0	0	0	0	0	0	0	0	0
1	0	1	0	0	0	0	0	1	0
1	1	0	0	0	0	0	1	0	0
1	1	1	0	0	1	1	1	1	1

It is important to notice that the physical realisation of these functions is different, although they produce the same result, as shown in Figures 2.1 and 2.2. The second realisation requires less gates and is therefore more economical.

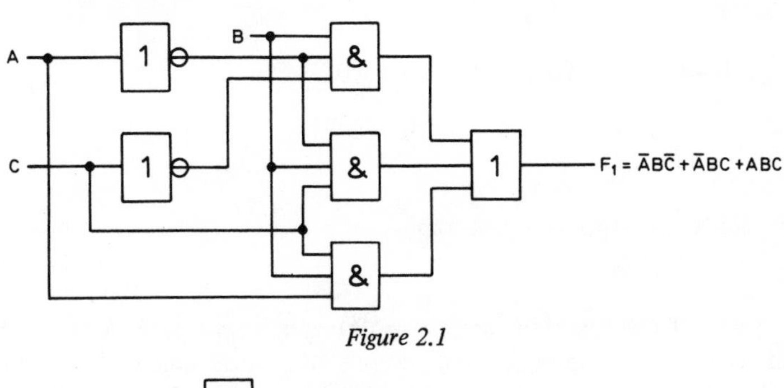

Figure 2.1

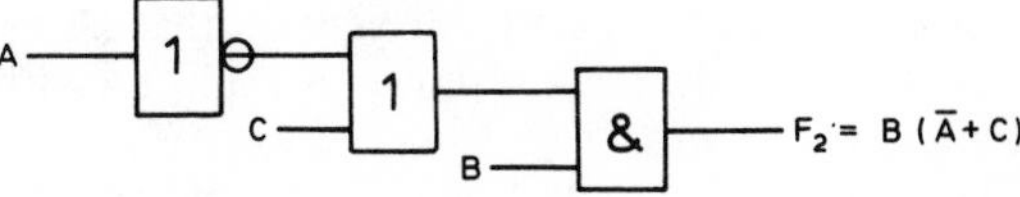

Figure 2.2

This introduces the idea of minimisation of the number of logic gates by manipulation of the Boolean expressions which is the most important practical application of switching algebra. One may also wish to find the most suitable expression for the type of gates available, or the input variables may not always be in the true or negated form, so that by modifying the expression, inverters may be eliminated.

Consider a problem which it is assumed may have occurred in the design of a digital device, in which we have as input a series of binary numbers 0–7 and we wish to have an output of 1 at the arbitrary numbers 0, 2, 4, 6 and 7. A truth table is first constructed as shown in Table 2.3.

Table 2.3

	A	B	C	F
0	0	0	0	1
1	0	0	1	0
2	0	1	0	1
3	0	1	1	0
4	1	0	0	1
5	1	0	1	0
6	1	1	0	1
7	1	1	1	1

Form an expression with sum of product terms by logically adding all the conditions in which F = 1

$$F = \overline{A}\overline{B}\overline{C} + \overline{A}B\overline{C} + A\overline{B}\overline{C} + AB\overline{C} + ABC$$

This can be simplified as follows:

$$F = \overline{C}(\overline{A}\overline{B} + \overline{A}B + A\overline{B} + AB) + ABC$$

$$= \overline{C}\,[\overline{A}(\overline{B} + B) + A(\overline{B} + B)] + ABC$$

$$= \overline{C} + ABC$$

whence by absorption this becomes

$$= \overline{C} + AB$$

Some of the functions of 2 variables have been shown. A and B can between them assume 4 combinations of values, and each function will thus have 4 columns in its truth table so that 2^4 or 16 different functions exist. The truth table is shown in Table 2.4 with descriptions of some common functions.

In general if n is the number of variables, the number of possible functions is 2^{2n}. It can easily be seen that this rapidly increases to an enormous number as n increases, which illuminates the fact that it becomes very laborious to manipulate functions with large numbers of variables.

Table 2.4

A B	0 0	0 1	1 0	1 1	FUNCTION DESCRIPTION	EXPRESSION
F_0	0	0	0	0		
F_1	0	0	0	1	AND	AB
F_2	0	0	1	0		
F_3	0	0	1	1		
F_4	0	1	0	0		
F_5	0	1	0	1		
F_6	0	1	1	0	Exclusive OR	$A \oplus B = A\overline{B} + \overline{A}B$
F_7	0	1	1	1	OR (inclusive OR)	$A + B$
F_8	1	0	0	0	NOR	$\overline{A + B}$
F_9	1	0	0	1	EQUIVALENCE	$AB + \overline{A}\overline{B}$
F_{10}	1	0	1	0		
F_{11}	1	0	1	1		
F_{12}	1	1	0	0		
F_{13}	1	1	0	1		
F_{14}	1	1	1	0	NAND	$\overline{AB}$
F_{15}	1	1	1	1		

Sum of Products and Product of Sums Expressions

A Boolean function may be expressed in two equivalent forms. The first type, already shown, is the sum of products form thus:

$$AB\overline{C} + \overline{A}BC$$

The terms in this form are sometimes called minterms. The other equivalent form is the dual of this or the product of sums expression

$$B(\overline{A} + \overline{C})(A + C)$$

and the terms within the brackets are called maxterms.

It is important to be able to convert from one form to the other, and for this the meaning of the canonical expression must first be defined.

A sum of products canonical expansion in n variables is an expression of a set of product terms logically added (OR'd), in which each product term contains each of the n variables in its true or complement form, or all literals. A variable occurring in either its true or complement form is called a literal.

A product of sums canonical expansion contains a set of terms logically multiplied (AND'd), in which each sum term contains all n variables in the true or complement form. Any expression can easily be converted to the canonical form. For example in the product of sums case

$$A + BC = A(B + \overline{B}) + BC(A + \overline{A})$$
$$= (AB + A\overline{B}) + (ABC + \overline{A}BC)$$
$$= (AB + A\overline{B})(C + \overline{C}) + (ABC + \overline{A}BC)$$
$$= ABC + A\overline{B}C + AB\overline{C} + A\overline{B}\overline{C} + ABC + \overline{A}BC$$
$$= ABC + A\overline{B}C + AB\overline{C} + A\overline{B}\overline{C} + \overline{A}BC$$

A product of sums example is as follows:

$$A(B + C) = [(A + B)(A + \overline{B})]\,[A + B + C)(\overline{A} + B + C)]$$
$$= [(A + B + C)(A + B + \overline{C})(A + \overline{B} + C)(A + \overline{B} + \overline{C})]$$
$$[(A + B + C)(\overline{A} + B + C)]$$
$$= (A + B + C)(A + B + \overline{C})(A + \overline{B} + C)(A + \overline{B} + \overline{C})$$
$$(\overline{A} + B + C)$$

The following two types of expressions represent different physical realisations of the same function, shown in Figures 2.3 and 2.4, which may be verified by a truth table

$$F = AB\overline{C} + \overline{A}BC = B(\overline{A} + \overline{C})(A + C)$$

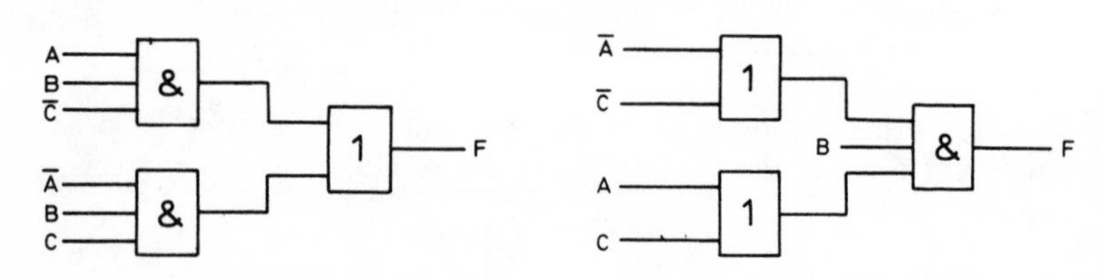

Figure 2.3 Sum of products realisation

Figure 2.4 Product of sums realisation

NAND and NOR Gates

NAND and NOR gates have simpler circuits, need less elements, and require less silicon area on an integrated circuit chip than AND or OR gates. From the logic point of view they are both universal functions in that all other functions can be created with them. For these reasons these circuits, particularly the NAND circuit, have become very widely applied in the design of modern computers. It is therefore necessary to convert expressions into a form which can be realised with NAND or NOR gates.

Suppose we have an expression in sum of products form, which we may have derived from a truth table, for example:

$$F_N = AB + CD + EF + \dots$$

This can be realised with AND and OR gates Figure 2.5. Using De Morgan's theorem we can represent the function as follows:

$$F_N = \overline{\overline{AB}} + \overline{\overline{CD}} + \overline{\overline{EF}} \dots$$
$$= \overline{(\overline{AB})\,(\overline{CD})\,(\overline{EF})} \dots$$

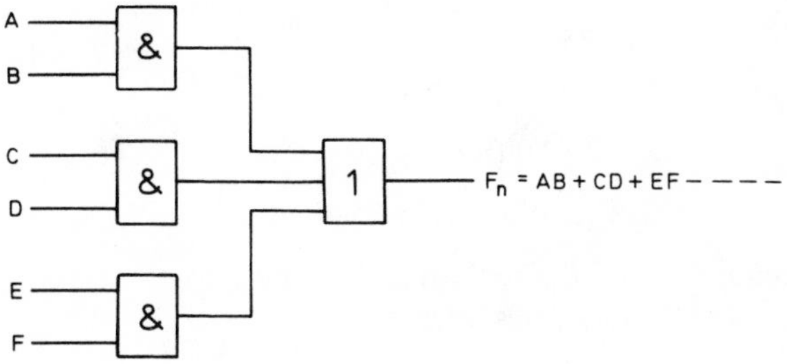

Figure 2.5

The terms $\overline{AB}$, $\overline{CD}$ etc. are the NAND function, so that we can realise the function as shown in Figure 2.6. Therefore a simple way of visualising the network is that the NAND circuits represent alternately AND and OR functions at each successive level.

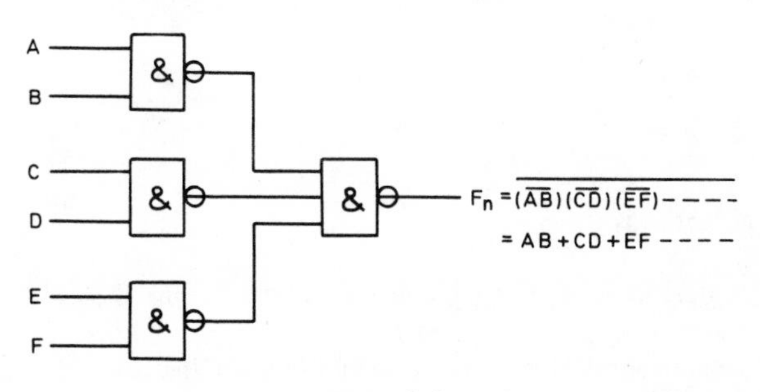

Figure 2.6

In the case of the NOR gate we can consider an expression in product of sums form

$$F_N = (A + B)\,(C + D)\,(E + F) \dots$$

which can be realised with AND and OR gates as shown in Figure 2.7.

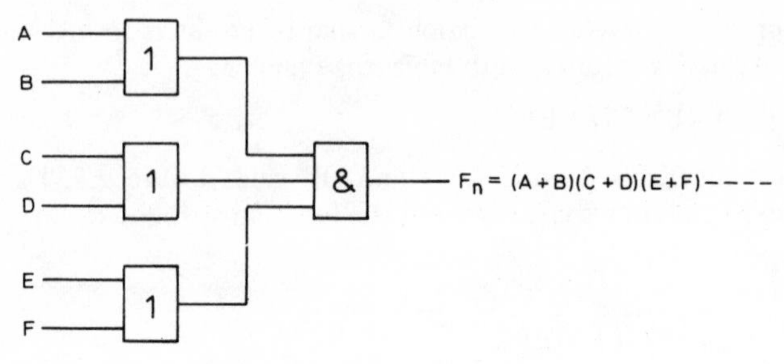

Figure 2.7

Again using De Morgan's theorem

$$
\begin{aligned}
F_N &= (A+B)\,(C+D)\,(E+F)\ldots. \\
&= \overline{\overline{(A+B)}}\,\overline{\overline{(C+D)}}\,\overline{\overline{(E+F)}}\ldots. \\
&= \overline{\overline{(A+B)}+\overline{(C+D)}+\overline{(E+F)}}\ldots.
\end{aligned}
$$

The terms $\overline{A+B}$ are the NOR function of A and B, and we can realise the network with NOR gates, Figure 2.8.

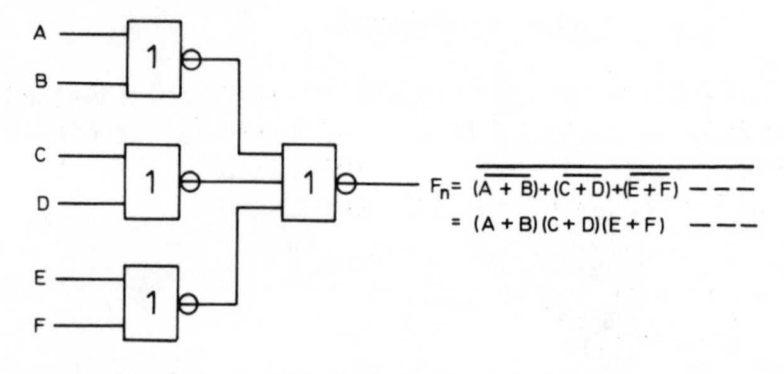

Figure 2.8

Mapping Methods

Boolean algebra is a formal way of manipulating the relationships between switching variables, and it is necessary to acquire skill in using expressions algebraically. However, in order to facilitate the handling of switching functions and to help in giving an insight into the operations of logical networks, engineers have looked for more descriptive ways of manipulating these functions. The map method was developed roughly simultaneously by Karnaugh and Veitch, and some confusion has arisen as both names are applied to similar maps. Veitch adopted a system in which the cells in the map were numbered in binary and therefore each cell was not always a distance of 1 from its adjacent cells. The Karnaugh arrangement, used here, is more convenient to use and has supplanted Veitch's numbering system.

To demonstrate the principle consider a two variable function of A and B. This can be shown on a map in the form Figure 2.9. Notice that B encloses the two right hand cells and A encloses the lower 2 cells. Where the areas A and B intersect we have the AND condition AB, and the condition of the other cells is as shown. Maps of some common functions of 2 variables are shown in Figure 2.10.

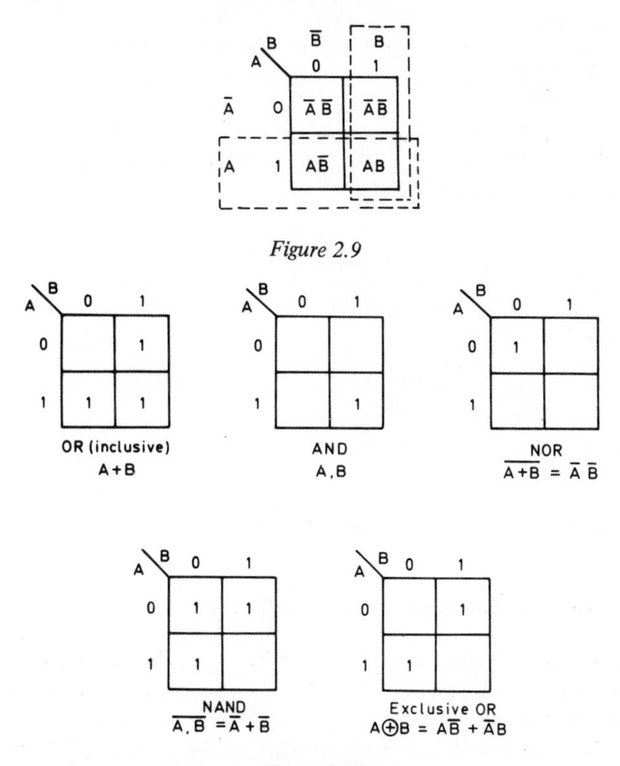

Figure 2.9

Figure 2.10

If the problem of simplifying a function of 3 variables is now considered, the map must contain either 4 rows and 2 columns or 2 rows and 4 columns. These maps are shown for the function F = AC + BC in Figure 2.11.

The sectioning of the map by the different variables is shown and the coding is also shown alongside the rows and columns. The binary coding of the rows and columns is convenient when converting from a truth table to the map. It also demonstrates the property of the

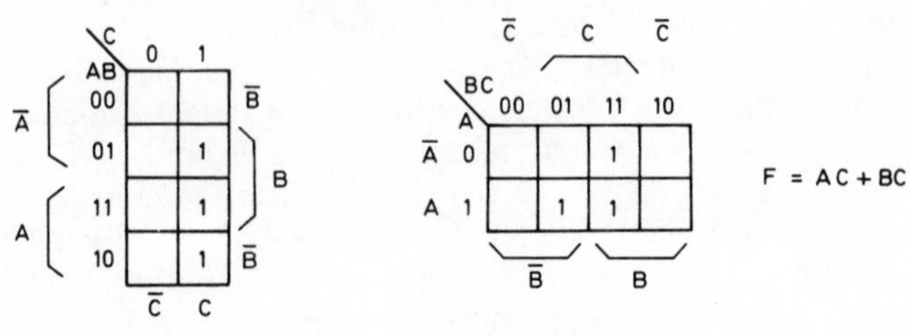

Figure 2.11

Karnaugh map that each cell is a distance of 1 from the next, i.e. there is a change of only a single bit in moving from one cell to an adjacent one.

The map for 4 variables is shown in Figure 2.12 for the function $F = BD + CD + \bar{A}BC + AB\bar{C}$. This map shows more clearly the unit distance property of adjacent cells.

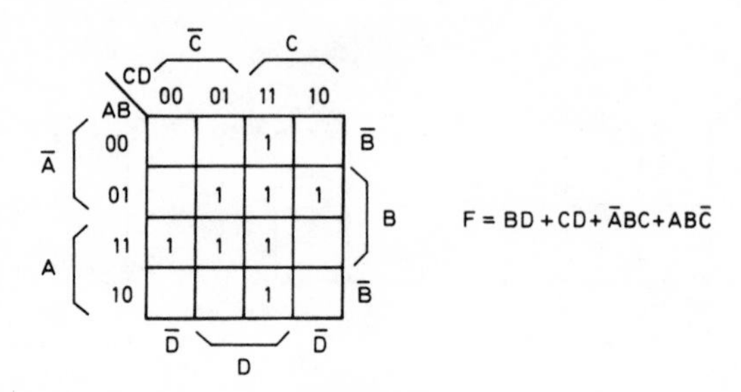

Figure 2.12

Minimisation of Functions by the use of Maps

To minimise the logical functions with Karnaugh maps we make use of the unit distance adjacency property of the maps to enclose subcubes of the maps having the fewest variables. Some examples of a single variable subcubes in a 3 variable map are shown in Figure 2.13. In each of these cases 4 cells of the map are adjacent and therefore can be represented by one term containing a single variable. The example $F = \bar{B}$ demonstrates the fact that opposing edges of the map are adjacent to each other, which can be shown by representing the 3 variable map as a loop, Figure 2.14. Both sides of the loop are also adjacent, but it becomes impracticable to show this three-dimensionally.

Referring to the function shown in the 3 variable map, Figure 2.15, this represents the function

$$F = AB\bar{C} + ABC + \bar{A}BC + A\bar{B}C$$

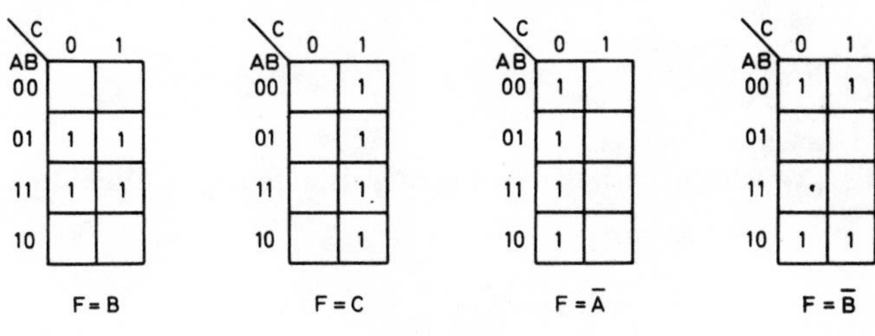

Figure 2.13

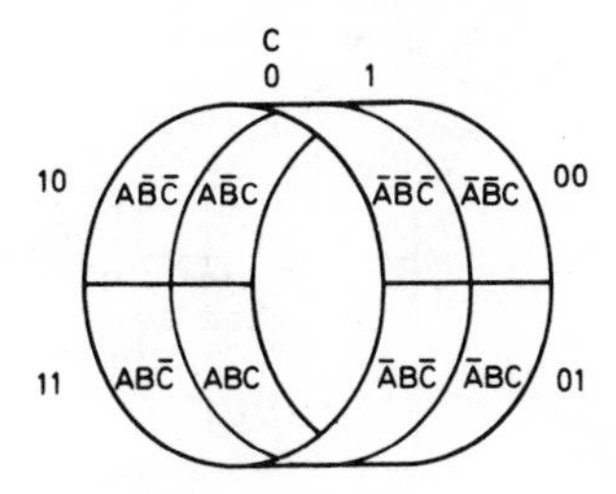

Figure 2.14

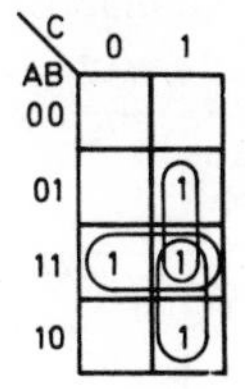

Figure 2.15

which can be simplified to

$$\begin{aligned} F &= (AB\overline{C} + ABC) + (\overline{A}BC + ABC) + (A\overline{B}C + ABC) \\ &= AB + BC + AC \end{aligned}$$

Notice that the three simplified terms are represented by encircled subcubes, and that the cell ABC (111) is enclosed 3 times, which also appears in the algebra as being written 3 times.

The aim in simplifying a function with a map is to draw subcubes which enclose as many cells in a subcube as possible (the subcubes having 1, 2, 4, 8, 16 cells etc.), and any one cell may be enclosed many times. Thus the function

$$F = ABC + \overline{A}BC + A\overline{B}C$$

simplifies to

$$F = AC + BC$$

and is shown in Figure 2.11.

The 4 variable map shown on Figure 2.12 representing the function

$$F = AB\overline{C}\overline{D} + AB\overline{C}D + ABCD + \overline{A}\overline{B}CD$$
$$+ \overline{A}B\overline{C}D + \overline{A}BCD + \overline{A}BC\overline{D} + A\overline{B}CD$$
$$= BD + CD + \overline{A}BC + AB\overline{C}$$

is simplified as shown in Figure 2.16.

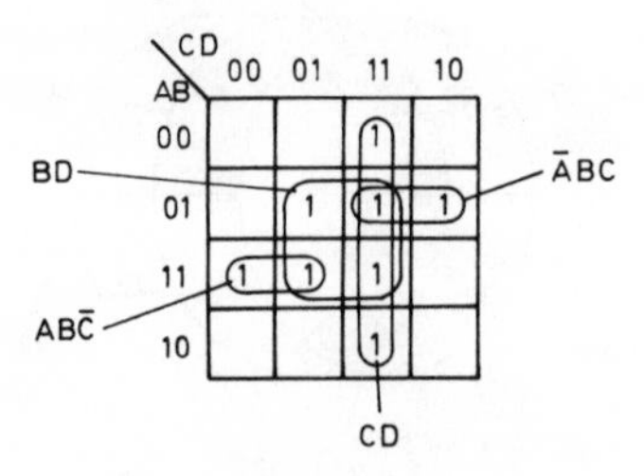

Figure 2.16

An interesting example is the map of the function shown in Figure 2.17. Looking first at the map on the left without the subcubes delineated, the temptation is to enclose the subcube $A\overline{C}$, however, it

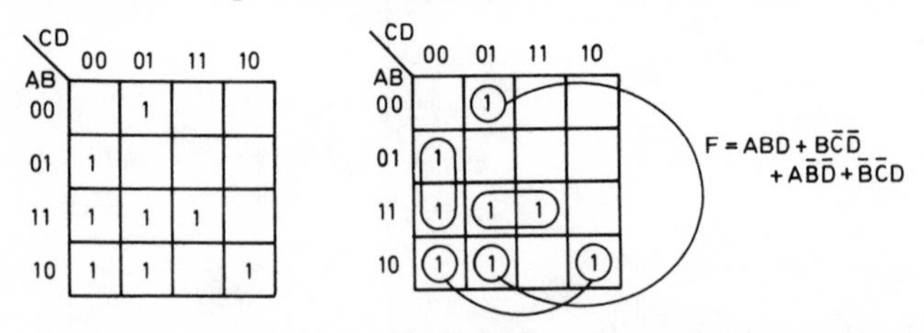

Figure 2.17

can be seen from the right map with subcubes enclosed that all four cells of $A\overline{C}$ must be enclosed by necessary small subcubes as shown, when the simplified function becomes

$$F = ABD + B\overline{C}\overline{D} + \overline{A}\overline{B}\overline{D} + \overline{B}\overline{C}D$$

It sometimes happens that a function can be simplified in more than one way, each of which is equally minimal, and an example of this is shown in Figure 2.18 which can be equally well given by

$$F = \overline{A}\overline{B}\overline{D} + \overline{A}B\overline{C} + ABD + A\overline{B}C$$

or $$F = A\overline{C}\overline{D} + B\overline{C}D + ACD + \overline{B}C\overline{D}$$

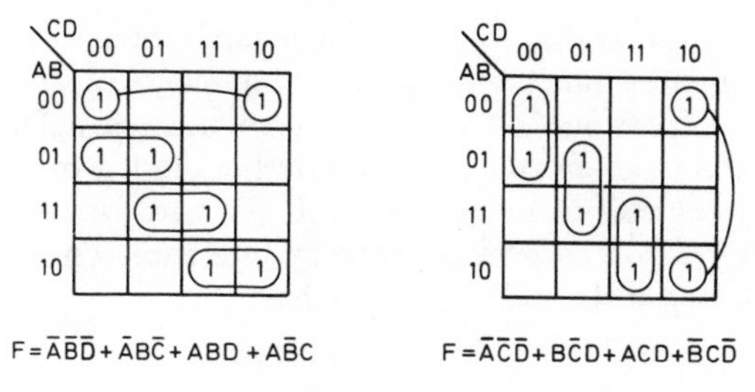

Figure 2.18

The Karnaugh map can be extended to higher numbers of variables, but it becomes less obvious to see all the adjacent cells as can be seen in Figure 2.19 which shows the 5 variable map with lines drawn for the adjacent cells. The map consists of 2–4 variable maps drawn side by side, but notice the numbering of cells is so arranged that the two halves of the map are also distanced 1 apart.

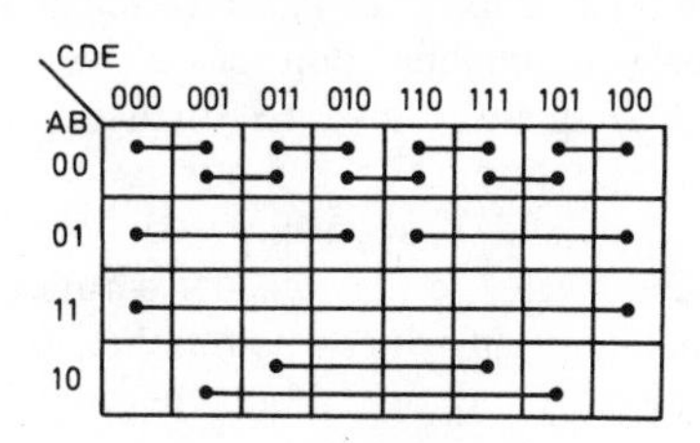

Figure 2.19

Another method is to make use of 2–4 variable maps effectively lying one above the other, and it has been suggested that three dimensional models of transparent plastic boards can be made, in which cells representing the function can be marked with coloured chips.

The map is most powerful for 4 variables. For 2 or 3 variables it is quite often as quick to simplify by algebra. For 5 variables and even more so for 6 variables the maps become too complex to be so convenient.

To simplify functions with more than 5 variables it is preferable to resort to chart methods. Historically these methods were evolved before the map technique. The chart technique was first developed at the Harvard Computation Laboratory, and the method is known as the Harvard Chart. The most popular chart is a development of a method by Quine extended by McCluskey and known as the Quine-McCluskey Chart. By using a chart it is possible to systematically minimise functions of higher numbers of variables than 5 with considerable labour.

Experience shows that in practice it is rarely necessary in computer design to minimise functions with larger numbers of variables. Where this is necessary some of the large computer manufacturers have developed computer programs to remove the burden of tedious work. For those who wish to or must do this the hard way, it is suggested that they refer to the several excellent references on the subject of switching theory at the end of this chapter.

Unconditional or Don't Care Terms

Functions frequently occur in which some of the terms are unconditional, or in other words, one does not care whether they are 1 or 0. For example, the input to some combinational logic network may be a binary decimal code in which only 10 out of 16 possibilities of functions can legitimately occur. The other 6 functions will either not normally appear or will signify an error which is separately deleted. It is particuarly easy to include 'don't care' terms on the Karnaugh map and this will frequently lead to further simplification of the expression for the function. The symbol used for the 'don't care' terms consists of a 1 and 0 superimposed (ɸ). As an example of minimising with 'don't care' terms consider a function defined by the 1248 binary decimal code, in which the numbers 0 through 9 can exist and produce functions of 0 or 1, but the numbers 9 through 15 represents erroneous functioning and therefore are considered as 'don't care' cases.

Table 2.5

	A	B	C	D	F
0	0	0	0	0	0
1	0	0	0	1	1
2	0	0	1	0	1
3	0	0	1	1	0
4	0	1	0	0	0
5	0	1	0	1	1
6	0	1	1	0	0
7	0	1	1	1	1
8	1	0	0	0	0
9	1	0	0	1	0
a	1	0	1	0	ɸ
b	1	0	1	1	ɸ
c	1	1	0	0	ɸ
d	1	1	0	1	ɸ
e	1	1	1	0	ɸ
f	1	1	1	1	ɸ

Suppose we wish, as an example, to derive a function which gives an output of 1 for the numbers 1, 2, 5 and 7, the truth table will be as shown in Table 2.5.

The map of this function is shown in Figure 2.20. When drawing the subcubes in this case, each of the 1 cells must be enclosed by subcubes, and likewise none of the 0 cells may be enclosed. However, it is permissible to enclose 'don't care' cases, denoted, ϕ, in the subcubes, if it leads to simpler expressions. In this case the function can be simplified to

$$F_1 = BD + \bar{A}\bar{C}D + \bar{B}C\bar{D}$$

if the 'don't care' cases are included. If they are not included the function becomes the more complicated

$$F_2 = \bar{A}BD + \bar{A}\bar{C}D + \bar{A}\bar{B}C\bar{D}$$

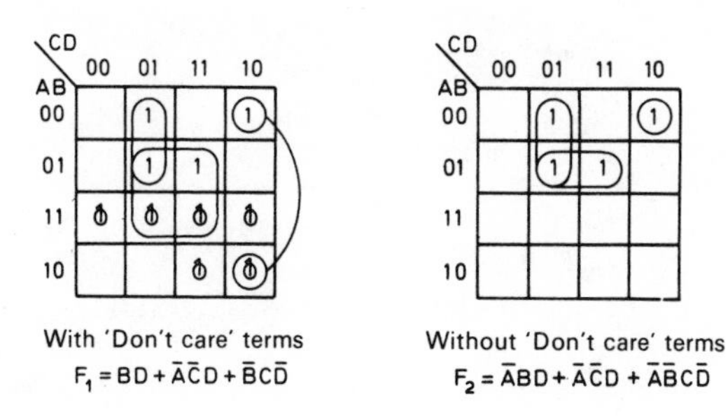

Figure 2.20

Networks with Multiple Outputs

The general case of a logical network may be considered as a box having n inputs and m outputs as shown in Figure 2.21. Both inputs and outputs can be any number greater than 1 and need not be equal. A Boolean function is applied to $X_1 \ldots X_n$ and generates another Boolean function on $F_1 \ldots F_m$. So far we have considered the case where n is more than one, but m is only one. In cases where m is greater than one and there are multiple outputs from the networks further reduction in gates is sometimes possible.

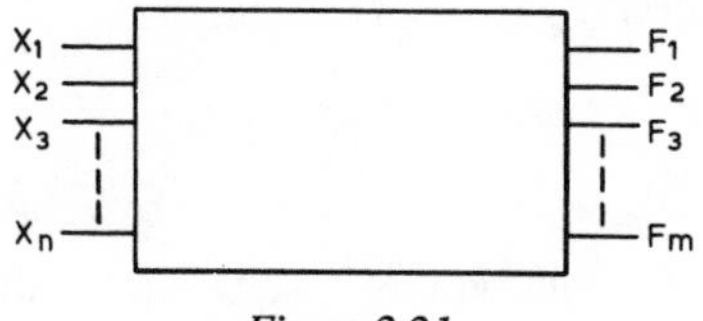

Figure 2.21

To design a multiple output network it is first necessary to derive the expressions for $F_1, F_2, \ldots F_m$ by the methods already described. Examination of the expressions for each of these functions may reveal that a certain term appears in more than one of the expressions for $F_1 - F_m$. It is therefore unnecessary to generate this term more than once. For example consider the expressions

$$F_1 = \overline{A}\overline{C} + B + E$$

$$F_2 = A + \overline{B}\overline{C} + DE$$

$$F_3 = \overline{A}\overline{B}\overline{C} + DE$$

Direct translation of this expression into a realisation with NAND gates would result in the diagram, Figure 2.22.

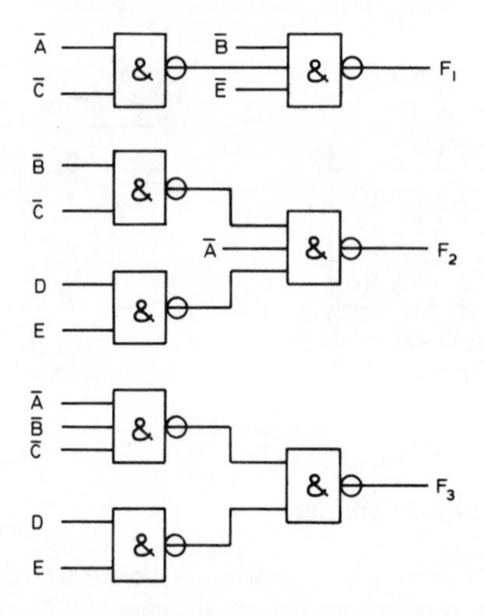

Figure 2.22 Requirement: Three 3 input NAND gates and five 2 input NAND gates

The first point to notice is that the term DE appears in both F_2 and F_3, and therefore need not be generated twice. An additional saving can be achieved by expanding the expressions for F_1 and F_2 using the law of absorption $A + B = A + \overline{A}B$.

Applying this identity we have

$$F_1 = B + \overline{B}(\overline{A}\overline{C}) + E$$

$$F_2 = A + \overline{A}(\overline{B}\overline{C}) + DE$$

$$F_3 = \overline{A}\overline{B}C + DE$$

The realisation of this function in NAND gates is shown in Figure 2.23 making use of the terms repeated in each expression.

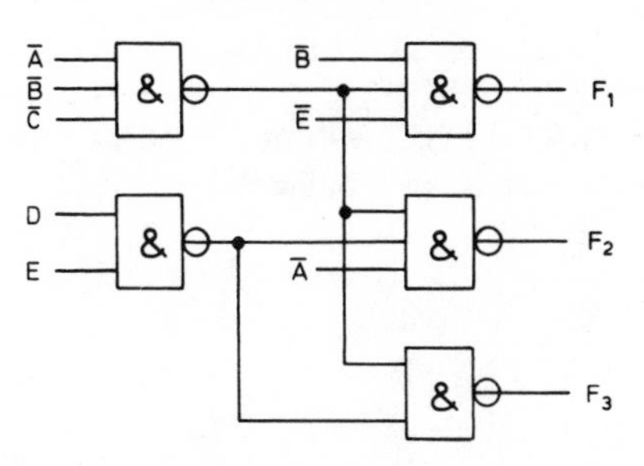

Figure 2.23 Requirement: Three 3 input NAND gates and two 2 input NAND gates

It can be seen that three 2 input NAND gates have been saved by the operations described. By manipulating the expressions to repeat terms several times it is therefore possible to obtain quite significant savings. This is particularly so when designing a complete system. It is easy when designing different sections of a computer, to find that the same function may be generated more than once for different purposes, and a careful watch for this may produce worthwhile savings.

Problems

1 Simplify the following expressions, first by using Boolean algebra, and then by Karnaugh maps. Confirm the correctness of the algebra by means of truth tables, and draw physical realisations of these expressions, first with AND and OR gates, and secondly with NAND gates:
   (a) $\bar{A}C + \bar{A}B + BC + AB + A\bar{C}$
   (b) $\bar{A}\bar{C} + B\bar{C} + A\bar{B}$
   (c) $\bar{A}\bar{B} + \bar{A}C + AC + A\bar{B}$
   (d) $\bar{A}\bar{C} + A\bar{B}\bar{C} + \bar{A}BC$
2. Convert the following expressions from sum of products form to product of sums form, and show which is the most economical form to realise with AND and OR gates:
   (a) $B\bar{C} + A\bar{B}C + \bar{A}BC$
   (b) $A\bar{B}\bar{C} + \bar{A}B\bar{C} + \bar{A}\bar{B}\bar{C}$
3. Convert the following expressions from product of sums form to sum of products form:
   (a) $(A + B)(\bar{A} + \bar{B} + \bar{C})(\bar{A} + B + C)$
   (b) $(\bar{B} + \bar{D})(\bar{A} + B)(\bar{B} + C)(\bar{C} + \bar{D})(\bar{A} + \bar{D})$
4. Using Karnaugh maps simplify the following expressions:
   (a) $\bar{A}\bar{B}\bar{C}\bar{D} + \bar{A}\bar{B}CD + \bar{A}B\bar{C}D + \bar{A}BC\bar{D} + AB\bar{C}D$
   $ABC\bar{D} + A\bar{B}\bar{C}\bar{D} + A\bar{B}CD$

(b) $AB\overline{C} + A\overline{C}D + \overline{A}\,\overline{C}\,\overline{D} + A\overline{B}\,\overline{C}\,\overline{D}$

(c) $PQS + PRS + QRS$

(d) $PRS + PR\overline{S}T + \overline{P}QST + \overline{P}\,\overline{Q}\,\overline{R}\,\overline{T} + \overline{P}\,\overline{R}ST\overline{} + \overline{P}\,\overline{Q}RST$

5. The excess three code is given below:

	A	B	C	D		A	B	C	D
0	0	0	1	1	5	1	0	0	0
1	0	1	0	0	6	1	0	0	1
2	0	1	0	1	7	1	0	1	0
3	0	1	1	0	8	1	0	1	1
4	0	1	1	1	9	1	1	0	0

This is presented as 4 parallel binary inputs ABCD to a logic network which must translate this code to binary coded decimal. Design the logic network using NAND gates and 2 levels of logic to give the binary coded decimal output on 4 terminals EFGH as shown in Figure 2.24.

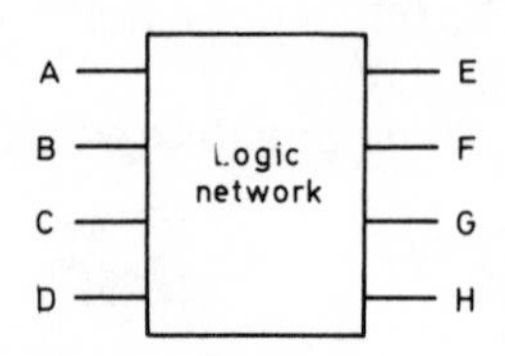

Figure 2.24

6. The numbers 0 to 9 appear in binary coded form on the input to a logic network. The numbers are to be displayed as decimal digits on a seven bar pattern of lights as shown (Figure 2.25), in which only the appropriate bars are to be illuminated.

Two types of light driving circuits can be made. With the first the lights are normally extinguished and are lighted by a binary 1 on the

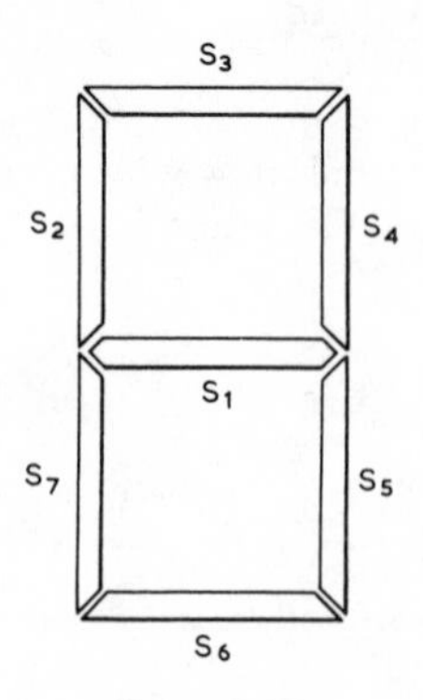

Figure 2.25

driver input. With the other driving circuit the bars are normally illuminated unless a binary 1 at the driver input causes them to be extinguished.

Design the bar patterns to show the decimal digits. Then design the decoding network to operate the lights for both types of light drivers, and demonstrate which type of driver results in the most economical logic network.

REFERENCES

1. DIETMEYER, D.L., *Logical Design of Digital Systems.* Allyn and Bacon., New York. 2nd (1978)
2. PETERSON, G.R. and HILL, F.J., *Introduction to Switching Theory and Logical Design.* John Wiley (1974)
3. MANO, M.M., *Digital Logic and Computer Design.* Prentice-Hall (1979)
4. PORAT, D.I., *Introduction to Digital Techniques.* John Wiley (1979)
5. GIBSON, J.R., *Electronic Logic Circuits.* Arnold (1979)
6. MORRIS, N.M., *Logic Circuits 2nd Ed.* McGraw-Hill (1976)
7. DOKTER, F., *Digital Electronics.* Macmillan. London (1973)
8. CRIPPS, M., *An Introduction to Computer Hardware.*, Arnold (1977)
9. HELLERMAN, I., 'A Catalog of Three-Variable Or-Invert and And-Invert Logical Circuit. *IEE Trans, Elect Comp.* **12** No 3, 198–223 (1963)
10. KARNAUGH, M., 'The Map Method for Syntheses of Combinational Logic Circuits.' *Com' Electr. Trans. AIEE* 72, Part 1, (1953)
11. MCCLUSKEY, E.J. Jr., Minimization of Boolean Functions. *Bell Sys. Tec. J.*, 35, 1417–44 (1956)
12. CATT, I, WALTON, D.S., and DAVIDSON, M. *Digital Hardware Design.* Macmillan

Chapter 3

Counters and Sequential Circuits

The logic circuits described in Chapter 2 have all had the property, when considered as a box with binary digital inputs and outputs, that the output can be represented as a Boolean function of the input at that particular instant, and is not affected in any way by previous events. This class of circuit contains no storage elements of any kind which could preserve any memory of what has gone before, and are termed combinational circuits. The output of a circuit which includes some type of memory as well as logical elements, and is a Boolean function not only of the input, but also of the binary number stored in its memory elements–which itself is also a function of previous events–is known as a sequential circuit.

A wide variety of memory devices are used in the design of computers, but, for the purpose of current design of the counters and sequential circuits embodied in the arithmetic and control systems of computers, the flip-flop is in general use for the temporary storage of digital data. It is constructed from similar circuits to those used in the logic gates, with which it is designed to be compatible in voltage, current and power, and has the advantage of providing an output as a dc level which can be used directly as an input to a succeeding network of logic gates. As will be described in Chapter 7 on memories the static RAM consists of a large array of flip-flops formed as microcircuits on a silicon chip. The flip-flops may be set to either the 1 or 0 state and are provided with addressing logic on the chip so that only selected flip-flops are set or reset. Essentially the whole operation of a computer system can be reduced to a problem of transferring digital information from one register to another, usually by way of more or less complicated interacting logic.

The Flip-Flop Register

To the computer designer, the flip-flop now usually arrives ready made as an integrated circuit, or indeed there may be a number of flip-flops

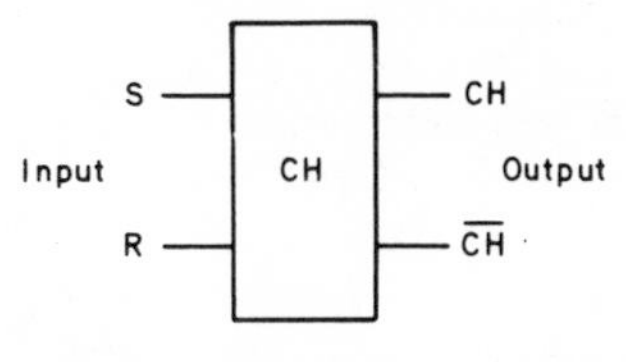

Figure 3.1

with inter-connecting logic designed to perform some predetermined function. The logic symbol for a SET-RESET flip-flop is shown in Figure 3.1. Usually each flip-flop has a name symbol which is often an abbreviation of its function, for example CH (short for CHECK), and the outputs which are in both true and complement form have the same name. The symbol might also have a number representing a bit number in a register or counter. The simplest flip-flop can be made from 2-NAND circuits as shown in Figure 3.2. The digital inputs can be at

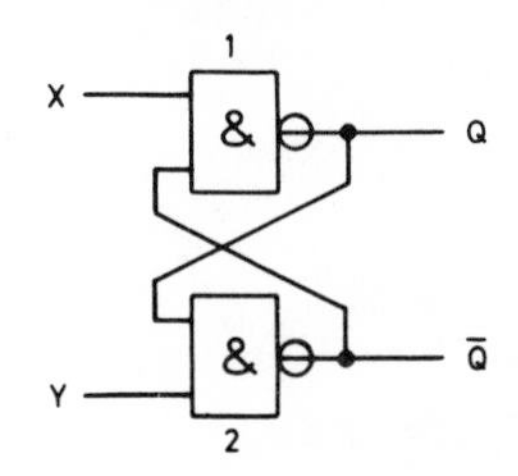

Figure 3.2

one of two levels, representing 1 or 0, which will also be called, high and low. Remembering that with the NAND circuit the output is low only when both of its inputs are high. Suppose that both X and Y are high. The circuit must then have 2 stable states and will settle with either Q high and $\overline{Q}$ low or vice versa. If we make the input X or Y low to the conducting NAND circuit i.e. with a low output, its output must become high, causing the opposite NAND to be put into the conducting state, and thus reversing the state of the flip-flop. If it is wished to set or reset the flip-flop at only a given time we can gate the S (set) or R (reset) inputs with a pulse that enables the flip-flop only when needed as shown in Figure 3.3. Notice that if both S and R are high together the flip-flop may be set into an indeterminate state, and it is necessary to ensure that simultaneous signals to S and R are never given.

The operation of the RS flip-flop can be conveniently described in Table 3.1. S and R are the conditions at the input and Q_n and Q_{n+1} are the states of the flip-flop before and after the enabling pulse.

An extension of this flip-flop is the D flip-flop (Figure 3.4), also called a latch, which uses a single input with an inverter for the reset input.

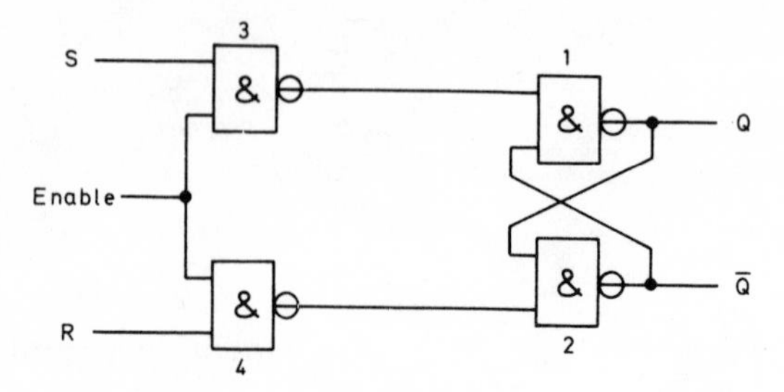

Figure 3.3

Table 3.1

Input conditions		*Present state*	*Next state*
S	R	Q_n	Q_{n+1}
0	0	0	0
0	0	1	1
1	0	0	1
1	0	1	1
0	1	0	0
0	1	1	0
1	1	0	indeterminate
1	1	1	indeterminate

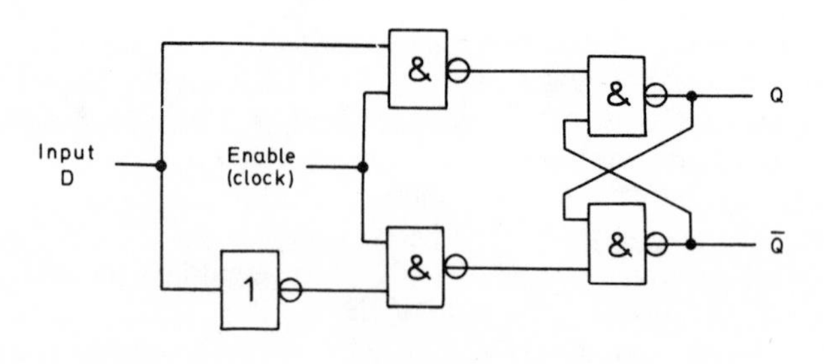

Figure 3.4

The Shift Register

The Shift Register is a device in universal use in computer circuits. Serial data entering a shift register can be trapped for subsequent manipulation, or it may be used for sending out serial data at a predetermined time and rate. By taking the output from each flip-flop in parallel it is a convenient way of converting data from serial form to parallel form, and conversely data entered in the flip-flops can be shifted out in serial form, performing a parallel to serial conversion. Speed conversion where data is received at one speed and transmitted at a different one is also easily accommodated. Long shift registers of hundreds or more bits are also used for storage purposes, where they may be regarded as variable speed digital delay lines.

A simple shift register is shown in Figure 3.5, constructed from a series of RS flip-flops, A, B, C, . . . The simplest transfer operation is to transfer the contents of A to B, the contents of B to C and so on. The register can be extended to any length.

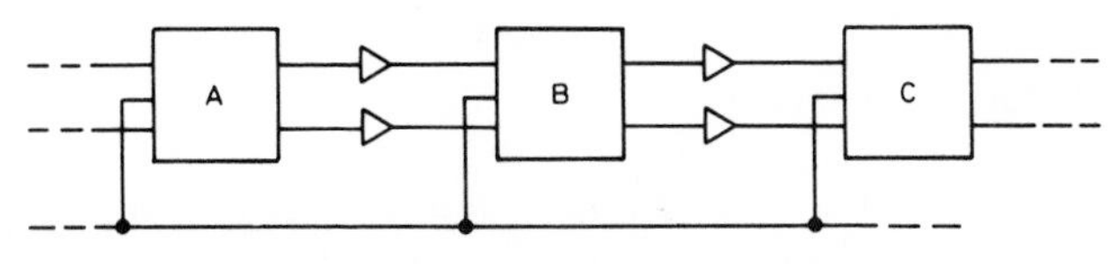

Figure 3.5

Normally the shift clock is low and no inputs are enabled so that there is no change in A, B, C, etc. To eventuate a shift, the shift pulse is raised to the enable condition, and it can be seen that B may be changing to the contents of A at the same time that its contents are being transferred to C. If the output of each flip-flop was connected to the input of the next, and the flip-flops changed instantaneously there would be ambiguity due to the input and output changing simultaneously. To overcome this delay circuits, which were often inadvertent in earlier circuits, can be introduced to prevent the following inputs changing until some period after the previous output has changed. This was an acceptable solution for a while, when circuit speeds were slower, but it has a serious disadvantage that the circuit operation becomes speed dependent.

This problem can be overcome by replacing the delay circuits by flip-flops, so that two flip-flops are now used per bit in the register. A two phase shift pulse is applied so that data is shifted alternatley to alternate flip-flops, as shown in Figure 3.6. With this means, information

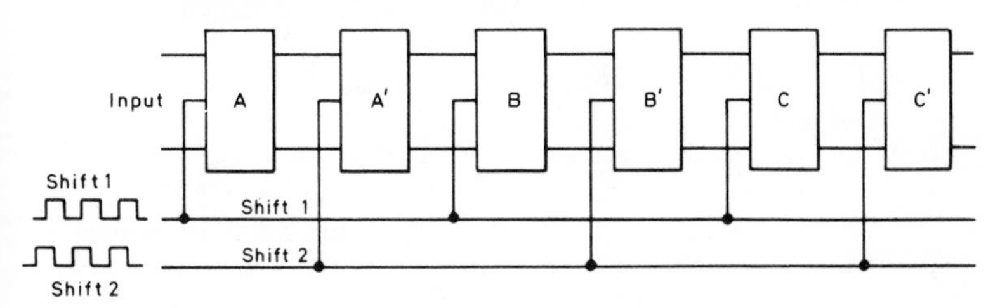

Figure 3.6

is transferred from A′ to B, and B′ to C while any change to A′, B′, C′ is prevented by shift 2 being off. Then the transfer from B to B′, and C to C′ is initiated, while any change of A, B, or C is prevented. The two flip-flops A A′, B B′ etc. are generally combined in a single circuit jointly called a 'master slave' or 'double rank' flip-flop.

Instead of using two separate shift pulses, the second shift pulse is the inversion of the first, so that a single shift pulse is used in which the transfer from A to A′ occurs at the leading edge of the shift pulse and the transfer from A′ to B, and B′ to C occurs at the trailing edge of the pulse.

The JK Flip-flop

Figure 3.7 shows the logic diagram of a double rank JK flip-flop constructed from NAND gates. Notice that two separate flip-flops of the RS type are embedded within the circuit, and that the inputs to the first flip-flop are enabled directly by the shift pulse, and the input to the second flip-flop is enabled by its inverse so that data is transferred alternately.

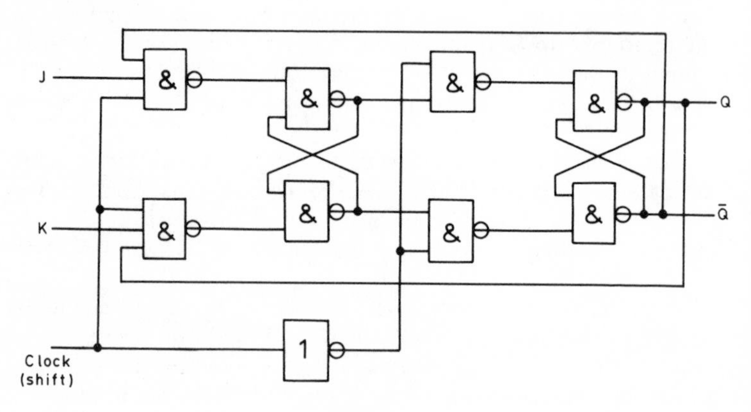

Figure 3.7

Lastly notice that the inputs to the first flip-flop are cross coupled to the outputs of the second flip-flop. By this means only the gate which will change the state of the input flip-flop is enabled and the indeterminate cases occurring when both set and reset pulses are simultaneously applied to the RS flip-flop are eliminated. Furthermore to make the flip-flop behave as a binary counter it is only necessary to make both J and K simultaneously 1. Table 3.2 describes the operation of the JK flip-flop.

Table 3.2

Input conditions		*Present state*	*Next state*
J	K	Q_n	Q_{n+1}
0	0	1	1
0	1	1	0
1	0	1	1
1	1	1	0
0	0	0	0
0	1	0	0
1	0	0	1
1	1	0	1

The internal logic circuits of a computer can be resolved into an interconnection of a large number of circuits as shown in Figure 3.8, where data is transferred from one set of flip-flops to a second set of flip-flops through a complicated interconnecting logic network. Also sometimes the combinational logic may transfer back into a flip-flop in the first set.

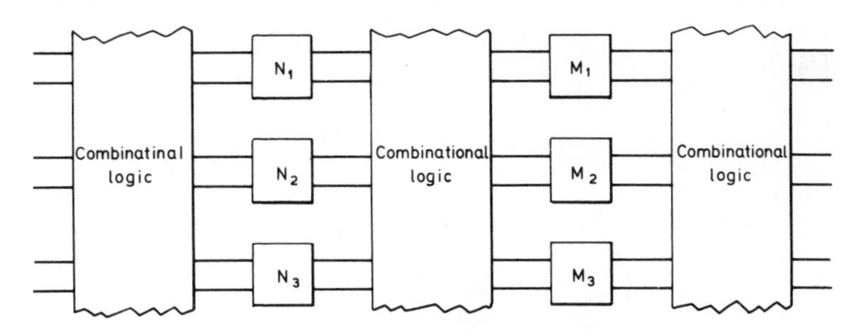

Figure 3.8

The transfer of data from flip-flop to flip-flop throughout the computer is caused to occur simultaneously by using a common shift pulse on all flip-flops, and this is generally known as the clock from its action as a master timer. By timing in this way problems engendered by pulses travelling with different delays by different paths in the combinational network are eliminated.

The clock timing diagram for a clocked logic system is shown in Figure 3.9. All the flip-flops in the system change state at the trailing edge of the clock pulse, and sufficient time must be allowed for all the logic levels in the system to establish themselves before the leading edge of the next clock pulse appears. Since this time is determined by the longest delay in the machine, much of the computer is operating at a

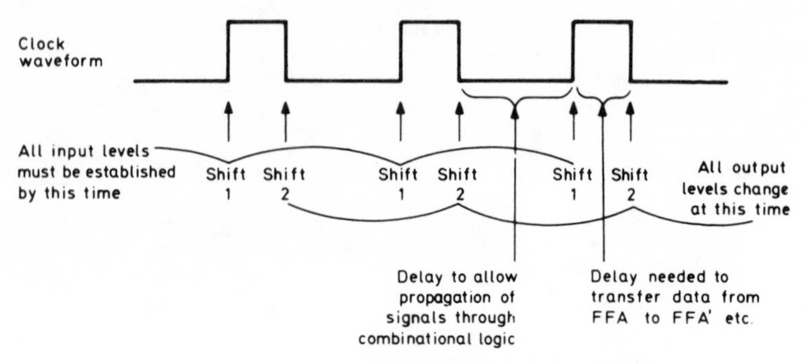

Figure 3.9

slower-speed than that of which it is capable. This is the price paid for eliminating the difficulties of differential delay times by alternate logic routes. It is possible to construct circuits without using a master clock, but it becomes extremely difficult to control the design except on a small system and the clocking principle is in general use in current computers.

The Sequential Circuit

It has been seen that it is possible to consider a digital computing machine as a collection of registers linked by combinational logic networks, in which the operation of the network consists of sequential transfers of the binary values in registers from one to another in combinationally translated form. In this sense a computer can be regarded as a large sequential circuit, but in practice it is necessary to consider smaller sequential circuits which can be analysed, and which can be assembled to perform more complex functions.

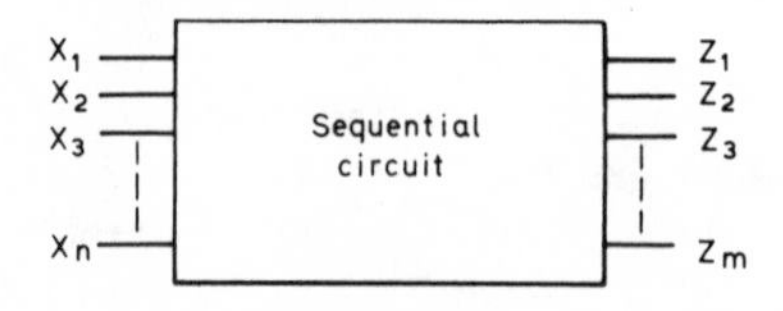

Figure 3.10

The generalised sequential circuit may be considered as a 'black box' containing both storage elements, or registers, and combinational logic as shown in Figure 3.10. The box has a number of inputs $X_1, X_2, \ldots X_n$, and a number of outputs $Z_1, Z_2, \ldots Z_m$. The outputs $Z_1, Z_2, \ldots Z_m$ are Boolean functions of $X_1, X_2, \ldots X_n$ and the contents of the storage elements, which themselves depend on the history of previous events.

The circuit can be assumed to be controlled by a timing signal, which is usually the clock signal, causing the circuit to change from one binary state to the next at discrete instants in time. The machine then proceeds through a series of distinguishable finite states, changing from one state to another at definite instants in time, and remaining in that state until the next instant of change. Ideally, it is assumed that change of state occurs instantaneously, and remains unaltered between changes. The next state to which the circuit changes is determined by its existing state and by the inputs $X_1, X_2, \ldots X_n$. There are some simpler sub-classes of the circuit shown in Figure 3.10. These are:

1. A network with a single input and multiple outputs. This is usually thought of as a type of counter or binary sequence generator. Examples are the binary counter or decimal counter, the pseudo-random number generator, or the program counter of a computer which is incremented to the next instruction at the end of each operation.
2. A network with a single input and single output. This device may receive one time sequence of input pulses and issue a different sequence of pulses from its output. Such a device might be used in the control system of a machine.
3. A network with multiple inputs and a single output. Such a device could be a decoding network which would emit an output pulse only after a correct predetermined series of input signals. A combination lock is a mechanical equivalent of this.

Sequential circuits can be synchronous or asynchronous. In synchronous, or clock driven circuits, the instant at which the change of state occurs is determined by a timing device or clock, as has been described for the J-K flip-flop. Most arithmetic and control circuits in processors are of this type. In asynchronous circuits, the instant at which the state changes is determined by a change of some input signal, and by internal delays, so they are also called 'event driven'.

Most of the present computers are controlled by a synchronous clock timing signal which causes the circuits to change state at equally spaced time intervals. However in some cases a circuit may be controlled by a signal from an external device, which is not synchronised to the internal computer clock. In these cases it is usual to pass the signal through a synchronising circuit which converts the signal from the asynchronous external environment to the synchronous internal environment of the computer. This may often be inherent in the timing of so called 'hand shaking' signals at the input-output of a processor. It should be added that in a synchronous system, there is no necessity for the timing signals to be at equal intervals, only that they occur simultaneously throughout the system. Sometimes circuit delays in the clock timing, can cause the timing signals not to happen simultaneously throughout. This is known as 'clock skew' and can cause problems if allowed to become too great.

The 'black box' representation of a sequential circuit may be separated into two segments consisting of a combinational network having no memory elements and a set of memory elements or register as shown in Figure 3.11.

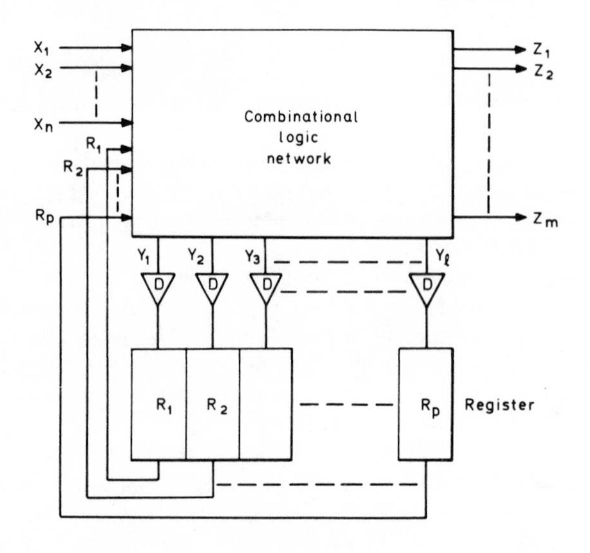

Figure 3.11

The combinational network now has inputs $X_1, X_2, \ldots X_n$, and $R_1, R_2, \ldots R_p$ and outputs $Z_1, Z_2, \ldots Z_m$ and $Y_1, Y_2, \ldots Y_l$, thus giving $n + l$ inputs and $m + l$ outputs. Notice that delay elements D have been introduced between the output of the combinational network and the register, and these are needed as shown in the foregoing treatment on the single rank flip-flop. If the registers R consist of double rank synchronously clocked flip-flops the diagram can be simplified to that shown in Figure 3.12, which may be applied to all double rank clocked flip-flop circuits. This circuit can be interpreted with the aid of the timing diagram of Figure 3.9 in which it is seen that the time between the leading (or rising) and trailing edge of the clock waveform is required for setting the register whose flip-flops actually change state at the trailing edge, and the time between the trailing edge

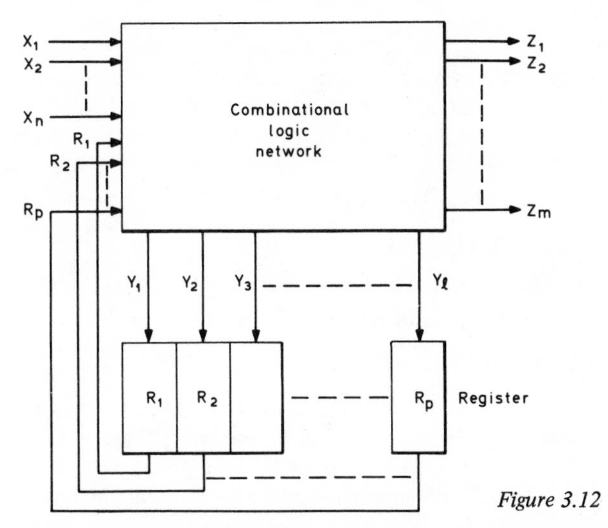

Figure 3.12

and the next leading edge is available for propagation delay of the signals through the combinational logic network.

Modern synchronous circuits use clocked double rank flip-flops, and the only changes of state considered are those occurring at the trailing edge of the clock and observable at the flip-flop outputs. The internal change of state during transfer from master to slave flip-flop does not appear in calculations. In circuits using single rank flip-flops every change of state must be included, and especially the effects at the inputs to flip-flops with different delays, leading to race problems, which are avoided with the double rank system. Because some of the state changes are omitted from the calculations, the design of synchronous circuits is less complicated. It is often necessary however, to design asynchronous circuits in input-output logic and ancillary circuits and these are treated later.

The Type 1 Circuit

It is assumed that the inputs $X_1, X_2, \ldots X_n$ in Figure 3.12 can only take the values of 0 or 1 at a given instant. It is appropriate here to define what is meant by 'state'. The Input state is a Boolean function of time of the input.

$$X(t) = [X_1(t), X_2(t), X_3(t) \ldots X_n(t)]$$

Where t changes in discrete steps, defined by the clock in the case of the synchronous circuit. In asynchronous circuits t defines instants when some input changes, usually in a random, but discrete, fashion.

The Output State is the Boolean function of time of the output.

$$Z(t)[= Z_1(t), Z_2(t) \ldots Z_m(t)]$$

It should be noted that there may be a different number of outputs to inputs.

The Internal State can easily be identified in this case, where the storage is in individual flip-flops, and is:-

$$R(t) = [R_1(t), R_2(t) \ldots R_p(t)]$$

The combinational network has a Boolean output function.

$$Y(t) = [Y_1(t), Y_2(t), \ldots Y_l(t)]$$

If we now assume that each clock pulse initiates a transfer Y→R, then the internal state of R at time interval t + 1 is given by:-

$$R(t + 1) = Y(t) = \alpha[R(t), X(t)]$$

Which is a Boolean function of the combinational network α and its inputs X(t) and R(t). This is called the Next State Function. In this simple case, which could for example be a binary counter. the output at time t is the contents of the flip-flop register, in which case

$$\begin{aligned} Z(t) &= R(t) \\ Z(t + 1) &= R(t + 1) \\ &= Y(t) \\ &= \alpha[R(t), Y(t)] \\ \text{or } Z(t) &= \alpha[R(t - 1), Y(t - 1)] \end{aligned}$$

Where α is a Boolean function of the combinational network. I will call this a Type 1 circuit.

Two more general cases of this network are common.

The Type 2 Circuit.

The flip-flop register can be followed by a second combinational circuit as shown in Figure 3.13, so that Z(t) ≠ R(t)

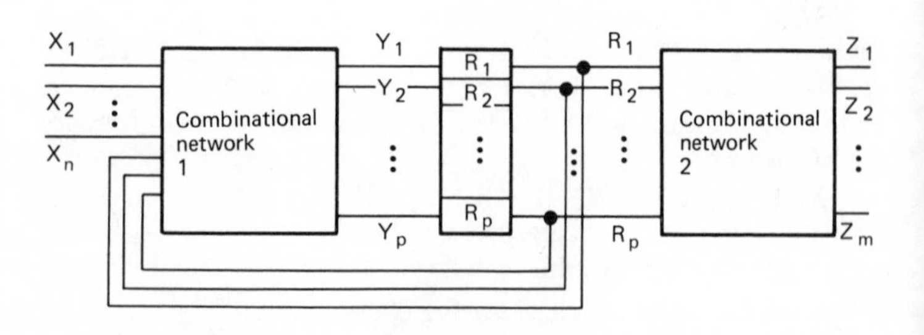

Figure 3.13

In this case

$$\begin{aligned} Z(t) &= \beta[R(t)] \\ R(t+1) &= \alpha[R(t), X(t)] \\ Z(t+1) &= \alpha[\beta(R(t), X(t)] \\ \text{or } Z(t) &= \alpha[\beta(R(t-1), X(t-1)] \end{aligned}$$

α is a Boolean function of combinational network 1 and β is a Boolean function of combinational network 2.

The Type 3 Circuit

In this variation a second combinational circuit is introduced which has as its inputs, the inputs $X_1, X_2 \ldots X_n$, as well as the register outputs $R_1, R_2 \ldots R_p$. This is shown in Figure 3.14.

In this case

$$\begin{aligned} Z(t) &= \alpha[R(t), X(t)] \\ \text{As before } R(t+1) &= \alpha[R(t), X(t)] \\ \text{So } Z(t+1) &= \alpha[R(t+1), X(t+1)] \\ &= \alpha[\{\alpha(R(t), X(t)\}\{X(t+1)\}] \\ \text{Or } Z(t) &= \alpha[\{\alpha(R(t-1), X(t-1)\}\{X(t)\}] \end{aligned}$$

The algebraic approach to the sequential circuit gives a concise mathematical description, which may help in classification and understanding, but is of little help in the actual design of the circuit. For this we turn to the use of the state diagram and state table, which are alternative and complementary ways of describing the circuit.

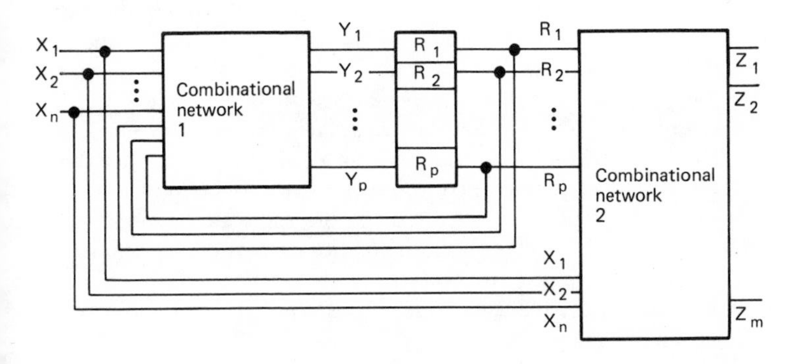

Figure 3.14

The State Diagram

To understand the behaviour of a sequential circuit, a convenient way is needed to represent the relations between different states, and input and output conditions, in graphical form. This can be done by means of a directed linear graph or digraph, which is known as the *state diagram*, in which the different states of the network are represented as nodes and the transitions between states as lines with arrows. Since digital networks are being considered they can only have a finite number of states.

Suppose as an example there is a network having three internal states Q_1, Q_2, Q_3 and two input conditions X_1, X_2 and two output conditions Z_1 and Z_2. This circuit can be represented by the diagram in Figure 3.15. The circles are the nodes of the graph, and inside are shown the different states Q_1, Q_2, Q_3, as are also the output for each state Z_1, Z_2, shown separated from the states by a slash. The directed lines represent the transitions and the input condition for the particular transition is written next to the line. Thus if the circuit is in the state

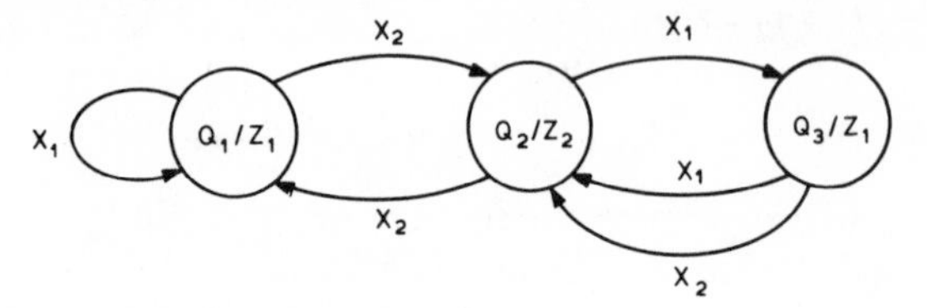

Figure 3.15

Q_1, there will be an output Z_1, and if an input condition X_1 is applied at the next change of state determined by the clock pulse, the arrow returns to the same node, and the state remains at Q_1. If however the input condition is X_2, the circuit will change from Q_1 to Q_2 and have an output Z_2. Now if the circuit is in state Q_2 with an input condition of X_1, the change will be from Q_2 to Q_3 with an output Z_1. And so on. If we assume the network is in state Q_1 at $t = 0$, the output sequence generated at times $t = 0, 1, 2, 3$ when the input sequence X_2, X_1, X_1, X_2, is applied, is Z_1, Z_2, Z_1, Z_2. Or again if the input sequence is X_1, X_2, X_2, X_1 then the output sequence is Z_1, Z_1, Z_2, Z_1. Since the two different input conditions may cause the same transition we may find more than one directed line between the same states, or it may be preferred to label one line for both conditions. Notice that this diagram is completely specified, in that for each input condition there is a directed line out of the state node. If this is not shown the next state is indeterminate, and we have an incompletely specified circuit.

Notice by the way, that the states Q_1, Q_2, are not the same as the flip-flops R, and for example with a circuit with 4 flip-flops it is possible to have 2^4 or 16 states. The circuit may be incompletely specified in another way, since the diagram shows 3 states, but for this 2 flip-flops are required giving $2^2 = 4$ states. This means in practice that there is a state Q_4 which never occurs but physically exists. This is quite legitimate, and the circuit will operate perfectly unless by some unforeseen circumstance it gets into state Q_4, where it will stay indefinitely. It is best practice therefore, to include all the states physically possible, with the directed lines for all input conditions.

The State Table – Synchronous Sequential Circuits

The state diagram is an excellent descriptive device and is a great help in understanding the sequence of operations. But for design, a formal method is needed for converting the description into switching functions, and hence into logical circuits. For this a state table is used which contains the same information as the state diagram in a form which is more easy to manipulate although less explanatory. Some may prefer to omit the state diagram and to construct the state table directly. The state table derived from the state diagram Figure 3.15 is shown in Table 3.3. The rows of the table correspond to the states of the network, and the columns to the input conditions. The output column shows the output for the present states.

Table 3.3

Present state	*Next states*		*Output*
	X_1	X_2	
Q_1	Q_1	Q_2	Z_1
Q_2	Q_3	Q_1	Z_2
Q_3	Q_2	Q_2	Z_1

As an example consider the design of a 2 bit up-down binary counter. When the input is X_1 corresponding to the 'up' condition the counter will continuously count the sequence 00, 01, 10, 11, 00 etc., and when the input is X_2 corresponding to the 'down' condition the counter will count continuously in the reverse sequence 00, 11, 10, 01, 00 etc. Let the input be a single line having binary 1 for X_1 and 0 for X_2, and the states Q_1, Q_2, Q_3, Q_4, correspond to outputs Z_1, Z_2, Z_3, Z_4, of 00, 01, 10, 10, 11, and R_1 represents 2^0, and R_2, 2^1. The state diagram describing this counter is shown in Figure 3.16.

For convenience the state table as in Table 3.3 is rearranged, Table 3.4, and in addition it is convenient to list the required inputs to the

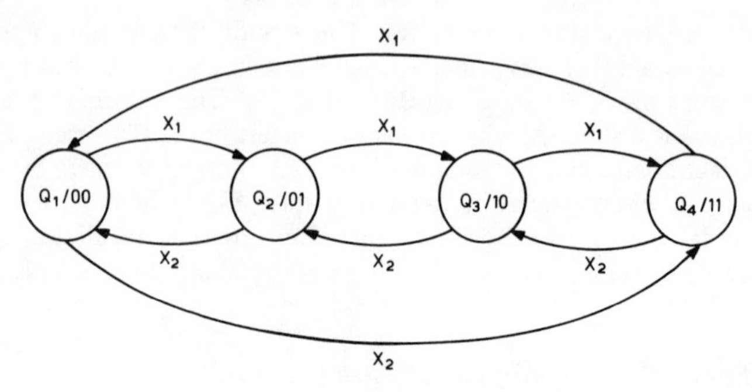

Figure 3.16

flip-flops in the counter in other columns. The counter is first designed with RS flip-flops, and then with JK flip-flops showing the saving in logic gates that can be obtained. The columns for R_A, S_A, R_B, S_B are constructed by reference to Table 3.1. The symbol Ø means that the particular flip-flop may receive either a 1 or 0 and is a 'don't care' condition. This occurs when a flip-flop which is already 0 must remain 0, but it does no harm if it is again set to 0, and likewise for a 1 remaining a 1.

Table 3.4

Input	*Present state*		*Next state*		*Output*					
X	Q_n		Q_{n+1}		Z		S_A	R_A	S_B	R_B
	A	B	A	B	A	B				
0	0	0	1	1	0	0	1	0	1	0
0	0	1	0	0	0	1	0	Ø	0	1
0	1	0	0	1	1	0	0	1	1	0
0	1	1	1	0	1	1	Ø	0	0	1
1	0	0	0	1	0	0	0	Ø	1	0
1	0	1	1	0	0	1	1	0	0	1
1	1	0	1	1	1	0	Ø	0	1	0
1	1	1	0	0	1	1	0	1	0	1

The S and R conditions can now be converted into logic networks in the conventional way (Figure 3.17). The logic diagram of this counter is shown in Figure 3.18, designed with NAND gates. If the counter is designed with JK flip-flops with reference to Table 3.2 there is a reduction in the number of gates needed due to the property of the JK flip-flop that it changes state when both J and K inputs are 1. The state table becomes that shown in Table 3.5.

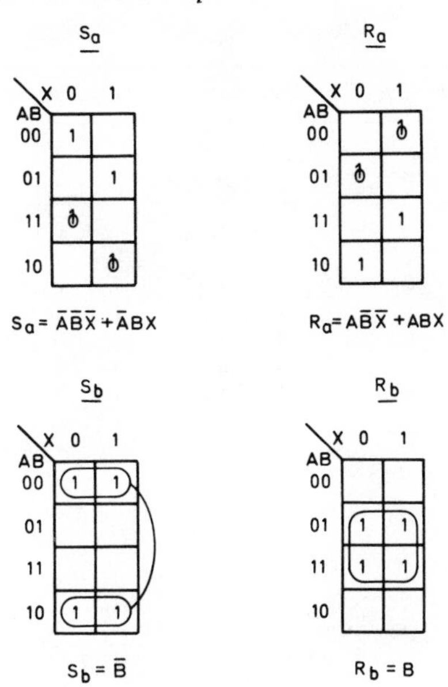

Figure 3.17

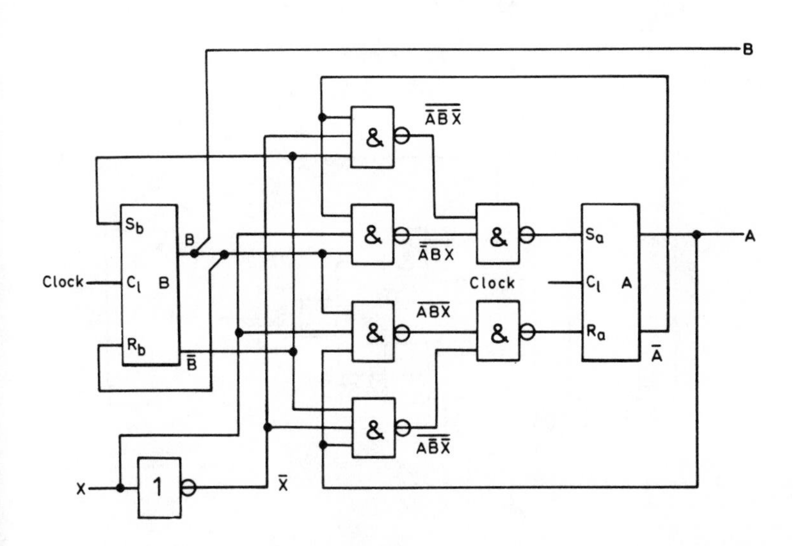

Figure 3.18

Table 3.5

Input	Present state		Next state		Output					
X	Q_n		Q_{n+1}		Z		J_A	K_A	J_B	K_B
	A	B	A	B	A	B				
0	0	0	1	1	0	0	1	ϕ	1	ϕ
0	0	1	0	0	0	1	0	ϕ	ϕ	1
0	1	0	0	1	1	0	ϕ	1	1	ϕ
0	1	1	1	0	1	1	ϕ	0	ϕ	1
1	0	0	0	1	0	0	0	ϕ	1	ϕ
1	0	1	1	0	0	1	1	ϕ	ϕ	1
1	1	0	1	1	1	0	ϕ	0	1	ϕ
1	1	1	0	0	1	1	ϕ	1	ϕ	1

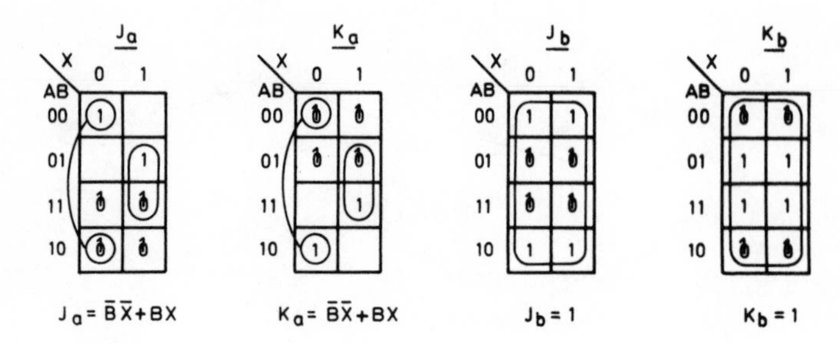

Figure 3.19

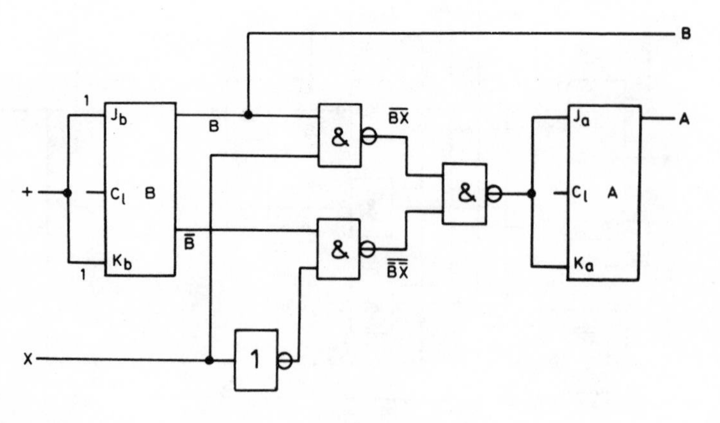

Figure 3.20

The logic functions for J_A, K_A, J_B, K_B, are then derived in Figure 3.19 whence we arrive at the logic diagram of Figure 3.20.

As a second example consider a more complicated network which has been constructed arbitrarily, but which might be required in the control system of a processor. Three input conditions occur X_1 ($\overline{A}\overline{B}$ or $\overline{A}B$), X_2 ($A\overline{B}$) and X_3 (AB), and the sequences can be seen from the

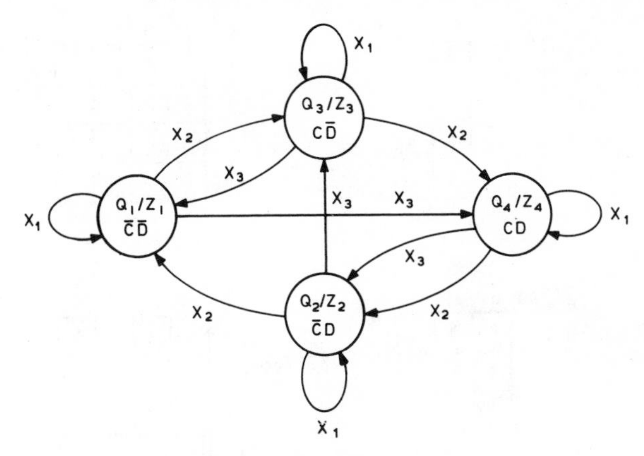

Figure 3.21

state diagram Figure 3.21 and the coding of the flip-flops C and D has been arbitrarily chosen as shown within node circles. Finally it is assumed that the outputs Z_1, Z_2, Z_3, Z_4, are the same as the flip-flop states.

Table 3.6

Input X		*Present state* Q_n		*Next state* Q_{n+1}		*Output* Z	*Flip-flop inputs*			
	A B		C D		C D	C D	J_C	K_C	J_D	K_D
X_1	00, 01	Q_1	0 0	Q_1	0 0	0 0	0	ϕ	0	ϕ
X_1	00, 01	Q_2	0 1	Q_2	0 1	0 1	0	ϕ	ϕ	0
X_1	00, 01	Q_3	1 0	Q_3	1 0	1 0	ϕ	0	0	ϕ
X_1	00, 01	Q_4	1 1	Q_4	1 1	1 1	ϕ	0	ϕ	0
X_2	1 0	Q_1	0 0	Q_3	1 0	0 0	1	ϕ	0	ϕ
X_2	1 0	Q_2	0 1	Q_1	0 0	0 1	0	ϕ	ϕ	1
X_2	1 0	Q_3	1 0	Q_4	1 1	1 0	ϕ	0	1	ϕ
X_2	1 0	Q_4	1 1	Q_2	0 1	1 1	ϕ	1	ϕ	0
X_3	1 1	Q_1	0 0	Q_4	1 1	0 0	1	ϕ	1	ϕ
X_3	1 1	Q_2	0 1	Q_3	1 0	0 1	1	ϕ	ϕ	1
X_3	1 1	Q_3	1 0	Q_1	0 0	1 0	ϕ	1	0	ϕ
X_3	1 1	Q_4	1 1	Q_2	0 1	1 1	ϕ	1	ϕ	0

From this state diagram the state table, Table 3.6 is produced and from this by orthodox techniques we derive the switching functions and the final logic circuit Figures 3.22 and 3.23.

It has been remarked that the states of the flip-flops were arbitrarily chosen. If the states had been chosen differently, it is possible that a simpler network would have resulted. The problem of optimum state

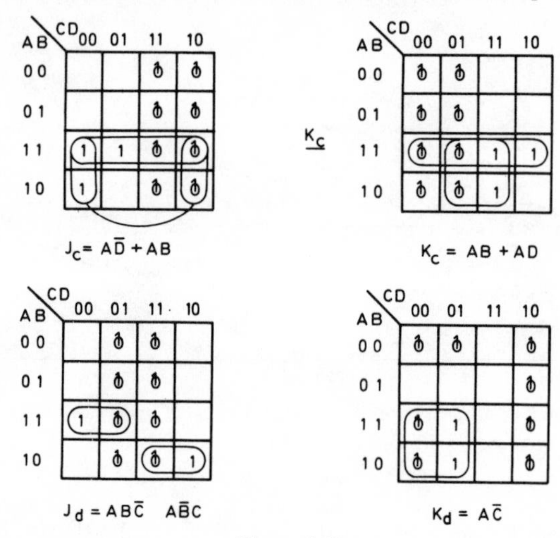

Figure 3.22

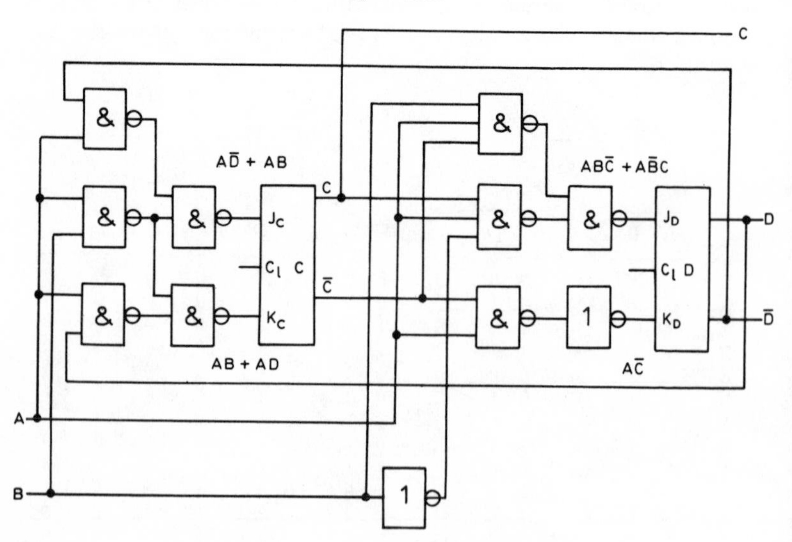

Figure 3.23

assignment is outside the scope of this book and those interested may wish to consult the references.

For simplicity the output functions Z_1, Z_2, Z_3, Z_4 were chosen to be the same as the flip-flop states. If they are different, further combinational logic must be designed having four inputs A, B, C, D to produce the desired Boolean output functions.

Asynchronous or Event Driven Sequential Circuits

It is not always possible to design in the tidy environment of synchronous clocked circuits, as in the control system of a processor. When dealing with peripheral circuits, signals are received at random times, and are not in synchronism with the computer clock, so that it may be necessary to synchronise the signal. In other cases, it may be necessary to design a sequential circuit, where no internal clock timing is available. In these cases, the circuits have to be designed to operate asynchronously.

The salient point of an asynchronous circuit is that the circuit changes state, at the moment an input signal changes. The flip-flops are not immobilised for the period while the clock is off, and unlike synchronous circuits no time is allowed for levels to be finally established before the clock pulse appears. It is also assumed that only one input can change at any instant. In practice this means two inputs cannot change within a short period in which the circuit fails to respond. Modern circuits are so fast that this is a very short time, and the probability of two inputs changing within this period is usually very small.

Design problems occur for two reasons. Two input signals may appear at approximately the same time, but in fact are slightly displaced from each other, so that sometimes one appears first, sometimes the other. This may cause the circuit to switch to a different state depending on which signal appears first. In a clocked circuit, this would not occur, because time would be allowed for both signals to be established before the clock pulse. The second difficulty is caused by differential delays in logic paths, which leads to input signals arriving in different order under different conditions. These so called race conditions, can be a source of unreliability in circuits if not properly understood.

An example of what can happen in an improperly designed circuit is shown in Figure 3.24, in the form of a state diagram.

It was required to set a circuit to give an output when X and Y were both 1. X and Y both set flip-flops of the type shown in Figure 3.2. Then, realising that X could arrive before Y, it was arranged that this

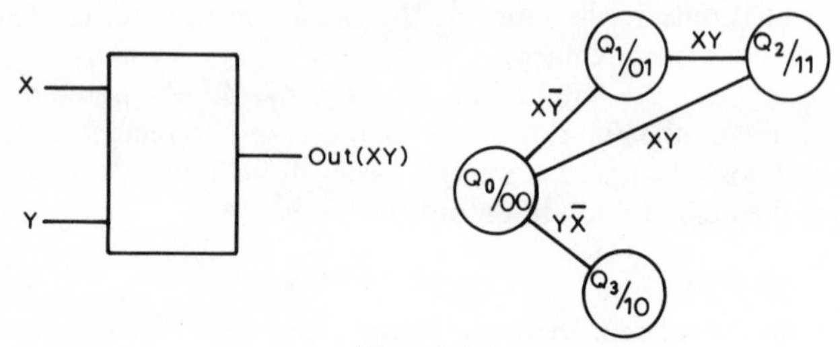

Figure 3.24

would set the circuit into state Q1 from Qo, and when Y became 1 the circuit would change to Q2 giving the required output.

However if Y arrived before X, the circuit was set into state Q3, from which no exit was provided, and the output for the input of X and Y together did not appear.

The principle adopted to overcome internal races in asynchronous circuits, is always to change only one flip-flop at a time. Thus in Figure 3.24 it is permissible to change from Qo with internal state 00 to Q1 with state 01, or from Q1 with state 01 to Q2 with state 11. But it is not permissible to transfer from Qo with state 00 to Q2 with state 11, because one is attempting to change two flip-flops simultaneously. By assigning the internal states appropriately this can be achieved, and the permissible transfers can be shown on race-free diagrams as shown in Figure 3.25 for 2, 3 and 4 bits.

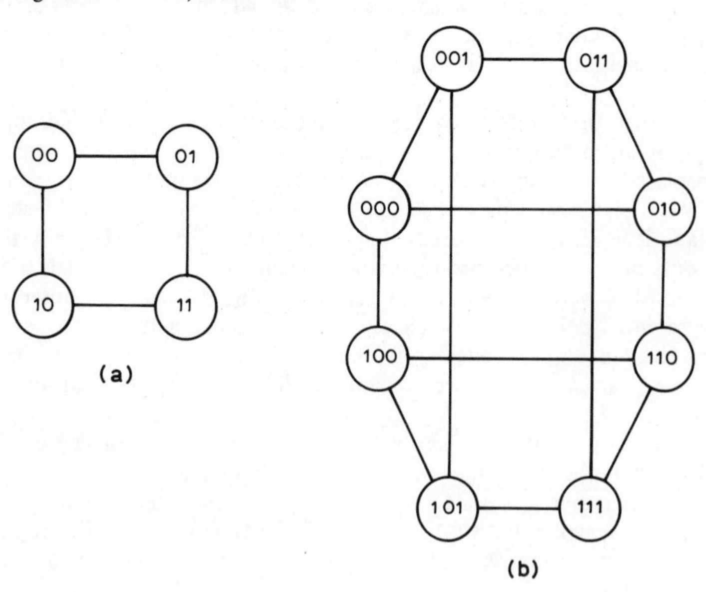

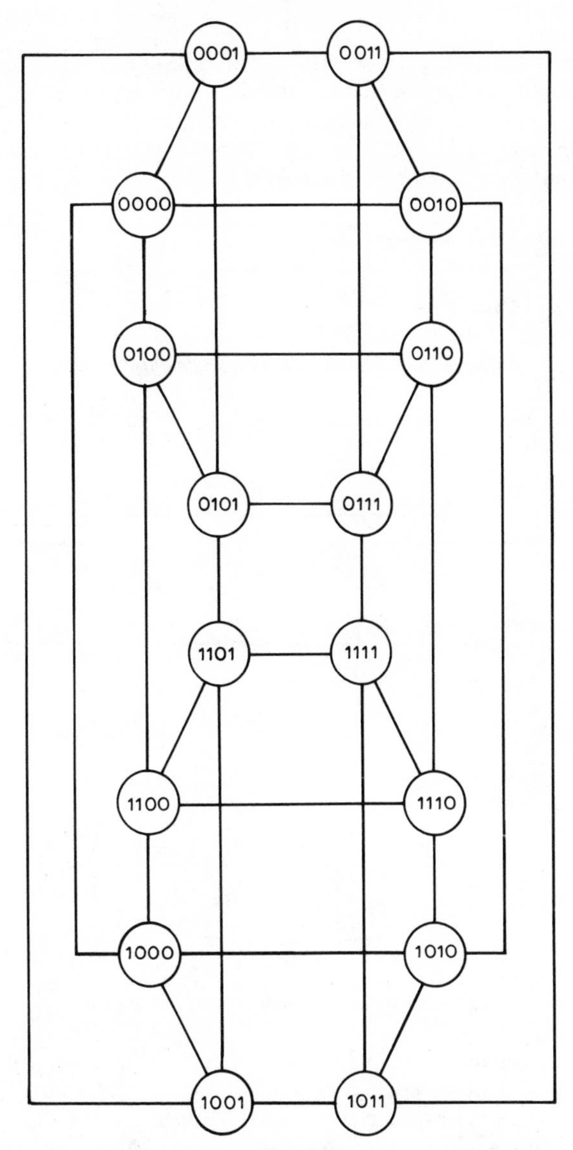

Figure 3.25

The procedure is explained best by the following examples. The first example shows a common problem that arises when operating a clocked system from an asynchronous input, such as a push button (assumed to have no bounce or noise), or a magnetic pick-up from a rotating shaft.

It is required to produce a single pulse, and only one, accurately aligned with the main timing clock. The clock is assumed to be at a high frequency of several megahertz, and the input signal is quite long, lasting for many clock periods. A schematic diagram of the system is shown in Figure 3.26, and a timing diagram explains the time relation of the input and output signals in Figure 3.27.

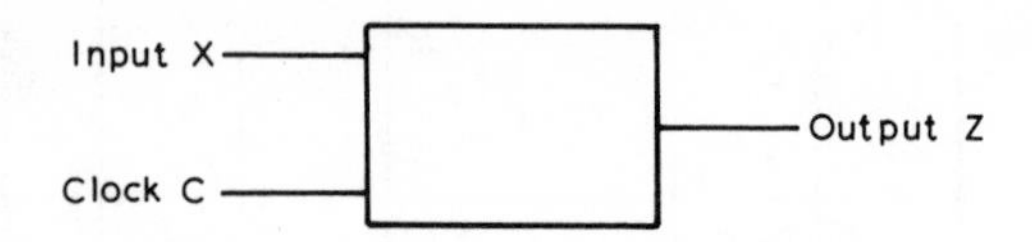

Figure 3.26 Schematic diagram, single pulse circuit

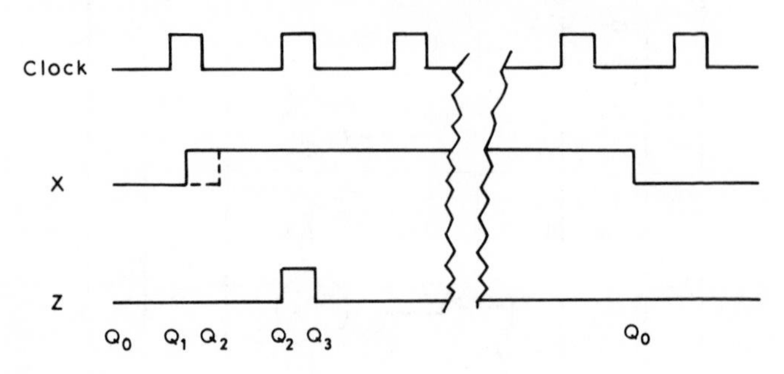

Figure 3.27

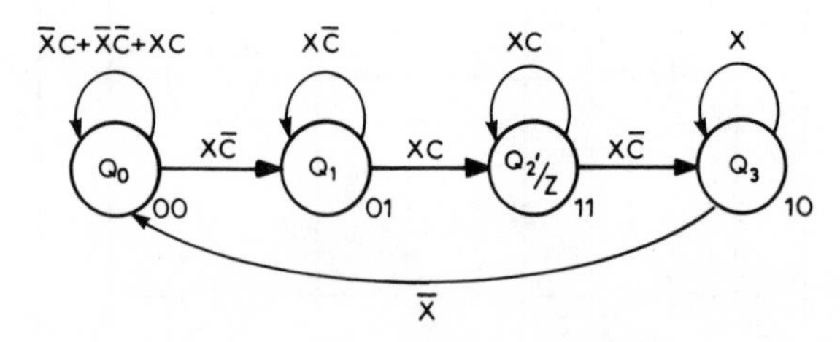

Figure 3.28 State diagram, single pulse circuit

A state diagram Figure 3.28, can now be developed, adopting a race free assignment of states. It is assumed that the circuit is initially in the Qo state. When the asynchronous signal X appears, it may, or may not, coincide with a clock pulse. An output signal cannot be emitted at this point, since being gated with the clock only a partial pulse might be generated, to which other circuits might respond unpredictably. Therefore, we first step to state Q1, at the point when the clock turns off. The circuit then waits until the next clock pulse and steps to state Q2, emitting an output. It remains in this state until the end of the clock pulse, and steps to state Q3. The circuit waits in this state until the input X turns off, and returns to its waiting state Qo for another input. In this way only one complete pulse, synchronous with the clock is emitted. The state diagram is a great help in understanding the circuit operation, and various arrangements can be tried.

Once the state diagram has been established, this can be converted into a state table in a similar way to a clocked circuit. The flip-flops will of course be of the Set, Reset type. This is shown in Table 3.7.

Table 3.7.

Input		*Present state*		*Next state*		*FF'A' inputs*		*FF'B' inputs*	
X	*C*	*A*	*B*	*A*	*B*	*R*	*S*	*R*	*S*
0	0	0	0	0	0	0	ϕ	0	ϕ
0	1	0	0	0	0	0	ϕ	0	ϕ
1	0	0	0	0	1	0	ϕ	1	0
1	1	0	0	0	0	0	ϕ	0	ϕ
0	0	0	1	0	1	0	ϕ	ϕ	0
0	1	0	1	0	1	0	ϕ	ϕ	0
1	0	0	1	0	1	0	ϕ	ϕ	0
1	1	0	1	1	1	1	0	ϕ	0
0	0	1	0	0	0	0	1	0	ϕ
0	1	1	0	0	0	0	1	0	ϕ
1	0	1	0	1	0	ϕ	0	0	ϕ
1	1	1	0	1	0	ϕ	0	0	ϕ
0	0	1	1	1	1	ϕ	0	ϕ	0
0	1	1	1	1	1	ϕ	0	ϕ	0
1	0	1	1	1	0	ϕ	0	0	1
1	1	1	1	1	1	ϕ	0	ϕ	0

Having evolved the state table it is now possible to use Karnaugh diagrams for the four flip inputs as shown in Figure 3.29. The flip-flop functions have been simplified by including the 'don't care' states.

The circuit diagram can now be drawn using simple flip-flops composed of two NAND gates. Since these require an inverted input, they can be set or reset directly from the NAND functions of R_A, S_A, R_B, and S_B. The result is shown in Figure 3.30.

The second example occurred in connection with a display for electrocardiograph waveforms. These were recorded on a portable tape recorder attached to the patient and are replayed at an accelerated speed of 60 times the original recording. The trigger signal for the CRT sweep is derived from the pulse (R wave) which is generated each time the ventricles contract, and the flyback occurs at each beat. Occasionally, however, the heart may behave abnormally, and a premature heart

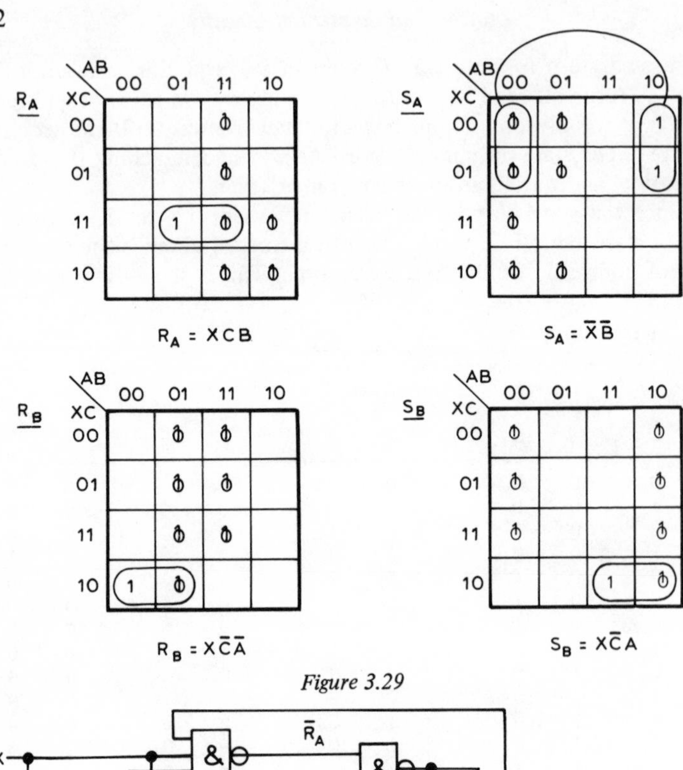

Figure 3.29

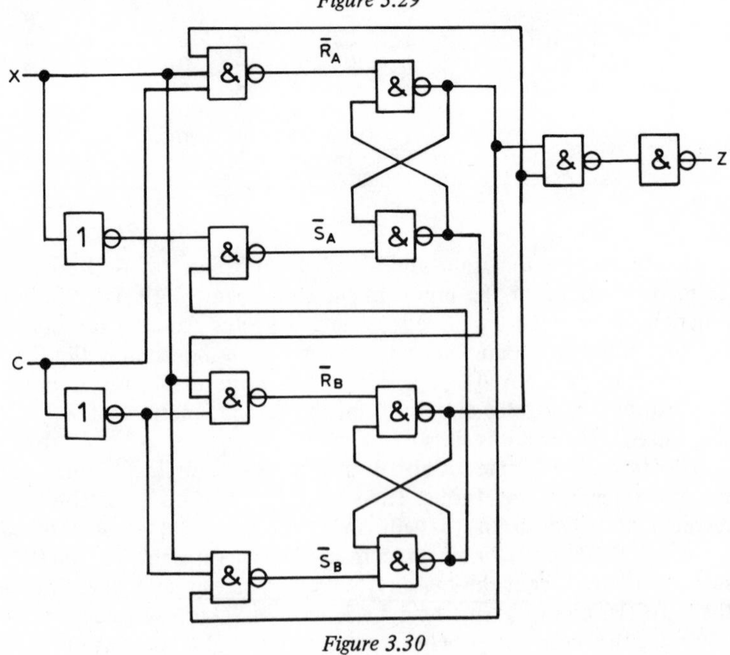

Figure 3.30

beat occurs, and then it is required that the sweep continues, without a flyback for the second, and premature beat.

For the design of the circuit, a heart trigger appears at each beat, and also a timed pulse is generated which represents the time within which a beat is classified as premature. This is a function of heart rate and is separately derived.

The output of the circuit starts and resets a binary counter, which, in turn is taken to a digital to analogue converter with the sweep waveform as its output.

A block diagram is shown in Figure 3.31.

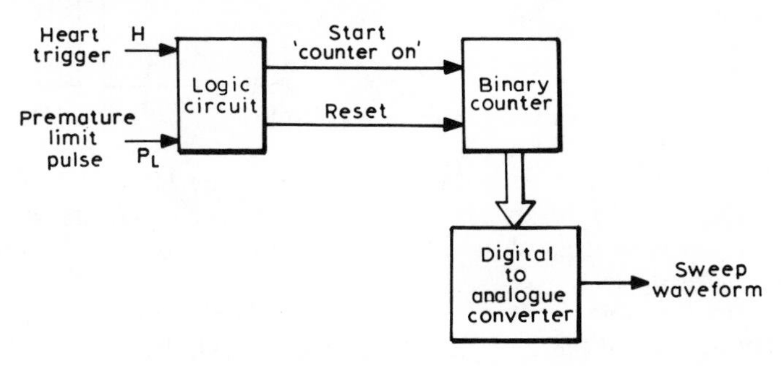

Figure 3.31

From the understanding of the circuit requirements, a state diagram can be constructed, as shown in Figure 3.32.

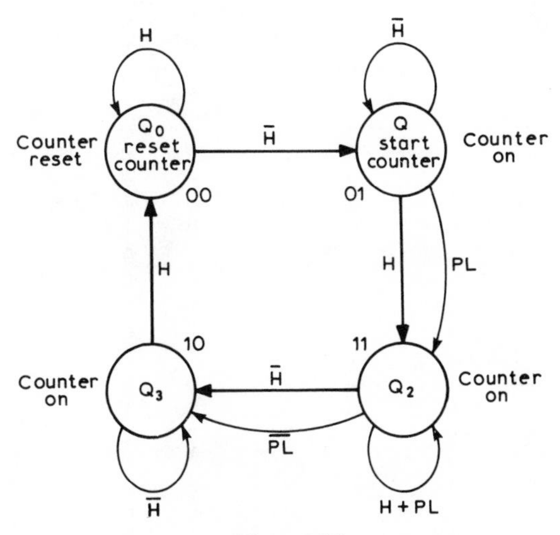

Figure 3.32

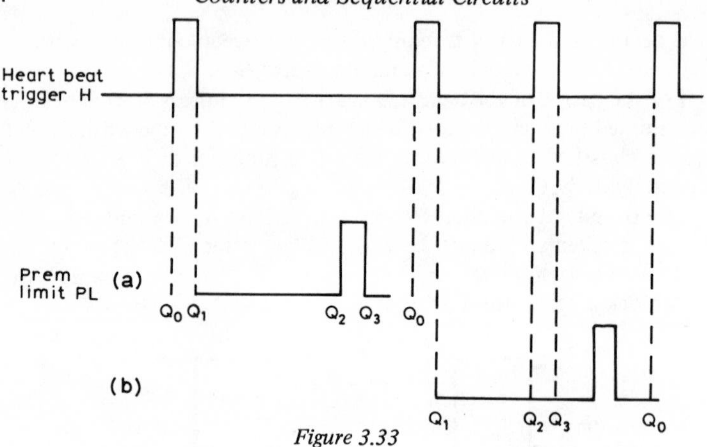

Figure 3.33

The timing is shown as pulse waveforms in Figure 3.33.

From the state diagram a state table can now be constructed. The states have been assigned to be race free, so that only one bit changes at any change of state.

From the table the Boolean functions for the flip-flop inputs can be obtained using the Karnaugh maps in Figure 3.34. This then leads to the logic diagram of Figure 3.35.

Table 3.8
From the table the Boolean functions for the flip-flop inputs can be obtained using the Karnaugh maps in Figure 3.34. This then leads to the logic diagram of Figure 3.35.

Input		*Present state*		*Next state*		*Flip flop A inputs*		*Flip flop B inputs*	
H	PL	A	B	A	B	R_A	S_A	R_B	S_B
0	0	0	0	0	1	0	ϕ	1	0
0	1	0	0	0	1	0	ϕ	1	0
1	0	0	0	0	0	0	ϕ	0	ϕ
1	1	0	0	0	0	0	ϕ	0	ϕ
0	0	0	1	0	1	0	ϕ	ϕ	0
0	1	0	1	1	1	1	0	ϕ	0
1	0	0	1	1	1	1	0	ϕ	0
1	1	0	1	1	1	1	0	ϕ	0
0	0	1	0	1	0	ϕ	0	0	ϕ
0	1	1	0	1	0	ϕ	0	0	ϕ
1	0	1	0	0	0	0	1	0	ϕ
1	1	1	0	0	0	0	1	0	ϕ
0	0	1	1	1	0	ϕ	0	0	1
0	1	1	1	1	0	ϕ	0	0	1
1	0	1	1	1	0	ϕ	0	0	1
1	1	1	1	1	1	ϕ	0	ϕ	0

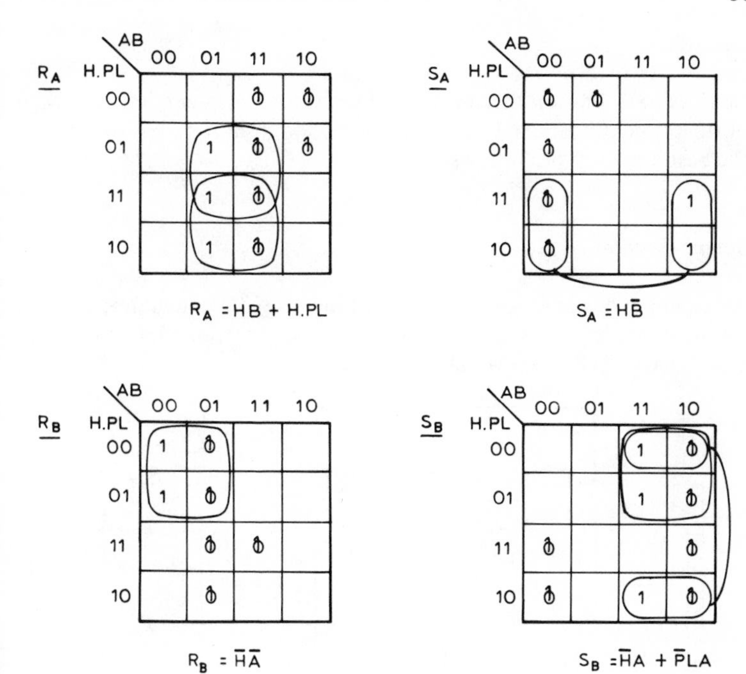

Figure 3.34

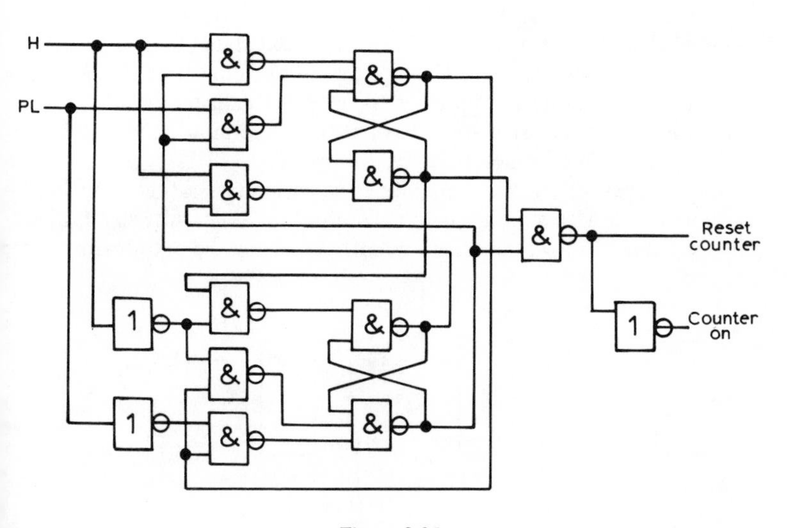

Figure 3.35

Counters

Counters are one of the most commonly used elements in the design of digital computers and other machines and a short survey of some of the best known types follows.

Binary Counter

An example has been given of a 2 bit binary up-down counter, and this can be extended to as great a number of bits as required. Consider the 4 bit binary counter shown in Figure 3.36.

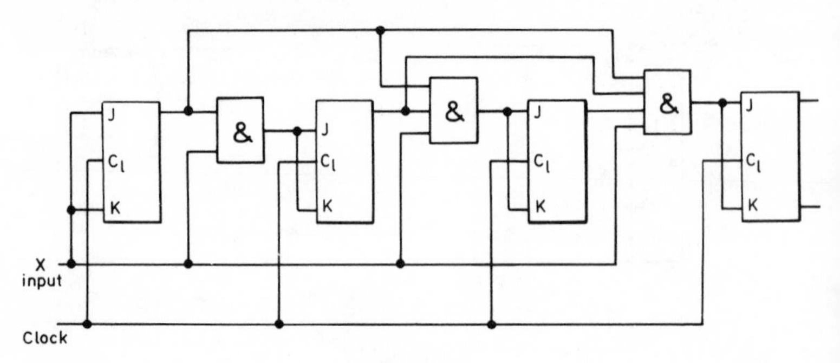

Figure 3.36

This counter is designed with a synchronous carry so that when the counter changes from the state 1111 to the next state 0000, all the flip-flops switch simultaneously. This is achieved by connecting the outputs from the less significant flip-flops to an AND gate to the next. This results in each successive stage having one more input, and in a large counter this soon becomes undesirably large.

Early types of binary were designed as circuits rather than logic networks, and with simple single rank flip-flops. The pulse signifying a change from 1 to 0 was obtained by differentiating the output from the

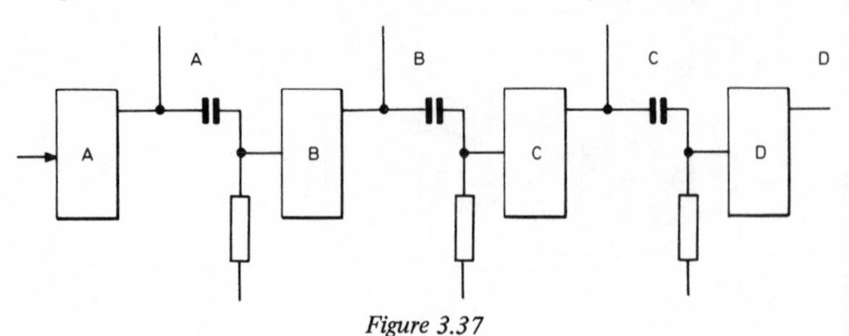

Figure 3.37

flip-flop by an *RC* circuit as shown in Figure 3.37. This circuit has the disadvantage that when a change from 1111 to 0000 occurs, the change ripples through the counter so that A first changes from 1 to 0, then B, and so on. But it does have the advantage of identical repetitive elements. Binary ripple counters are now being made with up to 16 stages on a single integrated circuit, and their speed is such that the carry ripples through the circuit so rapidly that the time taken causes no difficulty in many applications. The detection of the change from 1 to 0 is derived logically. Binary counters are the most economical in the number of components, and are widely used in computer design to perform a variety of functions.

It is frequently found necessary to count to some number which is not an exact binary value. This can be done by choosing the number of flip-flops to give the next higher binary number (2^n) than the count required, and then truncating the count before it is fully completed. As a simple example of this take the case of a counter needed to count to 5 and return to 0, the state diagram being as shown in Figure 3.38, and the logic network in Figure 3.39.

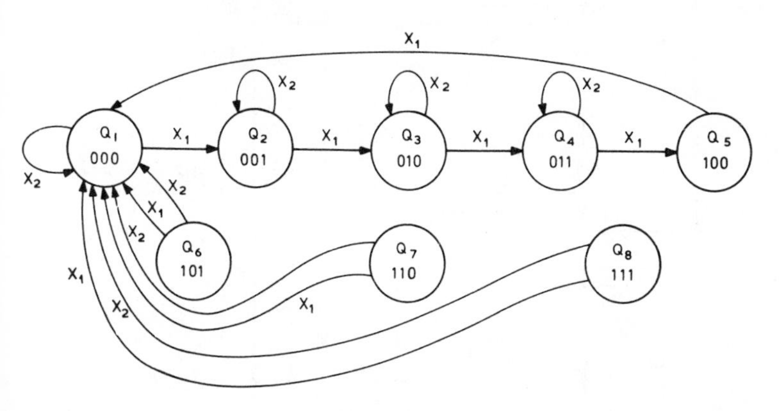

Figure 3.38

Notice that the redundant states Q_6, Q_7, Q_8 have been designed to return to state Q_1 immediately whether the input condition is X_1 or X_2. This causes the counter to immediately reset to state Q_1 if it accidentally gets into one of the redundant states. This can very easily happen when switching on, when the counter will be in a random state, and can also be due to an error in operation. The first effect can be circumvented alternatively by a forced reset before starting to operate, thus simplying the gating circuits. When designing a counter with redundant states these situations should be remembered.

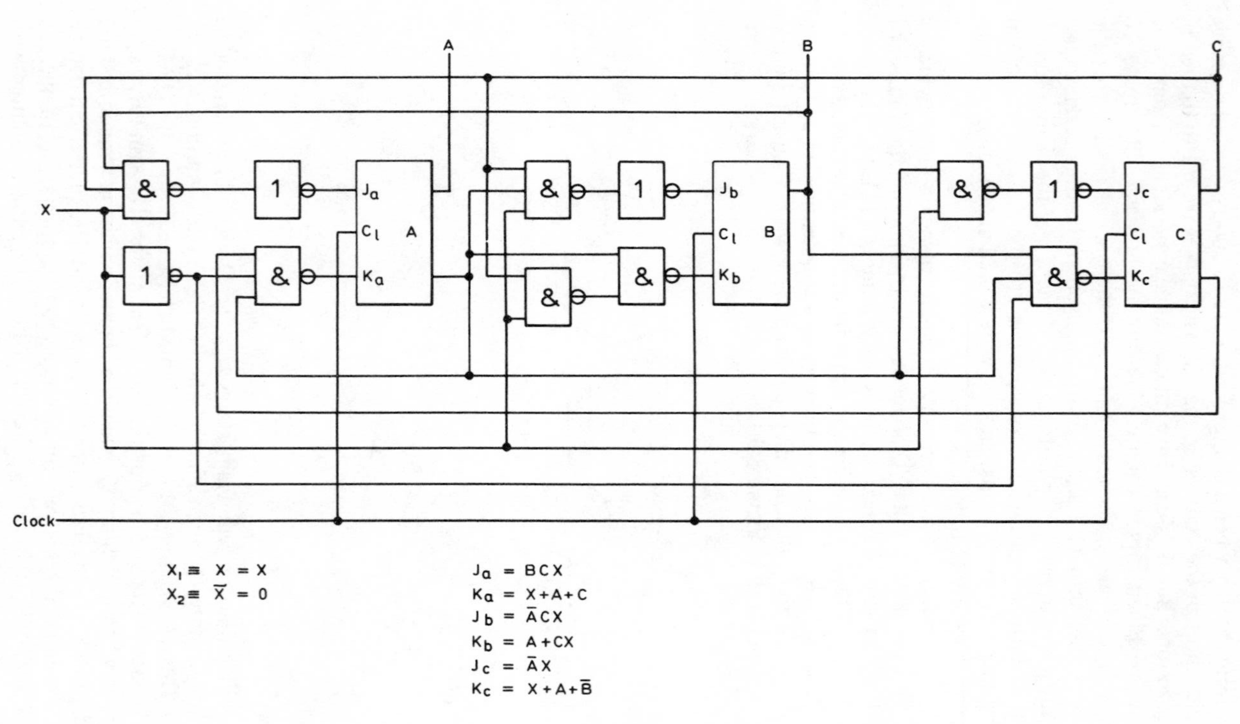
A
B
C
X
Clock
Ja
Cl
Ka
Jb
Kb
Jc
Kc
1
&
X1 ≡ X = X
X2 ≡ X̄ = 0
Ja = BCX
Ka = X+A+C
Jb = ĀCX
Kb = A+CX
Jc = ĀX
Kc = X+A+B̄

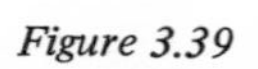
Figure 3.39

Counters with variable sequences

It is sometimes necessary to build a counter that can be truncated to a different sequence length depending on some external control signal. The block diagram of a counter truncated to produce 2 different sequence lengths is shown in Figure 3.40, and its state table in Table 3.9.

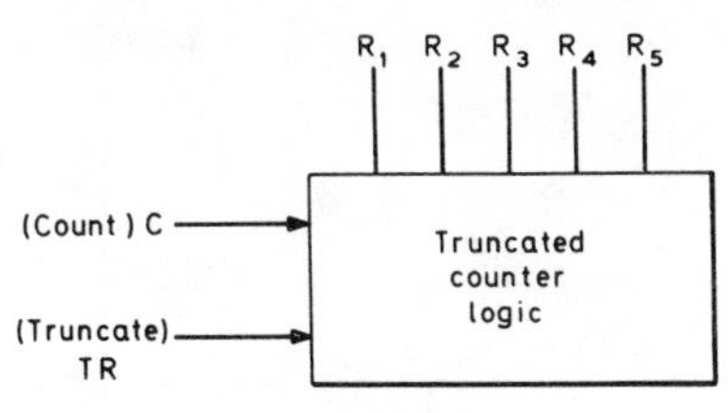

Figure 3.40

Table 3.7

Present state Q_n	*Next states* X_1	Q_{n+1} X_2
Q_1	Q_2	Q_2
Q_2	Q_3	Q_3
Q_3	Q_4	Q_4
Q_4	Q_5	Q_1
Q_5	Q_6	Q_1
Q_6	Q_1	Q_1
.	.	.
.	.	.
.	.	.
.	.	.
.	.	.
.	.	.
.	.	.
.	.	.
Q_m	Q_1	Q_1

The Bi-quinary Counter

The bi-quinary counter was popular in binary decimal computers and is still valuable. In the bi-quinary system the count of 10 is made by counting 2 × 5 as can be seen in the output code in Table 3.8 with its block diagram Figure 3.41. The divide by 5 counter is similar to the truncated counter previously described, and the divide by 2 stage is merely a single counter flip-flop. The arrangement can be reversed to produce the qui-binary counter.

Table 3.10

Number	A	B	C	D
0	0	0	0	0
1	0	0	0	1
2	0	0	1	0
3	0	0	1	1
4	0	1	0	0
5	1	0	0	0
6	1	0	0	1
7	1	0	1	0
8	1	0	1	1
9	1	1	0	0

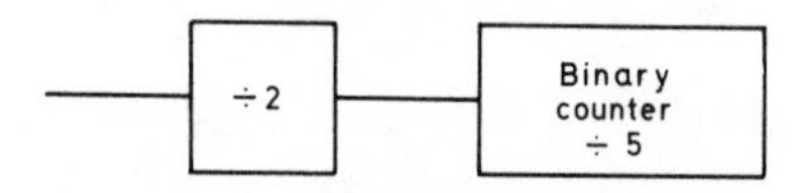

Figure 3.41

Constant Weight Counters

The term 'constant weight' refers to the fact that there are always the same number of 1's and 0's in the counting code. It is applicable when it is needed to keep a constant current load to some device, and thus reducing power supply requirements. An example is the 2 out of 5

Table 3.11

Number	A	B	C	D	E
0	1	1	0	0	0
1	1	0	1	0	0
2	1	0	0	1	0
3	1	0	0	0	1
4	0	1	1	0	0
5	0	1	0	1	0
6	0	1	0	0	1
7	0	0	1	1	0
8	0	0	1	0	1
9	0	0	0	1	1

counter. If we have 5 flip-flops ABCDE, we may choose 2 out of 5 in 5!/3!2! ways, which gives 10 combinations with 2 flip-flops in the 1 state (Table 3.11).

The Ring Counter

This is the oldest counting circuit, being analogous to the wheel counters used in mechanical calculating machines, and was originally designed as a special circuit. The ENIAC machine contained hundreds of these. It is still used to switch control points in time sequence and consists basically of a shift register in which a single 1 is set into the flip-flop and the rest to 0. Giving a shift pulse causes the 1 to be stepped down the register. If the end of the register is joined to the start, it forms a ring and the 1 will continue to circulate indefinitely, otherwise it will be lost when it reaches the end of the register.

The Johnson Counter

This counter can be very useful for generating timing control pulses, and is made by connecting the output of a shift register to its input in reverse as shown in Figure 3.42. With 5 shift register flip-flops the counting sequence is as shown in Table 3.12.

Table 3.12

Number	A	B	C	D	E
0	0	0	0	0	0
1	1	0	0	0	0
2	1	1	0	0	0
3	1	1	1	0	0
4	1	1	1	1	0
5	1	1	1	1	1
6	0	1	1	1	1
7	0	0	1	1	1
8	0	0	0	1	1
9	0	0	0	0	1

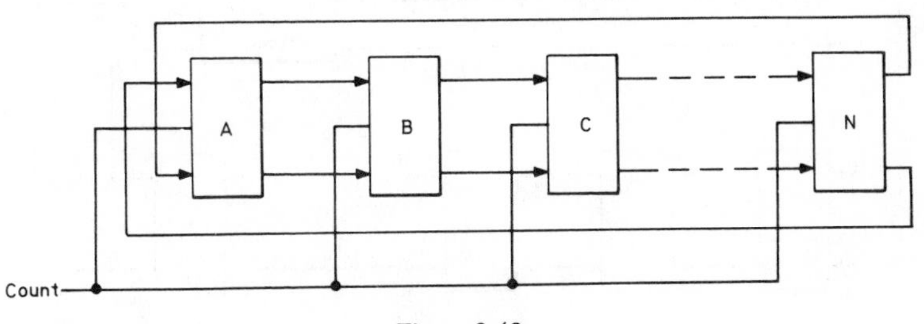

Figure 3.42

By taking the AND function of two inputs it is possible to obtain a timing pulse of any length up to 5 steps. For example the function AB gives a 1 output at No 1 only, but AE gives a 1 output for periods 1, 2, 3 and 4.

Shift Register Sequence Generators

These represent a class of circuit which have been investigated in detail by mathematicians. They have found application as pseudo-random number generators, for testing servo mechanisms and communication systems, and also in the generation and decoding of error correction

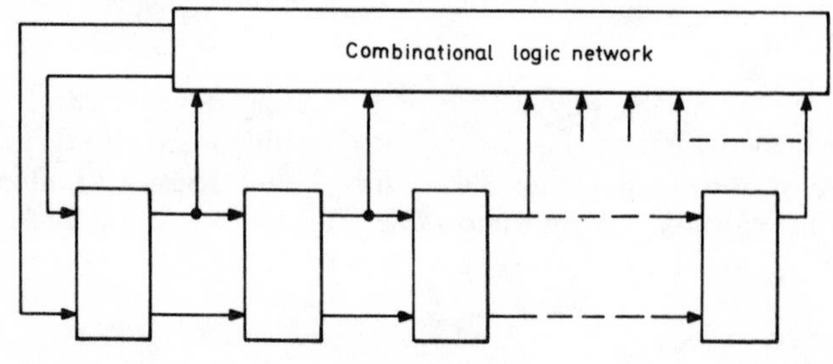

Figure 3.43

codes. Figure 3.43 shows the general block diagram of such a sequence generator. When the combinational logic network consists of only 'exclusive OR' gates, the output is the (modulo-two) sum of phase shifted versions of the register contents, then generators of this type are known as linear sequential networks. These are of interest in radar, communications systems, and control systems because they can be used to generate pseudo-random binary sequences. A simple example is shown in Figure 3.44 which generates a pseudo-random sequence of 15 bits in length. By suitable choice of the number of shift register stages, and feedback network, long pseudo-random sequences can be produced.

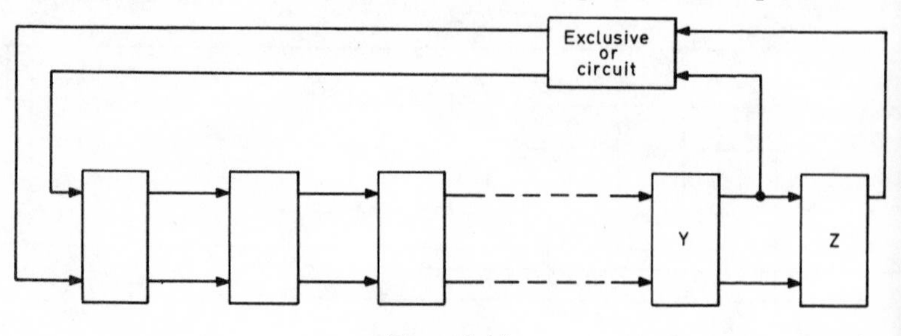

Figure 3.44

Problems

1. The excess 3 code is formed by adding 3 to the decimal value and converting to the binary equivalent and is as shown below:

0	0011
1	0100
2	0101
3	0110
4	0111
5	1000
6	1001
7	1010
8	1011
9	1100

   It has the important property that its decimal complement can be obtained by changing all ones to zeros and all zeros to ones.

   Design a counter using NAND logic and JK flip-flops and having three inputs. (a) Count–which causes the counter to step to the next higher number. (b) Complement–which causes the counter contents to be changed to its complement and (c) Clear–which causes the counter to be set to decimal zero (0011). Derive the state table and hence derive the gating structure for each flip-flop.

2. An integrated circuit is needed for an electronic watch. The counter should be able to count clock pulses in binary coded decimal from 0 to 9, or by the change of a single connection from the positive level to earth to be truncated to count in scale of 6. There should also be a 'clear' input. Draw a state diagram and derive the state table. By means of Karnaugh maps derive NAND circuits with JK flip-flops to achieve this.

3. A counter is to be built with a single binary input X and two outputs A and B using NAND gates and clocked JK flip-flops to perform as

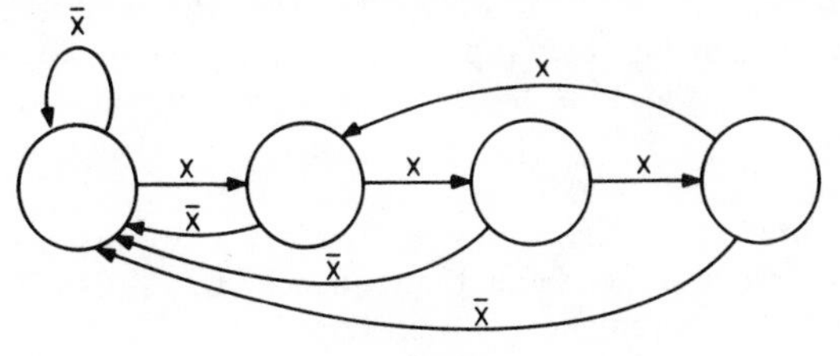

Figure 3.45

shown in the state diagram Figure 3.45. Write a state table and hence using Boolean algebra or Karnaugh maps produce a minimised logic diagram of the counter.

4. A synchronous clocked sequential circuit contains two JK flip-flops A and B, and has two inputs X and Y as shown in Figure 3.46. The circuit cycles continuously in one of four different sequences determined by the input condition, which can change synchronously at the instant when A and B both become 0. When X = 0 and Y = 0, the sequence is 00, 01, 10, 11, 00 etc; when X = 0 and Y = 1 the sequence is 00, 11, 10, 01, 00 etc., when X = 1 and Y = 0 the sequence is 00, 10, 01, 11, 00 etc., and when X = 1 and Y = 1 the sequence is 00, 11, 01, 10, 00 etc.

   Design a circuit to perform the required sequences under the various input conditions, by means of a state diagram and state table using JK flip-flops and NAND logic.

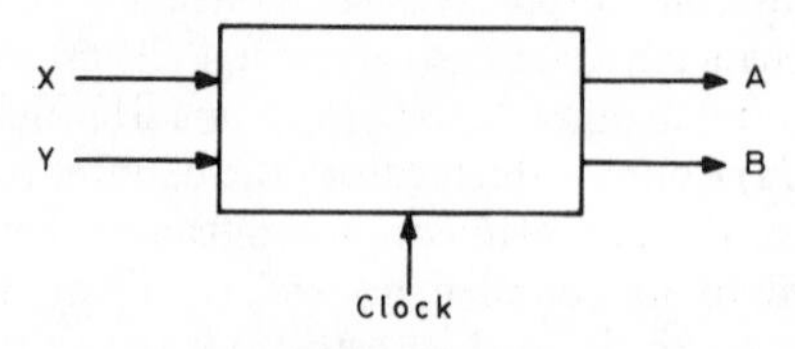

Figure 3.46

5. A sequential circuit has a single input and output. A synchronous random binary sequence is applied to the input, and the output is required to emit a single pulse every time the serial binary number 7 is detected. That is, when the sequence. . . XXXX 1110 XXXX is found (X's mean either 1 or 0).

   Draw a state diagram for the circuit showing the transitions and internal and output states, and from this derive the state table. Hence design a circuit to perform the desired function.

6. A clocked sequential circuit has two inputs and two outputs, and it is assumed that the inputs change synchronously with clock. If all input states can occur, it is required that the output indicates by being 1, which input or inputs last changed state. By means of a state diagram and state table, design a logic circuit to perform this function.

7. A sequential circuit has an input C and two outputs A and B. When C = 1, the circuit generates the sequence 00, 11, 01, 10, 00. When C = 0 the circuit remains in its existing state. Assume that the circuit is constructed with clocked JK flip-flops and NAND gates.

Draw the state diagram for this circuit, and write the state table. Hence derive a logic circuit which will produce the above sequence.

8. A pseudo-random number generator has four flip-flops in its shift register. By the addition of suitable gates, cause the counting sequence to be shortened to some chosen number, say 11.

9. Show the number of gating elements that are saved in problems 4 and 7 by using the property of the JK flip-flop to change state when both J and K are 1, compared with the use of RS flip-flops.

10. A clocked sequential circuit has two synchronous binary inputs A and B and a single output. It is required that the circuit delivers a single output only, whenever the sequence A = 1, B = 1, A = 1 occurs. If A and B are both 0, the circuit remains in its existing state, and A and B can never be 1 at the same time.

    Design a circuit by means of a state diagram and table to perform this function and implement it with clocked JK flip-flops and NAND gates.

11. The circuit shown in Figure 3.47 consists of a shift register having four flip-flops A, B, C, D. The Input to the shift register is the 'exclusive OR' function of the contents of the two final stages. The outputs of the four flip-flops are connected by way of combinational logic to four output lines W, X, Y, Z. Shift pulses are supplied to the register, which starts in the initial state 0001. It is required that the lines W, X, Y, Z, repeatedly produce the sequence of binary coded decimal digits for π (314159265358979) or e.

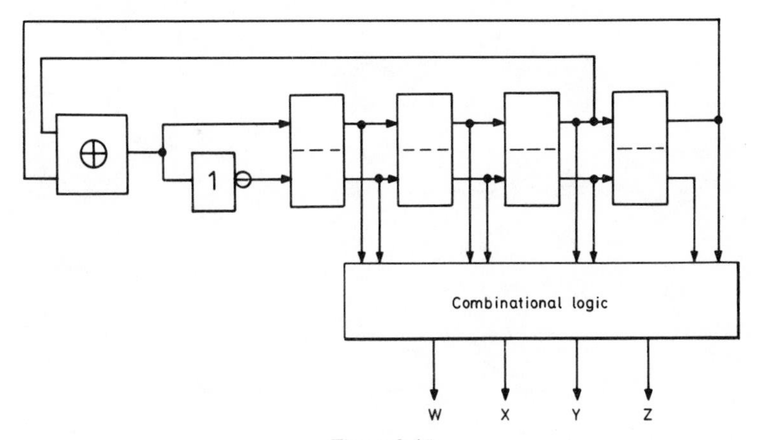

Figure 3.47

Derive the sequence produced in the shift register and design the minimised combinational logic to generate the required sequence on WXYZ. The problem can be varied by using either NAND gates only, or other logic elements.

REFERENCES

1. CLARE, C.R., *Designing Logic Systems Using State Machines.* Mc.Graw-Hill (1973)
2. LIND, L.F., *Analysis and Design of Sequential Digital Systems.* Macmillan (1977)
3. PETERSON, G.R. and HILL, J.F., *Introduction to Switching Theory and Logical Design.* John Wiley (1974)
4. PORAT, D.I., *Introduction to Digital Techniques.* John Wiley (1979)
5. MANO, M.M., *Digital Logic and Computer Design.* Prentice-Hall (1979)

Chapter 4

Number Representation in Computers

Number Systems

The number systems, with which we are most familiar, all use positional notation to represent a number. Although various number bases have been used by different races and nations throughout history, the base of 10 has been commonly accepted and is now universally established in the decimal system. It appears to have its origin in counting on the fingers, and the word 'digit' is derived from the Latin word for finger. The procedure of counting numbers greater than the base is to increase the digit which is one place to the left by one, each time the digit is increased by ten steps. One can therefore represent a decimal number: $a_n \ldots a_3 a_2 a_1 a_0$ in the form:

$$N = a_0 10^0 + a_1 10^1 + a_1 10^2 + a_3 10^3 \ldots + a_n 10^n .$$

The ordering of the coefficients is reversed in the polynomial in contrast to the number, which is a relic of the fact that our number system came to us from Arabia, in which writing is normally from right to left.

The system can be generalised for a uniform system of any base as the polynomial

$$N = a_0 b^0 + a_1 b^1 + a_2 b^2 + a_3 b^3 \ldots + a_n b^n$$

where b is the base, and the coefficients are $a_0 \ldots a_n$ which are normally written down to represent the number.

A step further in complication are the nonuniform based number systems which are now happily being outmoded, but some of which we still have with us for a time, such as tons, hundredweights, and quarters; seconds, minutes, hours and days; and these can be represented as the polynomial.

$$N = a_0 b_0 + a_1 (b_0) b_1 + a_2 (b_0 b_1) b_2 + a_3 (b_0 b_1 b_2) b_3 \ldots \text{where } b_0 = 1$$

Table 4.1 shows the numbers up to 16 represented in bases up to 10,

Table 4.1

Base	2	3	4	5	6	7	8	9	10
	0000	000	00	00	00	00	00	00	00
	0001	001	01	01	01	01	01	01	01
	0010	002	02	02	02	02	02	02	02
	0011	010	03	03	03	03	03	03	03
	0100	011	10	04	04	04	04	04	04
	0101	012	11	10	05	05	05	05	05
	0110	020	12	11	10	06	06	06	06
N	0111	021	13	12	11	10	07	07	07
	1000	022	20	13	12	11	10	08	08
	1001	100	21	14	13	12	11	10	09
	1010	101	22	20	14	13	12	11	10
	1011	102	23	21	15	14	13	12	11
	1100	110	30	22	20	15	14	13	12
	1101	111	31	23	21	16	15	14	13
	1110	112	32	24	22	20	16	15	14
	1111	120	33	30	23	21	17	16	15

and these have been given names. The common bases being (2) binary, (3) ternary, (5) quinary, (8) octal or octonary, (10) decimal or denary, and (12) duodecimal or duodenary.
Fractional numbers are represented by the use of a negative exponent thus:

$$N = a_{-m}b^{-m} + \ldots + a_{-2}b^{-2} + a_{-1}b^{-1} + a_0b^0 + a_1b^1$$

As an example the number 127.384 would be represented by the polynomial:

$$(127.384)_{10} = 4 \times 10^{-3} + 8 \times 10^{-2} + 3 \times 10^{-1} + 7 \times 1$$
$$+ 2 \times 10 + 1 \times 10^2.$$

The separation between the fractional portion of the number and the integer is called the point in the base in use, so that one may have a binary point, ternary point or decimal point.

Conversion of Numbers to other Bases

Numbers can be converted from one base to another, and the conversion to decimal can be easily done by evaluating the polynomial. Thus the binary number 10110.101 is converted to decimal as follows:

$$(101110{\cdot}101)_2 = 1 \times 2^{-3} + 0 \times 1^{-2} + 1 \times 2^{-1} + 0 \times 2^0 + 1 \times 2^1$$
$$+ 1 \times 2^2 + 1 \times 2^3 + 0 \times 2^4 + 1 \times 2^5$$
$$= 1/8 + 1/2 + 2 + 4 + 8 + 32$$
$$= 46.625$$

In the conversion of numbers from decimal to another base, the integer portion and fraction are treated separately. To convert the integer portion, this is divided by the base to which the number is to be converted and the remainder is the least significant integer digit. Repeated divisions give the higher digits as remainders, and the process is repeated until the remaining integral part is zero. Thus to convert the decimal number 27 to binary we have:

	Binary Remainder
2 | 27	
2 | 13	1
2 | 6	1
2 | 3	0
2 | 1	1
0	1

Thus $(27)_{10} = (11011)_2$.

The fractional portion is converted by multiplying by the base to which the number is converted. If the result of this multiplication is greater than 1, the most significant digit in the fraction is 1; if it is less than 1, then the digit is zero. Repeated multiplications produce successive digits until the remaining fractional portion to be multiplied is zero. Thus converting the decimal fraction 0.34375 to a binary fraction we have:

	Converted result
0.34375 X 2 = .6875	0.0
0.6875 X 2 = 1.375	0.01
0.375 X 2 = 0.75	0.010
0.75 X 2 = 1.5	0.0101
1.5 X 2 = 3.0	0.01011

The Binary Number System

From engineering circuit design considerations it is found that the maximum immunity to circuit noise, and to variations in device parameters, is obtained by restricting the devices to just two levels, or 'on' and 'off'. This implies a natural preference for binary devices, and thus the binary number system has been generally adopted for computer arithmetic. It can also be shown that the binary system is the most efficient way of storing and representing numbers. In binary arithmetic units the same type of logic devices can be used as in the control system, so that they are ubiquitous throughout the machine. There have been attempts to introduce decimal counting devices, but these have not been successful because they were special only to the arithmetic unit, as well as being more inefficient.

A binary integer is therefore represented in the form $a_n a_{n-1} \cdot \ldots a_4 a_3 a_2 a_1 a_0$, where the coefficients a_0, a_1, etc. may be either 1 or 0, and in the computer it would appear as:

Binary integer X - - - - - - X X X X X

a_n a_4 a_3 a_2 a_1 a_0

where X can be either 1 or 0. ↑ binary point here

A positive binary fraction would appear within the computer as:

Binary fraction ↑ X X X X X - - - - - X

a_{-1} a_{-2} a_{-3} a_{-4} a_{-5} a_{-n}

binary point here

Binary numbers are added in a similar way to decimal numbers, but the sum for each digit can be only 1 or 0, and there is a carry to the next higher digit if the sum in that position is greater than 1. This can be summarised in a table for two binary digits A and B and a carry from the previous position.

A	0	0	0	0	1	1	1	1
B	0	0	1	1	0	0	1	1
Carry from next lower position	0	1	0	1	0	1	0	1
Sum	0	1	1	0	1	0	0	1
Carry out to next higher position	0	0	0	1	0	1	1	1

As an example we have:

	1	1	0	1	0	0	1
	1	0	1	1	0	1	0
Sum 1	1	0	0	0	0	1	1

The term binary digit has been abbreviated to 'bit' throughout the computer world.

Decimal Codes

Whatever base it may be decided to use for calculation within the computer, we are faced with the fact that in the outside world human beings prefer to think and work with numbers represented in decimal, or perhaps in one of the other units of weights and measures. It is therefore necessary to translate from decimal to binary, and vice versa, if binary is chosen as the internal number system. The translation of large numbers requires either a computer program, or a fairly elaborate hardware converter and this could not be justified for each input-output human interface, but large scale integrated circuits may make this feasible in the future. The usual solution is to split the problem into two parts, first, representing the decimal digit as a binary code, which can be done with fairly simple coding and decoding networks; and second, translating from the coded form to the true binary form by means of a program.

There are a large number of possible decimal codes, but experience has eliminated all but a few, the most important being binary coded decimal (BCD), in which each decimal digit is represented by its binary equivalent, which can be seen in Table 4.1. Thus the number 437 would appear as 0100, 0011, 0111, in BCD, whereas in pure binary it would appear as 110110101, which is found by the decimal to binary conversion given earlier.

The Teletype code embodies the BCD code within it, but with the added complication of extra codes for representing letters and symbols. So that in this case the BCD code is used as a communication code. The 1 out of 10 hole code used in punched cards is easily converted to BCD for input-output purposes.

Another binary decimal code with important applications is the Excess 3 code. This code is formed by adding 3 to the decimal digit and converting it to binary, and has the useful property of being a self-complementing code. This means that when all 1's are changed to 0, and all 0's changed to 1's the code becomes the nine's complement of the decimal number. This is useful in devices which operate directly in coded decimal arithmetic, such as small calculators.

Gray Code

Up to this point we have described only weighted number systems or codes, except for Excess 3 code which is not weighted for the decimal code itself. In a weighted code each bit or digit represents a given weight or value and the magnitude of the number can be found by adding the weights. For the purposes of performing and instrumenting arithmetic operations it is almost essential to use weighted codes.

There is a large body of knowledge on codes for varying purposes which cannot be explored here, but a code which is of importance to the ordinary computer user, and should be described is the Gray code.

A useful application of Gray codes is in connection with position transducers, such as shaft encoders, in which the value representing the angular position of the shaft is read from a disc, either by optical means with photocells, or by brush contacts on a commutator. If the natural binary code is engraved on the disc, it can be seen that in certain cases many bits can change together when counting from one number to the next. For example counting from 7 to 8 in binary requires that 4 bits change, and 1023 to 1024 requires that 10 bits change simultaneously. Large errors can ensue if all the bits do not simultaneously change due to small misalignment. The Gray code overcomes this problem by arranging that only one bit changes state when counting from one number to the next, so that the maximum error cannot be greater than 1.

Gray codes are a class of codes which have the property that they have 'unit distance' i.e. a single bit change, between one number and the next. However it is also necessary to be able to easily translate from the Gray code to natural binary code for arithmetic purposes, and this property is found with one particular Gray code called 'reflected binary code' and often called the Gray code.

The unit distance behaviour can be clearly demonstrated on a Karnaugh map, as shown in Figure 4.1, in which each step in counting causes a change to an adjacent cell in the map. The pattern shown is

AB \ CDE	000	001	011	010	110	111	101	100
00	0	1	2	3	4	5	6	7
01	15	14	13	12	11	10	9	8
11	16	17	18	19	20	21	22	23
10	31	30	29	28	27	26	25	24

Figure 4.1

for a 5 bit 'reflected binary code', but it is clear that many different patterns could be fitted into the map all exhibiting the unit distance attribute. The reflected binary code for the numbers 0–15 is shown in Table 4.2. The important property of the 'reflected binary code' is that a simple mathematical relation exists between it and binary code. If we denote binary code bits by

$$b_n, b_{n-1}, b_{n-2}, \ldots b_1,$$

and Gray or reflected binary code bits by

$$g_n, g_{n-1}, g_{n-2}, \ldots g_1,$$

the reflected binary code bits are found by the following rules:

$$g_n = b_n$$

$$g_{n-1} = b_n \oplus b_{n-1}$$

$$g_{n-2} = b_{n-1} \oplus b_{n-2}$$

$$g_1 = b_2 \oplus b_1$$

Where $\oplus$ means the 'exclusive OR' function.
It can be seen that a 'reflected binary code' of any size can be constructed, and it will have the same number of bits as the natural binary code.

The inverse operation of conversion from the reflected binary code to the natural binary code is found by

$$b_n = g_n$$

$$b_{n-1} = b_n \oplus g_{n-1}$$

$$b_{n-2} = b_{n-1} \oplus g_{n-2}$$

.

.

$$b_1 = b_2 \oplus g_1$$

In both cases the computation starts at the most significant or most left hand bit and proceeds to the least significant bit.

Table 4.2

0	0000
1	0001
2	0011
3	0010
4	0110
5	0111
6	0101
7	0100
8	1100
9	1101
10	1111
11	1110
12	1010
13	1011
14	1001
15	1000

Signed Numbers

It is clearly essential to be able to represent both positive and negative numbers within the computer, and several different methods of representing signed numbers have been used.

Sign and Magnitude

This representation is the simplest to understand and the least commonly used. It is analogous to the way in which one writes a number by hand with a + or – in front, but in the computer the convention is to indicate + by a 0, and – by a 1. This 'sign bit' can be at either end of the binary number, but it is usually placed at the left hand end. The number part is always either a positive binary integer or fraction, thus

$$+7 \equiv \underset{\substack{S \\ +}}{0}\,\underset{7}{0111}$$

$$-9 \equiv \underset{\substack{S \\ -}}{1}\,\underset{9}{1001}$$

$$-0.6875 \equiv \underset{S}{1}\,1011$$
$$-0.6875$$

This system has advantages at the input and output devices, since the number is in the positive form with a separate sign as in the manual convention. The disadvantage appears in the arithmetic unit, where the decision to add or subtract depend not only on the function of addition or subtraction, but also on the sign of the number, and this leads to complications in the control circuits. Furthermore, it is necessary to know the sign of the number before the operation, so that the sign bit

Table 4.3

Coded form	*Value represented*	
1111	−7	
1110	−6	
1101	−5	
1100	−4	negative numbers
1011	−3	
1010	−2	
1001	−1	
1000	−0	
0111	+7	
0110	+6	
0101	+5	
0100	+4	positive numbers
0011	+3	
0010	+2	
0001	+1	
0000	+0	

must be inspected first. In a serial machine, which must have the number presented to the adder with the least significant bit first, the sign bit would have to be ahead of the least significant bit of the number. The sign and magnitude system for binary numbers in the range –7 to +7, with the sign bit at the left hand end is shown in Table 4.3.

Negative Numbers represented in Complementary Form

The arithmetic unit of a machine can be simplified if only an adder is needed instead of an adder-subtractor, and it is possible to do this by using complement representation for negative numbers in which subtraction is performed by addition of the complement. The method of operating with negative numbers represented by their complements has a history going back to mechanical calculators and electro-mechanical punched card machines which operated with numbers in base 10, and this continues with modern processors with numbers in the binary system.

Two types of complement representation are in use, and are sometimes known as the *range complement* and the *digit complement.*

Range Complement Representation

Considering first the range complement representation, the largest number that can be represented with n digits is given by:

$$N = b^n - 1$$

where b is the base and n the number of digits. A constant is now attached to the number to indicate the sign and this is chosen as

$$K = b^{n+1}.$$

The range of the number then becomes b^{n+1}, in which

$$(b^n - 1) \geqslant x \geqslant 0$$

are called positive numbers, and

$$(b^{n+1} - 1) \geqslant x \geqslant b^n$$

are negative numbers. If b is 10 this is called the 'ten's' complement system and if b is 2 it is called the 'two's' complement system. This will become clearer in Table 4.4 where the complement system for binary numbers in the range $2^4 = 16$ is shown.

Table 4.4

Natural value	*Two's complement form*	*Value represented*	
	range $\equiv b^{n+1} \equiv (10000)_2$		
15	1111	−1	Complement forms
14	1110	−2	
13	1101	−3	
12	1100	−4	
11	1011	−5	
10	1010	−6	
9	1001	−7	
8	1000	−8	
7	0111	+7	True forms
6	0110	+6	
5	0101	+5	
4	0100	+4	
3	0011	+3	
2	0010	+2	
1	0001	+1	
0	0000	+0	

A simple algorithm is needed for calculating the complement, and this is done, by subtracting the number x from b^{n+1} (or in our example $16–x$). The complementation process is performed separately for each digit, and consists of subtracting each digit from the base, which in the case of binary, consists of changing all 1's to 0, and all 0's to 1; a final correction of 1 is then added to the least significant digit or bit. In the decimal case the operation consists of subtracting each digit from 9 and adding a correction of 1 to the least significant digit.

In the binary example $16 - x$ can be written as

$$16 - x = (15 - x) + 1.$$

Thus the 16's complement of 7 is given by

$$16 - 7 = 9 \equiv 1001 \equiv -7$$

The algorithm is then

$+7$	$\equiv 0111$
Invert 1's and 0's	1000
Add 1	$1001 \equiv -7$

A further complementation of a negative number gives its true value:

-7	$\equiv 1001$
Invert 1's and 0's	0110
Add 1	$0111 \equiv +7$

To subtract b from a, b is first complemented and then added to a. Any carry appearing from the most significant digit is discarded. The following examples show a positive and negative result:

```
Example: (5–4)                 +4   0100
   (Two's complement of 4)     –4   1100

                               +5   0101
                               –4   1100
                                    ----
        carry discarded             ←
                                    0001 ≡ +1
                                    ↑
                                    S
                                    +

Example: (4–5)                 +5   0101
   (Two's complement of 5)     –5   1011

                               +4   0100
                               –5   1011
                                    ----
                                    1111 ≡ –1
                                    ↑
                                    S
                                    –
```

Since we see that this is a negative number from its sign, we recomplement it to find its true value.

```
             Thus    1111
Invert 1's and 0's   0000
            Add 1       1
                     ----
                     0001  true value is 1.
```

The system is easy to implement in the binary case since it is merely necessary to gate the binary number through inverters and add 1 to the least significant bit, which is usually done by presetting the input carry flip-flop to 1.

To illustrate the system in other bases an example is given in ten's complement. Suppose the range to be 1000, and 0 to 99 are positive, while 900 to 999 are negative numbers represented in ten's complement. The thousands complement is given by

$$1000 - x = (999 - x) + 1.$$

To find the ten's complement of $027 \equiv +27$:

$$1000 - 27 = 973 \equiv -27$$

and this can be formed by subtracting 027 from 999 digit by digit and adding one.

	999
	027
Subtracting each digit from 9	972
Add 1	1
	973

To subtract 27 from 83 we can add the complement

	083
	973
	056
discard the carry	←

A special case always exists in the range complement system, which is half the range constant, (represented in our binary example as –8), to which no positive true form exists. Complementation of this number gives an incorrect result, in fact the same number, and it must be considered as unusable.

Digit Complement Representation

The alternative system is called the digit complement system, and is represented in binary systems as the one's complement, or in decimal systems as the nine's complement. In this case the complementation constant is

$$K = b^{n+1} - 1$$

and the complement is found by

$$(b^{n+1} - x) - 1$$

or in our example

$$(16 - x) - 1.$$

This gives the simplest possible procedure for complementation in binary, the 1's and 0's are merely inverted and it is not necessary to add 1 as in the two's complement. But the procedure for addition is more complex, since any carry from the most significant bit must be added into the least significant position; this is known as the 'end around carry'. The values for positive and negative complementary numbers with a range of 16 represented in one's complement is shown in Table 4.5.

Table 4.5

Natural value	*One's complement form*	*Value represented*	
15	1111	−0	complement of 0 (−0)
14	1110	−1	
13	1101	−2	
12	1100	−3	complement form negative numbers
11	1011	−4	
10	1010	−5	
9	1001	−6	
8	1000	−7	
7	0111	+7	
6	0110	+6	
5	0101	+5	
4	0100	+4	true form positive numbers
3	0011	+3	
2	0010	+2	
1	0001	+1	
0	0000	+0	True form of 0 (+0)

To form the one's complement of 7 we change 1's to 0, and 0's to 1 thus:

$$+7 \equiv 0111$$
$$-7 \equiv 1000$$

To subtract 4 from 5, we first complement 4, then add it to 5, and add the 'end around carry' to the least significant bit.
Thus

$$+4 \equiv 0100$$
$$-4 \equiv 1011$$

```
                  +5   0101
one's complement  −4   1011
                      ------
                      ⌐0000
                      └→  1
                      ------
                       0001 ≡ +1
                       ↑
                       S
                       +
```

```
Example: (4–5)    +4   0100
                  −5   1010
                      ------
                       1110
                       ↑
                       S
                       −
```

Since this is seen to be negative, we can recomplement to find its true value:

	1110
complementing	$0001 \equiv +1$

Overflow Detection

It is not always possible for a programmer to foresee the size of the numbers which will occur in his calculations. If the number becomes larger than the number of bits provided, it causes an overflow and produces an error, the effect being that a carry is propagated into the sign bit incorrectly. This can be easily detected by simple logic when two's complement representation is used, which causes an overflow flip-flop to be set. When an overflow occurs, the carry from bit n (the sign bit) is different to that from bit $n-1$; if these two carries are both 1, or both 0 the result is correct. This does not apply in the one's complement system.

Multiple Precision Arithmetic

When it is necessary to handle numbers that require a greater number of bits than are provided in the arithmetic unit, it may be necessary for the programmer to divide the number into two or more parts, each of the size available in the machine. A small program is written which causes the least significant portions of the number to be added first. There may be a carry from the lower significant parts to the more significant parts, and this is stored in the carry flip-flop of the adder, where it can remain until the next more significant parts are added, when this carry is automatically added.

Floating Point Numbers

When it is necessary to represent very large or very small numbers, or numbers which vary very widely in magnitude, floating point representation can be used. On moderate sized machines this is handled by means of programs, but in the largest machines, particularly those used for scientific calculations, floating point arithmetic units are incorporated, some of which are as large as fair sized processors in themselves.

Everyone is familiar with decimal floating point notation, in which a number is represented by two portions, the exponent and mantissa, plus the sign. The exponent describes the order of magnitude of the number, in decimal the power of 10, and the mantissa describes the size of the number within the range. For example, the mass of the electron is given as 9.108×10^{-31} kilograms. It is equally possible to represent both the exponent and mantissa as binary numbers.

As an illustration, consider the floating point representation on the IBM 360 system. The floating point data can occupy a full word of 32 bits or a double length word of 64 bits. It consists of a sign bit, seven bits to represent the exponent, and either 24 or 56 bits to represent the mantissa, as shown in Figure 4.2.

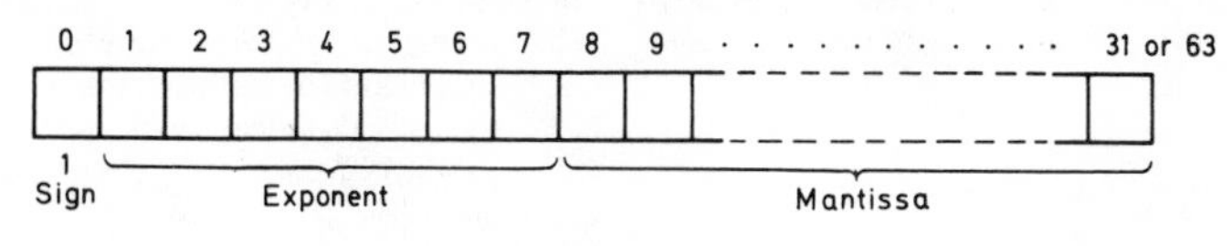

Figure 4.2

The binary point of the mantissa is considered to be to the left of its most significant bit. The exponent portion in bits 1 to 7 indicates the binary power having a range of –64 to +63, which corresponds to the values 0 to 127, and 64 must be subtracted to find the actual exponent. It is thus possible to represent numbers in the range

$$(\pm)2^{-64} \text{ to } (\pm)2^{+63}$$

to an accuracy of 24 or 56 significant bits.

The subject of floating point arithmetic is too complicated to pursue further here, and the interested reader is referred to references 1, 2 and 3.

Comparison of One's and Two's Complement systems

The one's and two's complement are compared in Table 4.6

Binary Coded Decimal Arithmetic

It is often desirable in calculators, electronic cash registers and other small special purpose computing devices to perform arithmetic directly in binary coded decimal form and avoid the necessity for conversion to and from binary code. The addition of two digits in any base, must result in a number less than twice the base, so that only one carry can be generated, the largest sum in decimal being 9+9 = 18. The natural

Table 4.6

Two's complement	*One's complement*
Rule for complementation	
(a) Change 1's to 0 and 0's to 1. (b) Add 1 to least significant bit.	(a) Change 1's to 0 and 0's to 1.
Rule for addition with complementary numbers	
(a) Add in binary and discard the carry from the most significant (or sign) bit.	(a) Add in binary. (b) If there is a 1 carry from the most significant (or sign) bit, add this to the least significant bit, and propagate any further carries if necessary.
Advantages and disadvantages	
(a) Complementation more complicated due to need for adding 1 to least significant bit. But this can easily be implemented by setting carry input flip-flop to 1.	(a) Simplest process for complementation.
(b) Addition simple. Most significant carry just discarded.	(b) Addition more complicated due to 'end around carry'.
(c) Convenient for serial arithmetic.	(c) Inconvenient for serial arithmetic due to 'end around carry'.
(d) Simple for multiple precision arithmetic.	(d) Difficult for multiple precision, because 'end around carry' must be from most significant portion to least significant portion of the number.
(e) One value for zero.	(e) Two values for zero, positive and negative.
(f) Overflow detection simple.	(f) Not good for overflow detection.

binary and binary coded decimal (BCD) representation of the sum of two numbers with results 0 to 18 are shown in Table 4.7.

It can be seen that the BCD and binary sums are the same for 0 to 9. From 10 to 18 a correction has to be made, being the binary addition of 6 to the sum, i.e. the difference between 10 and 16. This correction must be added in a second addition operation depending on the result of the first sum, and the conditions where it is necessary to add the correction must be detected from it. The results 16, 17 and 18 in the binary sum are signified by a binary carry from bit 4. Results in the range 10 to 15 have to be found by a logical test on the binary sum bits, or by experimentally adding 0110 (6) in a separate adder and testing again for a carry from bit 4. The first and simplest way is shown

Table 4.7

Sum a+b	*Natural binary code*		*BCD representation*	
	01234567		0123 4567	
00	00000000		0000 0000	Binary and BCD the same—no correction
01	00000001		0000 0001	
02	00000010		0000 0010	
03	00000011		0000 0011	
04	00000100		0000 0100	
05	00000101		0000 0101	
06	00000110		0000 0110	
07	00000111		0000 0111	
08	00001000		0000 1000	
09	00001001		0000 1001	
10	00001010		0001 0000	Correction add 6 (0110)
11	00001011		0001 0001	
12	00001100		0001 0010	
13	00001101		0001 0011	
14	00001110		0001 0100	
15	00001111		0001 0101	
16	00010000	Binary carry occurs from bit 4	0001 0110	
17	00010001		0001 0111	
18	00010010		0001 1000	

in the implementation of a BCD adder in Chapter 5. An example of addition in BCD is:

Decimal sum			3807		
			5924		
			9731		
BCD 3807	0011	1000	0000	0111	
BCD 5924	0101	1001	0010	0100	
Binary Sum	1001 ←	0001	0010	1011	
Add correction due to carry between groups ←		0110		0110	→ Add correction, sum greater than 9
	1001	0111	0011	0001	
BCD result	9	7	3	1	

Subtraction is performed by the addition of the nine's or ten's complement. It is clear that the generation of the nines complement of the BCD code is not straightforward, but several decimal codes have been discovered that can be easily complemented, the best known being the excess 3 code. The principle of this code is that half the correction constant of 6 is added to the BCD value, and the nine's complement is generated by merely inverting 1's and 0's, as in the binary case, as shown in Table 4.8. When two excess 3 digits are added, the total added excess is 6, and this causes a binary carry to the next decimal group if the sum is greater than 9, and a correction of 3 must be added to the result to form the correct new excess 3 code. If the sum is less than or

Table 4.8

True value	*Excess 3 code*		*Nine's complement*
0	0011	1100	9
1	0100	1011	8
2	0101	1010	7
3	0110	1001	6
4	0111	1000	5
5	1000	0111	4
6	1001	0110	3
7	1010	0101	2
8	1011	0100	1
9	1100	0011	0

Table 4.9

Decimal sum	*Binary sum of excess 3 codes*	*Correct excess 3 sum*	*Correction*
0	0110	0011	Subtract 3 (add 1101)
1	0111	0100	
2	1000	0101	
3	1001	0110	
4	1010	0111	
5	1011	1000	
6	1100	1001	
7	1101	1010	
8	1110	1011	
9	1111	1100	
10	carry 0000	carry 0011	Add 3 (0011)
11	,, 0001	,, 0100	
12	,, 0010	,, 0101	
13	,, 0011	,, 0110	
14	,, 0100	,, 0111	
15	,, 0101	,, 1000	
16	,, 0110	,, 1001	
17	,, 0111	,, 1010	
18	,, 1000	,, 1011	

equal to 9, it contains twice the excess and 3 must be subtracted. This is shown in Table 4.9.

An example of addition in Excess 3 code is now shown. Notice that 3 is subtracted by adding the 16's complement of 3, i.e. 13 in binary and discarding the carry between groups.

Decimal Sum	
	3807
	5924
	9731

Excess 3 3807	0110	1011	0011	1010	
Excess 3 5924	1000	1100	0101	0111	
Binary Sum	1111 ←	0111	1001 ←	0001	
	1101	0011	1101	0011	←(+ 3 where carry between groups
	← 1100	1010 ←	0110	0100	−3 where no carry between groups)
	↑ Discard		↑ Discard		
	9	7	3	1	

Choice of the Operating Base for the Processor

A major decision in the design of a processor is whether the machine should operate directly in decimal, or in a simpler base, probably binary, and convert to and from decimal to binary. As no decimal computing elements have emerged to compete successfully on the grounds of speed, cost, and reliability with binary elements, decimal machines must be designed for binary decimal codes, which require four bits to represent the numbers 0–9.

Although mathematical computation is still very important, computers are now widely used for handling symbolic data, such as large data retrieval systems, and much business data also contains alphabetic and symbolic information. This symbolic data must in any case be converted to some coded form to be stored in a binary memory. Furthermore it is becoming progressively less expensive to increase the power of a processor, and the cost of conversion becomes much less significant than in earlier machines. It is also possible to design arithmetic units which can operate in both binary or BCD under program control, so that a processor can do both forms of arithmetic.

It is possible to make a numerical comparison of the efficiency of binary versus decimal operation. If it is assumed that a calculation is being performed on a set of numbers N, each of which has an equal probability of occurrence, the self-information associated with selecting a number from the set is given by

$$I = \log_2 N.$$

If the set N_b consists of 2^b consecutive integers from 0 to $2^b - 1$, then

$$I_b = \log_2 2^b = b \text{ bits}$$

and any number in the set may be represented by a binary number of b bits.

Now suppose we have a set N_d, consisting of 10^d consecutive integers from 0 to $10^d - 1$, and represented by d decimal digits. The self-information in the selection of a number from this set is given by

$$\begin{aligned} I_d &= \log_2 10^d \\ &= d \log_2 10 \\ &\triangleq d\ 3.322 \text{ bits} \end{aligned}$$

So that a decimal digit has roughly the information equivalent of 3.322 bits. As a convenient example, 2^{10} = 1024, which is approximately equal to 999, (and in fact is often referred to as a 'K' in computer jargon when referring to memory capacity, such as 8K, meaning 8192). Therefore 10 bits are roughly equivalent ot 3 decimal digits.

As has been seen in the description of binary decimal codes, 4 bits are needed to represent a decimal digit, and bits cannot be split. So that a decimal processor requires at least 4/3.322 = 1.204 times as many storage and arithmetic elements as a binary processor.

But the assumption that all the numbers in the set are equiprobable, is also not true, since in practice the capacity of a storage word in the memory is invariably greater than the largest number appearing in a calculation, some of the numbers available in the complete set are never used, and the information involved with the selection of a number is less than b bits.

Suppose the numbers in the range 0–220 appear in the calculation, then

$$I = \log_2 220 = 7.8 \text{ bits}.$$

As bits cannot be divided, at least 8 bits are needed to represent this range of numbers, and this gives an efficiency 7.8/8 = 97%.

But to store the same number in coded decimal, would require 3 decimal digits, and 12 bits, resulting in an efficiency of 7.8/12 = 65%. Or, relative to the binary processor for this range of numbers, the decimal machine has an efficiency of 65/97 or 68%.

If all integers above 10 are considered, for both binary and coded decimal representation, the maximum efficiency for binary is at 16, 32, 64 etc. and is 100%; the minimum efficiency is for the number 17 and is 82%. For decimal the maximum efficiency occurs at 10, 100, 1000 etc. and is 3.32/4 = 83%. The minimum efficiency is for the number 11, which is equivalent to 3.46 bits, but needs 8 bits to represent it in coded decimal giving an efficiency of 43.5%.

By making some dubious assumptions, it can be shown that 2 is close to an optimum base for storage and arithmetic. Suppose the number N is represented in the base x and requires q digit positions.

$$\text{Then } N = x^q$$

$$\text{and } q = \frac{\log_e N}{\log_e x}.$$

A reasonable assumption, but one which cannot be substantiated, is then made, that the cost of an arithmetic element or storage position is proportional to the base x. Therefore the cost of physically storing or handling N is given by

$$C = kxq \quad \text{where } k \text{ is a constant}$$

$$= kx\,\frac{\log_e N}{\log_e x}.$$

For the purpose of calculation x and q are then assumed to vary continuously instead of in discrete steps. Making $dC/dx = 0$ then gives a minimum when $x = e = 2.718$. The nearest base to e are 2 and 3. The possibility of designing ternary devices has only been of research interest, and has not led to any commercial devices, so that binary is confirmed as the most efficient choice of base.

Representation of Symbolic Data

A processor does not only handle numerical data, but a large amount of the data is symbolic and non-numerical in character. In particular much of the contents of the memory may be program instructions. There are special types of coded words which are interpreted by the processor to indicate what the next operation is to be, and where data is to be found or to be transferred. (See Chapter 8). There may also be other types of symbolic data, such as a row of bits indicating the state of switches in an external bit of apparatus, alphanumeric data, or the pattern for setting lights on another device.

It is important to have a convenient method of writing and typing or printing such strings of bits. Writing these down as strings of ones and zeros becomes both tedious and prone to error.

Two methods are in general use, the hexadecimal code, and octal code. The octal code is shown in Table 4.10, and the hexadecimal in Table 4.11. In both cases the string of bits is cut up into groups of bits,

Table 4.10

3 bit group	*Octal equivalent*
000	0
001	1
010	2
011	3
100	4
101	5
110	6
111	7

Table 4.11

4 bit group	*Hexadecimal equivalent*
0000	0
0001	1
0010	2
0011	3
0100	4
0101	5
0110	6
0111	7
1000	8
1001	9
1010	A
1011	B
1100	C
1101	D
1110	E
1111	F

3 bit groups for octal, and 4 bit groups for hexadecimal. These groups are then written in their code equivalents, which are easily memorised. Two examples will illustrate this, for the same string of bits. Commas are used to separate the groups of bits in each case. Both methods are common, but the hexadecimal representation seems to have gained in popularity, because words of binary numbered length such as 8, 16 or 32 are more conveniently cut up into groups of 4 bits.

Octal:

The octal equivalent of
1, 010, 011, 111, 100, 001, is 123741 and of
1, 111, 101, 001, 111, 100, is 175174.

Hexadecimal:

The same strings of bits are now shown in hexadecimal representation.
The hexadecimal equivalent of 1010, 0111, 1110, 0001 is A7E1 and of 1111, 1010, 0111, 1100 is FA7C.

Problems

1. Convert the following binary numbers to decimal numbers: (a) 1101, (b) 1011, (c) 00010101, and (d) 11001101.
2. Convert the same numbers to their decimal equivalents, assuming they are in binary coded decimal.
3. Convert the following integers to binary numbers: (a) 29, (b) 67, (c) 721, (d) 437, (e) 233.
4. Convert the following fractions to binary fractions of 8 significant bits: (a) $\frac{1}{3}$, (b) $\frac{1}{5}$, (c) 0.625, (d) 0.03725.
5. Convert the numbers in (3) to ternary integers and write the polynomials for these.
6. Write the polynomial representation for the non-uniform number systems of: (a) time in the range of milliseconds to 10 days in terms of milliseconds as the unit, and also of seconds as the unit. (b) Length in yards, feet and inches from $\frac{1}{16}$ of an inch to 10 yards in terms of $\frac{1}{16}$ inch as a unit or one inch as a unit.
7. The following sums should be done using complementary numbers in: (a) Nine's complement notation; (b) Ten's complement notation.

(i)	(ii)	(iii)	(ix)
+721	+437	−721	−437
+437	+233	−233	−721

(v)	(vi)	(vii)	(viii)
−437	+721	−233	+437
+233	−437	+437	−721

8. Having converted the numbers in (7) (i) to (viii) to binary using ten bits, do the same sums in; (a) 1's complement representation; (b) 2's complement representation.
9. Calculate the efficiency in binary and decimal representation, and also their relative efficiencies for the number ranges: (a) 0–20, (b) 0–99, (c) 0–10002 and (d) 0–16385.

10. An early computer was designed using the 'millesimal' system in which numbers 0 to 999 were represented by 10 binary bits, and using a group base of 1000 (one thousand). A correction filler constant was added for sums exceeding 999. Evolve the rules for addition and subtraction in this system, showing the correction constant needed and how it should be added, and develop the criteria for doing this.

11. Is it possible to devise an 'Excess *N*' system around the millesimal base which would lead to simpler rules for complementation and would be easier to implement?

REFERENCES

1. FLORES, I. *The Logic of Computer Arithmetic.* Prentice Hall (1960)
2. BUCHHOLZ, W. et al. *Planning a Computer System.* McGraw-Hill (1962)
3. REZA, F.M., *An Introduction to Information Theory,* McGraw-Hill (1961)
4. BECKENBACH, E.F. Ed., *Applied Combinatorial Mathematics.* John Wiley (1964)
5. HWANG, K., *Computer Arithmetic.* John Wiley
6. McCLELLAN, H.J. and RADER, C.M. *Number Theory in Digital Signal Processing,* Prentice-Hall

Chapter 5

Addition and Subtraction

Binary digits are physically represented within the arithmetic unit of a modern computer as voltage levels, which may of course be present in pulse form for only a very short time, due to the high speed circuits now in use. A binary number can be represented in parallel where all the bits of a number appear simultaneously on a number of lines. Alternatively it can appear on a single line as a train of pulses. These are shown in Figure 5.1; notice that in the serial case the least significant bit is first in time, and the bit significance progresses with time. This is necessary because carries must propagate upwards in significance, and can be delayed to be added to the position of the next higher significance. Also since time is usually shown increasing from left to right the least significant bit is shown on the left.

Various combinations of serial and parallel representation may also be found in different parts of a computer. So one may find a 16 bit number represented in full parallel in one place; and say 4 bits in parallel, but serial by group in 4 timing periods in another; and in complete serial form in another. This is often done to match the speeds of different sections of the machine to each other and to reduce the cost of logic circuits and interconnections. The serial method requires the minimum of circuits and connections and is also the slowest method of data transfer and addition. The parallel method is the fastest, and it is necessary to find an optimum compromise between speed and cost. An 8 bit serio-parallel number in 2 time periods would appear as shown in Figure 5.2.

Data streams can be changed from serial to parallel by shifting the data serially into a shift register, and unloading all the flip-flops in the register simultaneously in parallel. The reverse process obtains if the shift register flip-flops are parallel loaded, and the data is then shifted out in serial.

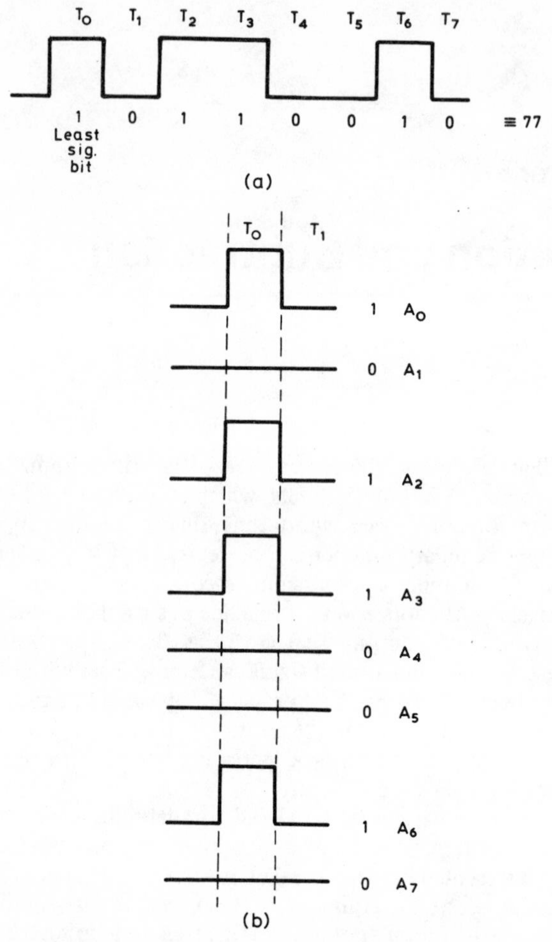

Figure 5.1 (a) Serial and (b) parallel binary number

Terms used in Describing Arithmetic Functions

Addend	The number to be added.
Augend	The number to which the addend is added.
Sum	The resultant sum of augend and addend.
Subtrahend	The number to be subtracted.
Minuend	The number from which the subtrahend is subtracted.
Difference	The result of subtracting the subtrahend from the minuend.

Multiplicand	The number to be added respectively according to the multiplier.
Multiplier	The number which controls the number of times the multiplicand is added.
Product	The result of multiplying the multiplier and multiplicand.
Dividend	The number to be divided.
Divisor	The number into which the dividend is to be divided.
Quotient	The result of dividing the dividend by the quotient.

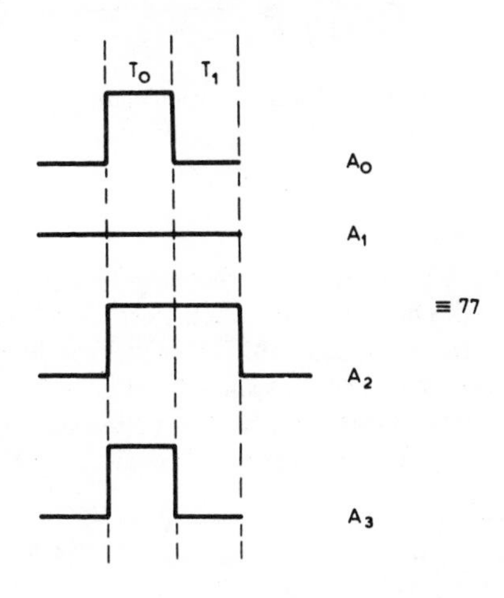

Figure 5.2 Serio-parallel binary number

The Half Adder

The simplest possible case is the addition of 2 bits, A and B, resulting in a sum and carry. The truth table is derived from the rules for binary arithmetic and is shown in Table 5.2. This is known as a half adder and can be simply realised with NAND gates, as shown in Figure 5.3.

Table 5.1 BINARY HALF ADDER TRUTH TABLE

A	B	*Sum* $A\bar{B}+\bar{A}B$	*Carry* AB
0	0	0	0
0	1	1	0
1	0	1	0
1	1	0	1

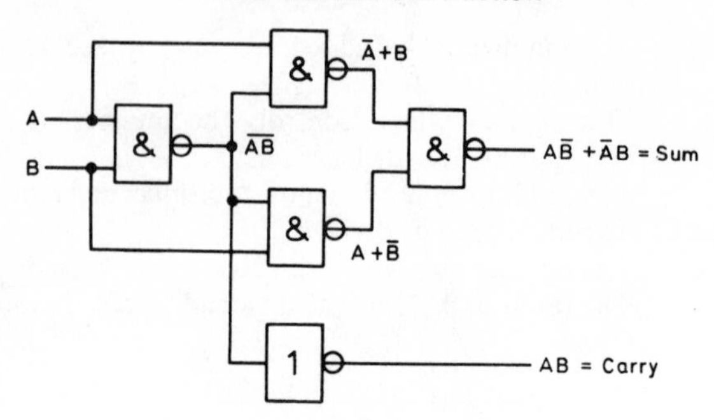

Figure 5.3 Binary half adder

The Full Adder

When adding two binary numbers of many bits it is necessary to add the augend and addend bits from each number plus the carry bit, so that a 3 input adder is needed, which is called the Full Adder. This can be realised with two half adders as shown in Figure 5.4, with the NAND logic circuit. This realisation only requires the true values of the input variables and has only nine 2 input NAND gates, but has the disadvantage

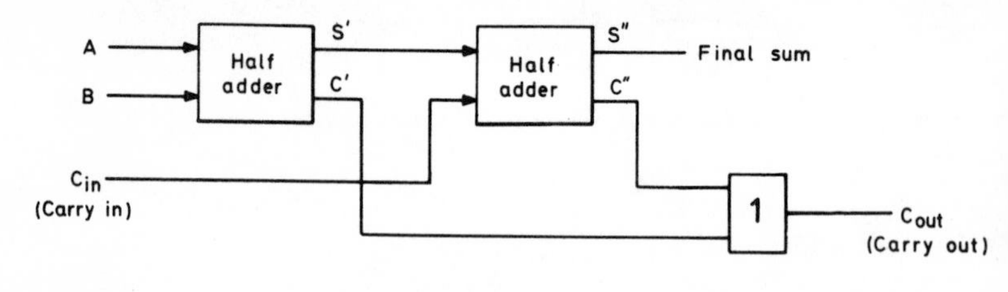

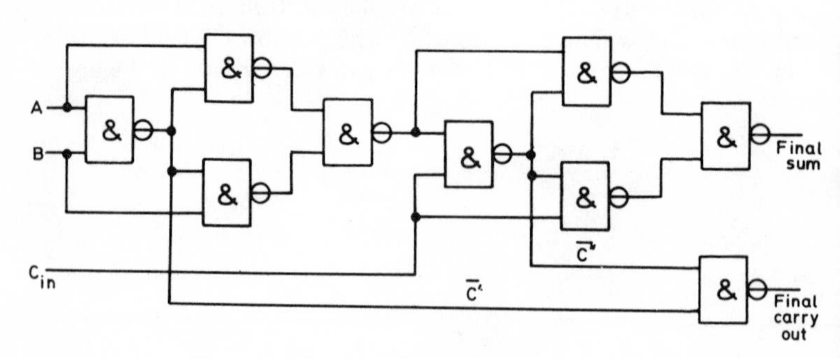

Figure 5.4 Binary full adder from half adders

that an input signal may have to propagate through 6 levels of gates before the sum terminal, or 5 gate levels before the carry terminal, which is not the fastest arrangement. In most cases both the true and negated input variables are available from a flip-flop, and this makes it possible to design a circuit having only 2 gating levels. From the truth table in Table 5.2 the expressions for the final sum and carry can be derived directly as shown with the Karnaugh maps, Figure 5.5. The carry function can be minimised, but no minimisation can be found for the sum. The realisation with NAND gates is shown in Figure 5.6.

Table 5.2 BINARY FULL ADDER TRUTH TABLE

A	B	C	*Sum*	*Carry*
0	0	0	0	0
0	0	1	1	0
0	1	0	1	0
0	1	1	0	1
1	0	0	1	0
1	0	1	0	1
1	1	0	0	1
1	1	1	1	1

AB \ C	0	1
00		1
01	1	
11		1
10	1	

Sum = $\bar{A}\bar{B}C+\bar{A}B\bar{C}+ABC+A\bar{B}\bar{C}$

AB \ C	0	1
00		
01		1
11	1	1
10		1

Carry = AB + BC + AC

Figure 5.5 Karnaugh maps for binary full adder

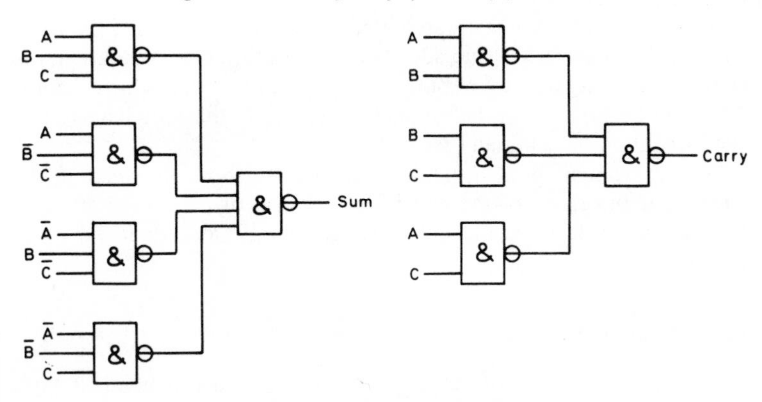

Figure 5.6 Binary full adder

Serial Binary Addition

In the addition of two serial binary numbers, these are applied to two of the inputs of a full adder shown in Figure 5.7, which has as its output the sum and the carry. The carry must be added to the next two bits of higher significance, which are due to arrive in the next time interval. This can be implemented by passing the carry signal through a time delay equal to the time interval between the bits of the serial data streams. This has the drawback that it only operates correctly at

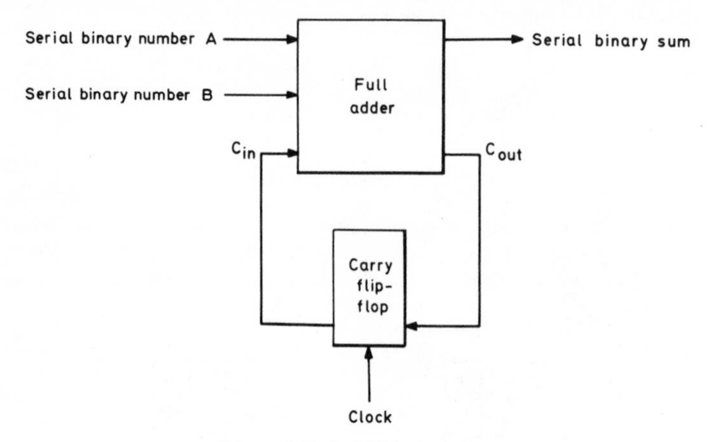

Figure 5.7 Serial binary adder

one bit frequency, and it is usual now to enter the carry into a clocked flip-flop, which is essentially a one bit shift register, so that the flip-flop output is always delayed by one bit time at all speeds within the operating range.

In the case of numbers represented in two's complement, the carry flip-flop is set to zero before addition. In the subtraction operation, the subtrahend is negated by passing it through an inverter, which changes 1's to 0's and 0's to 1's, before adding, to create the complement, and the carry flip-flop is initially set to 1.

The maximum speed of addition is determined by the delay in the adder and the speed of the carry flip-flop, and of course the addition time is the cycle time multiplied by the number of bits in the serial number.

Parallel Binary Addition

To increase the speed of addition and subtraction it is usual to work in the parallel mode. A diagram of a simple parallel binary adder is

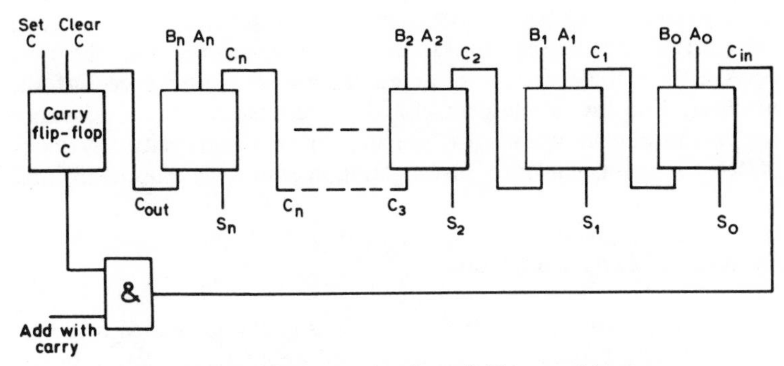

Figure 5.8 Conventional parallel binary adder

shown in Figure 5.8. The carry output from each full adder is now connected to the input of the adder of next higher significance. The carry into the least significant adder C_{in} is received from a carry flip-flop C which is set to 0 before addition and 1 before subtraction, and the final carry out from the most significant position sets the same flip-flop C. The two numbers A and B will normally be residing in parallel flip-flop registers and are gated to the adder inputs at the appropriate time.

Carry signals propagate from right to left through the whole adder. Each binary adder can be considered to be in one of three different states, which can also be interpreted in terms of their inputs:

1. G_0 – Generating no carry or generating zero carry
$$[\overline{A}\overline{B} \equiv 0.0].$$
2. G_1 – Generating a 1 carry
$$[AB \equiv 1.1]$$
3. P – Propagating a carry from input to output
$$[\overline{A}B + A\overline{B} \equiv 1.0 + 0.1]$$

In a typical situation a carry may be generated at one position, propagate through several more significant positions, and then be absorbed in a non-generating position. However in determining the time taken to complete the addition, one must consider the worst case which can arise, which happens when a number 0000......0001 is added to 1111.....1111. In this case all adders except the first are in the P state, and the first is in the G_1 state, and the carry signal will propagate the full length of the whole adder before the sum bit S_n and C_{out} are completed. Thus if the time delay in each adder to produce the sum bit is t_s, and the carry t_c, the time taken to complete the operation on the sum bit S_n is $(n-1)t_s + t_c$ and the time for the C_{out} to be completed is nt_c.

The time taken for the carry to propagate through a parallel adder is quite often the longest operation in the processor, and therefore becomes a critical factor in determining the overall speed of the machine. With the simple parallel adder one must allow sufficient time for the maximum worst case propagation to occur. Naturally much effort has been put into investigating methods of improving this.

Detection of Carry Completion

It was recognised very early that if means could be devised to detect when the carry propagation was completed a considerable improvement in the average speed could be found. This was investigated by Burks, Goldstine and Von Neumann[1] who derived the bound of $\log_2 N$ for the average number of carry stages that must be traversed for an N bit two's complement binary adder. This has been reinvestigated most recently by Briley[5] who obtains more exact expressions and derives tables for the average worst case carry for adders of up to 64 bits for both one's and two's complements. These were verified 'experimentally' by computer simulation. Some examples are tabulated in Table 5.3.

Table 5.3 AVERAGE WORST CASE CARRY

n	*One' complement adder*	*Two's complement adder*
8	2.552	2.162
16	3.527	3.239
32	4.473	4.288
48	5.027	4.888
64	5.424	5.311

In the carry completion adder, each binary full adder must be provided with a 'zero carry' output 0C and a 'one carry' output 1C. These outputs are inspected by logic, and only when either is present on every carry position is the overall carry propagation signified as being complete. The diagram of this adder is shown in Figure 5.9. The 'one' and 'zero' carries from each adder are logically added, and the AND function of all stages indicates completion. A realisation with NAND gates of a binary adder stage with a carry completion signal requiring only 2 levels of gating is shown in Figure 5.10.

Although this means of improving the speed of addition is interesting from the theoretical aspect, it does not seem to be used in modern machines. This appears to be because the time for any addition operation is dependent on the values of the operands to be added, which can result in a widely varying addition time, from the minimum

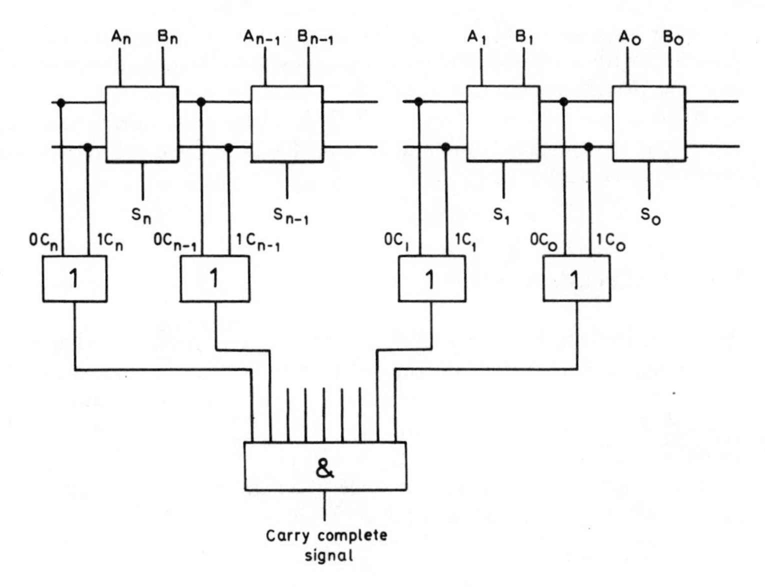

Figure 5.9 Carry completion adder

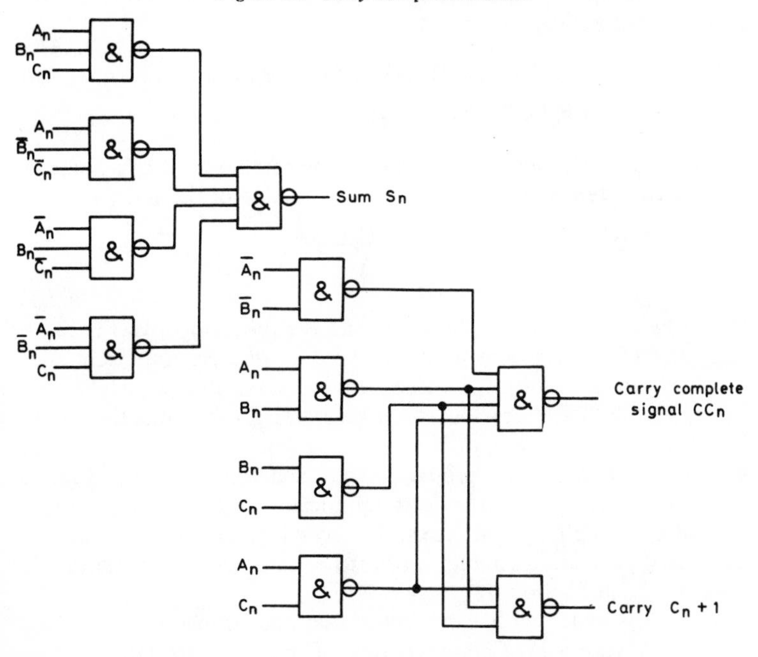

Figure 5.10 Binary adder element for carry completion adder

to the worst case time, although the average speed is much improved. An adder with a variable addition time does not dovetail conveniently into the overall system design of the machine because provision must again be made for the longest time. This means that other machine operations have to be movable in time or that the time is just lost, thus destroying the advantage gained.

The Carry Lookahead Adder

An alternative method of speeding up the addition process is to employ additional logic to anticipate the production of carry signals without waiting for them to propagate through a chain of adders. In this adder the signals needed are 'generate', the '1 carry' and the 'propagate' signals which are denoted as G_n, C_n and P_n.

If the carry output of the *n*th stage of a parallel adder is considered in terms of the previous stage it is found that:

$$C_n = G_n + P_n C_{n-1}$$

It is then possible to define this carry in terms of the carry in the two previous stages giving:

$$C_n = G_n + P_n [G_{n-1} + P_{n-1} C_{n-2}]$$
$$= G_n + P_n G_{n-1} + P_n P_{n-1} G_{n-2}$$

By continued iteration in this manner, the carry output of a stage can be defined in terms of the least significant section of the adder as:

$$C_n = G_n + P_n G_{n-1} + P_n P_{n-1} G_{n-2} +$$
$$\ldots . + P_n P_{n-1} P_{n-2} \ldots . P_1 C_0$$

C_0 is the carry input to the adder and is equivalent to G_0. It can be seen that each term consists of the product of a generate term and a series of propagate terms. In other words a stage n has a carry if one is generated, or if the previous stage generates a carry and the stage n is in the propagate state, or if stage $n - 2$ generates a carry and stages n and $n - 1$ are in the propagate state and this continues down to stage 0. Starting from the least significant stage, the first carry is formed by combining two terms, the second by three terms and so on. The carry generating circuits for up to 4 stage adders are shown with NAND logic in Figure 5.11.

A binary adder with carry generation and propagation circuits is shown in Figure 5.12. Combining four of these circuits with the carry generating circuit of Figure 5.12 forms a 4 bit lookahead adder.

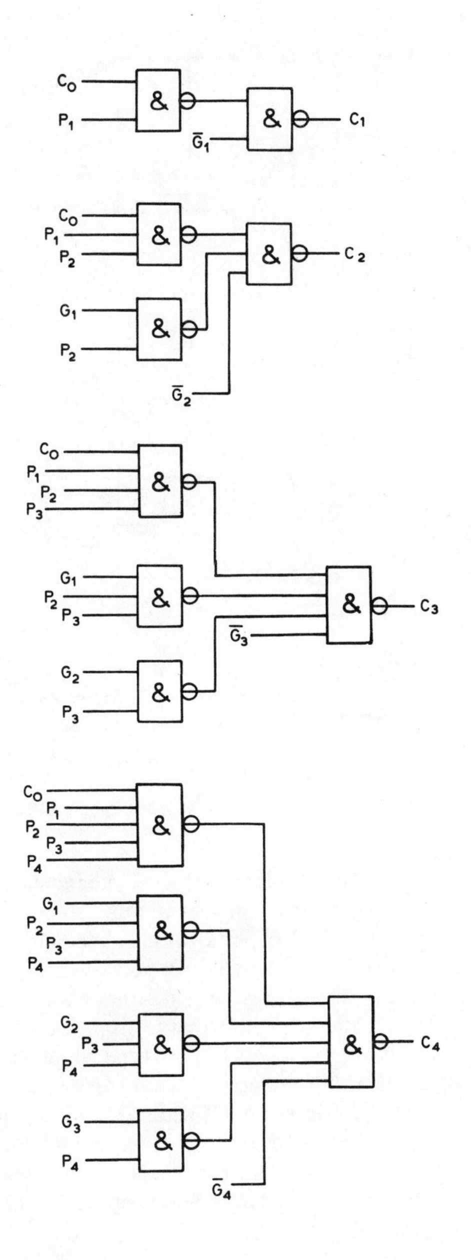

Figure 5.11 Carry generating circuits for lookahead adder

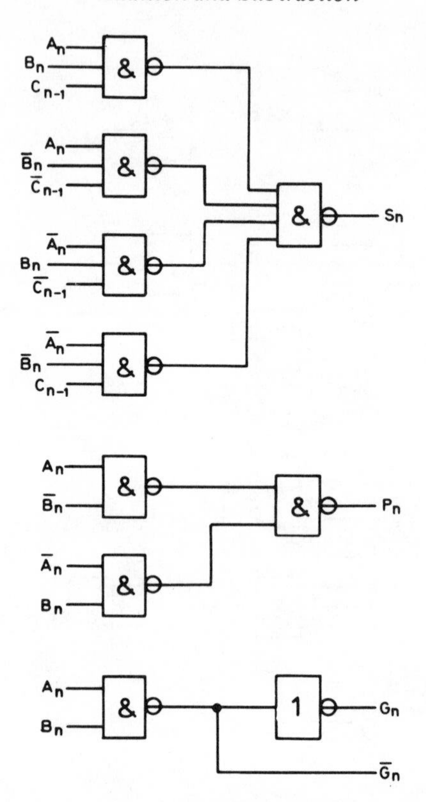

Figure 5.12 Binary adder element for lookahead adder

It can be seen that the complexity of the logic increases rapidly with the number of bits in the adder, so that to build a complete lookahead adder with a large number of bits would become excessive. This problem can be reduced to reasonable proportions by arranging blocks of complete lookahead adders, say of 4 bits linked in the usual way as shown in Figure 5.13, allowing the carry to ripple between blocks, but having lookahead within the blocks. This type of adder is convenient since 4 bit lookahead adders are now available on a single chip, and it is still very fast. By the addition of extra gates group lookahead functions can be generated and combined with the internal lookahead within the group. The group lookahead can be considered as a higher radix (or base) adder, and appropriate generate and propagate functions derived. The group propagate function is given by

$$P_g = P_1 P_2 P_3 P_4$$

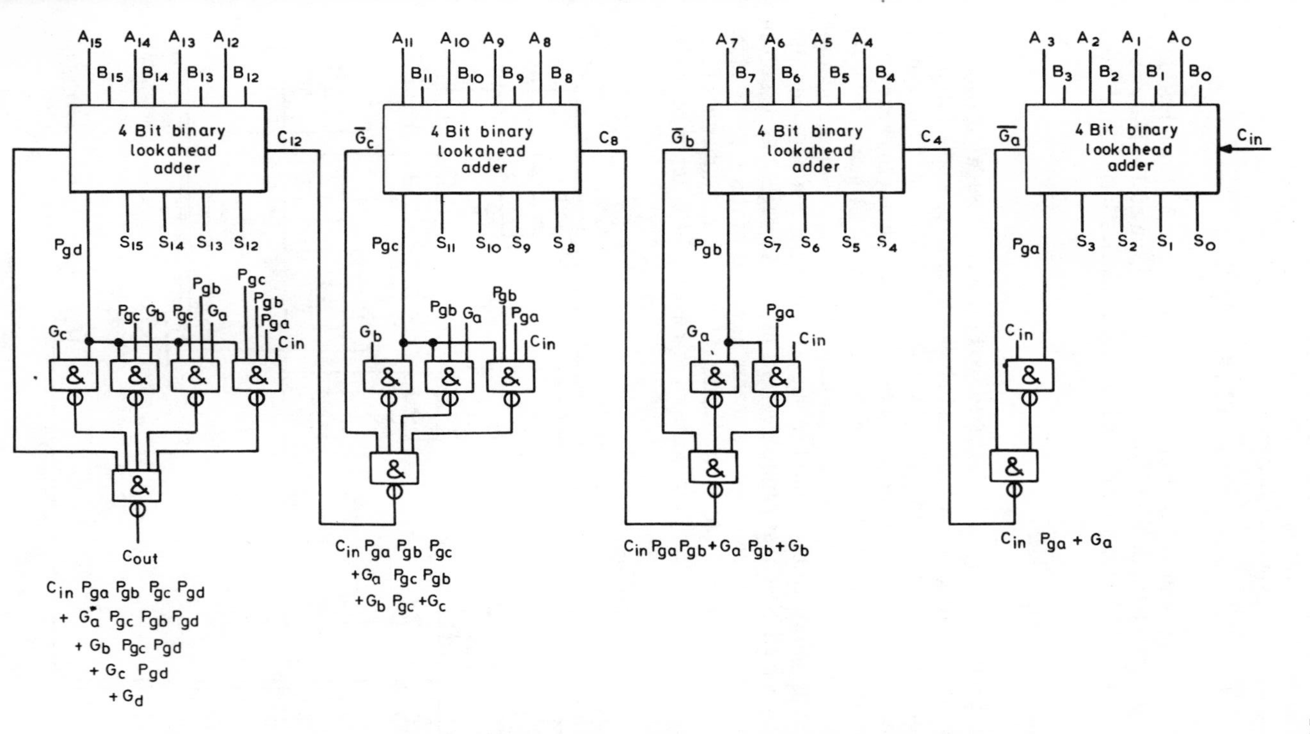

Figure 5.13 Parallel binary adder with group lookahead functions

and the group generate function by

$$G_g = G_4 + G_3P_4 + GP_3P_4 + G_1P_2P_3P_4$$

which is the same as the final C_{out} from the group. A second level look-ahead system can then be formed as shown in Figure 5.13. The idea can be extended to successive levels, but becomes increasingly complicated.

The Carry Skip Adder

An alternative approach described by Lehman and Burla[7] is to divide the adder into groups of bits and allow the carry to ripple within the group, but detect whether there will be a carry propagated through the whole group, and generate a skip carry immediately for the next higher group.The important feature of this circuit is the economy achieved, since only 2 extra gates need be added for a group, but the addition time is shown to be reduced to about 25% of the conventional ripple carry adder. Now that gating elements may be of negligible cost on an integrated circuit chip the arguments in favour of this type of adder, compared to the full lookahead adder, tend to convey rather less force. A skip circuit of this type is shown in Figure 5.14 in terms of NAND elements.

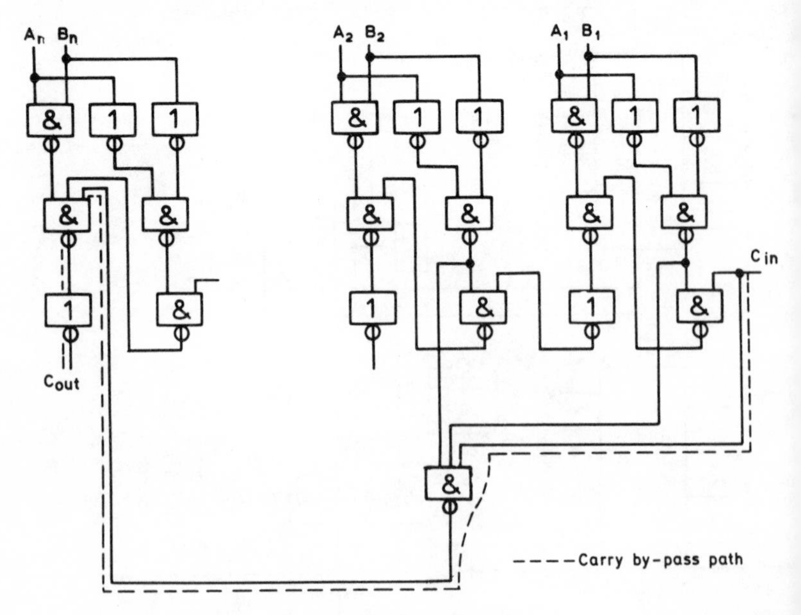

Figure 5.14 Carry skip adder

Lehman and Burla have investigated the size of groups needed and whether these should be equal or nonequal, and also whether there is an advantage to be gained from intergroup kips. If the adder is divided into K equal skip groups each of n bits, the adder length being $(m + 1)$ bits.

$$nK = m + 1$$

It is then shown that the optimum size of a group should be

$$n = \sqrt{\left(\frac{m+1}{2}\right)}$$

or $K = 2n$.

An interesting result is found that the speed of the adder is increased if the groups of which the adder is constructed are made nonequal, the larger groups being in the middle and grading to smaller groups towards each end. By introducing skips within the groups the full lookahead adder is eventually arrived at.

Other High Speed Adders

Various other types of high speed binary adders have been investigated. The conditional sum adder is described by Sklansky[10] which is based on the determination of the conditional sums and output carries that can arise from all possible arrangements of input carries for a group of bits. The appropriate information is passed through a series of networks and the number of sum bits that are unconditionally determined can be doubled in each of a sequence of steps. The time to derive the sum is approximately proportional to the logarithm of the number of bits in the number.

A somewhat different approach to the problem of fast binary addition has been adopted by the Manchester University Computer Group, and others. With this point of view the adder and the accumulator register are considered as a single combined device in which the objective is to place the result in the register in the shortest time. In the adder for the Atlas computer[11] a special purpose circuit is designed which derives its speed from the fast propagation of the carry signal from the collector to the emitter of a saturated symmetrical transistor. However this technique is no longer suitable for modern integrated circuit technology.

The need for high speed binary adders becomes most important on very large and fast computers having word lengths of 50 to 100 bits, in which the carry propagation time with a conventional ripple carry adder has a serious effect on the performance. With the availability of small lookahead adders complete on integrated circuits, it is now worth while to incorporate these in minicomputers. In any case, the speed of integrated circuit logic gates is continually rising, which makes for a very high performance with conventional methods. The lookahead adder seems to be the preferred method for improving speed on modern large machines.

Binary Coded Decimal Adders

Most modern processors operate with pure binary numbers, but decimal arithmetic units are still of interest in electronic calculators and special purpose devices, such as point of sale cash registers. The decimal numbers are usually represented as a binary code, the commonest being the straightforward BCD or 1248 weighted code. The 'excess 3' code has been widely used in the past, and is still popular in some applications.

The rules of binary coded decimal arithmetic with the BCD and 'excess 3' codes have been described in Chapter 4. Each decimal digit requires 4 bits to portray it, and these can be physically represented on 4 parallel lines in the form of serial by digit and parallel by bit, or the number may be completely parallel or completely serial.

In binary coded decimal addition, the operation must proceed in two stages. First the binary codes are added in the usual way in a conventional binary adder. The result of the addition is then examined to see if it is greater than or equal to 10 and if so a correction factor of 6 must be added. If the sum of the 2 decimal digits exceeds 15 there is a carry from the 4th bit of the binary sum. If the sum lies between 9 and 15 it must be detected by logic gates. Alternatively 6 can be added experimentally to test if there is a carry.

A block diagram of a serio-parallel BCD adder is shown in Figure 5.15. The two groups of 4 bits representing the decimal digits are presented simultaneously to the first 4 bit binary adder, and a 'carry out' from this adder indicates that the sum is greater than 15. The sum outputs of this adder are tested by logic gates for the sum being between 9 and 15. Either of these conditions indicates that a correction of 6 should be added, and these are logically added and generate the code for 6 (0110) which is added to the binary sum in the second adder. Any carry from the 4th bit in the second adder resulting from the correction operation is discarded. The least significant binary adder section can be omitted from the second adder since no correction is added to the least significant bit. The detection function can be seen from inspection to be $BS_4(BS_3 + BS_2)$, and is shown with NAND gates. The decimal carry is given by the same function that generates the

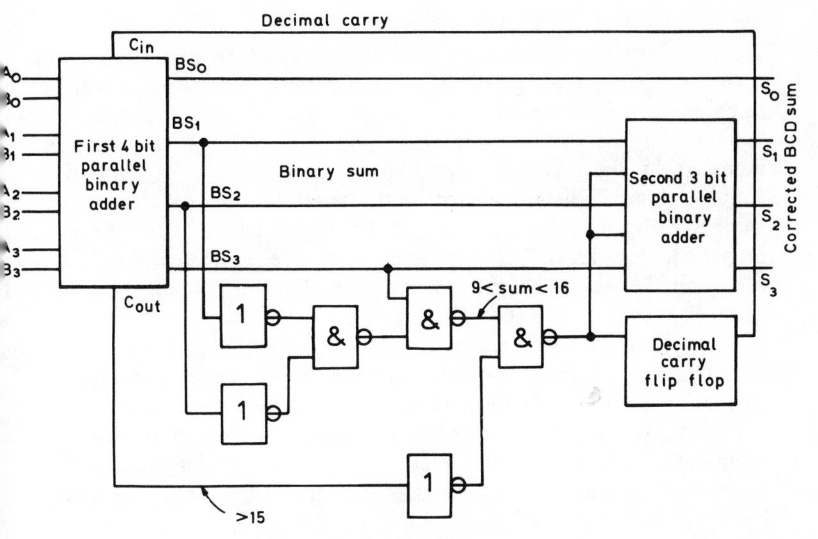

Figure 5.15 Serio-parallel binary coded decimal adder

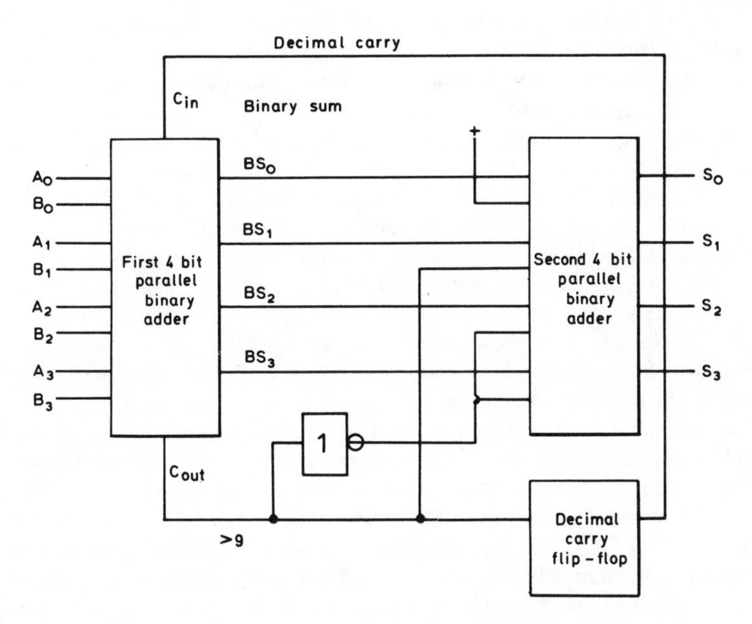

Figure 5.16 Serio-parallel excess 3 coded decimal adder

correction signal. This sets a carry flip-flop whose output is added into the next decade after the delay of one parallel shift period.

In the 'excess 3' code half the difference between 10 and 16 is added as an excess to the binary equivalent of the number, so that when two 'excess 3' digits are added a correction factor of 6 is automatically included in the addition. This makes the detection for corrections simpler, since, if there is a carry from the 4th bit after binary addition, the corrective 6 has been added, but there is no 'excess 3' and this must be added. Contrariwise, if there is no carry, the sum contains an excess of 6 and 3 must be subtracted, which is done by adding the binary two's complement of 3 (or 1101).

A diagram of a serio-parallel 'excess 3' adder is shown in Figure 5.16. The C_{out} signal from the first parallel binary adder provides the correction of 3 (0011) and its inverse $\overline{C_{out}}$ provides the correction of –3 or (1101) in two's complement. Since 1 is added to the least significant bit in both cases the correction to the least significant bit is connected to add 1 always. Again the final carry from the second binary adder is discarded.

Serial Binary Coded Adders

The same fundamental principles apply to adding binary coded decimal in serial form, but a different problem supervenes, in that the result of the first binary addition cannot be known until after 4 timing periods when the serial sum of the 2 serial decimal digits has been completed. Therefore it is necessary to store the group of 4 bits representing the first binary sum in a 4 bit shift register. At the end of the 4th bit C_4 can be sampled, as also the stored code in the shift register. If the sum is greater than 10 the serial correction factor can then be added to the output of the 4 bit shift register in a second serial binary adder.

Figure 5.17 shows a full serial binary coded decimal adder[14] in which the correction is added to the sum of the 2 serial decimal digits. The correction is sometimes known as the 'filler', as it fills up the number from 10 to 16 to give the correct final digit plus a decimal carry. In this adder both the 'filled' and 'unfilled' sums are generated. At the end of the group of 4 bits a carry from either of the 2 binary adders indicates that the 'filled' sum should be selected. No carry from either means that the 'unfilled' sum should be selected.

The interesting feature of this adder is that it can add in any base or radix of notation by choosing the appropriate filler, including non-uniform number systems such as minutes and seconds which have a different base for different positions. It is thus a completely universal adder. Each group of 4 bits can contain any number up to 16, and it

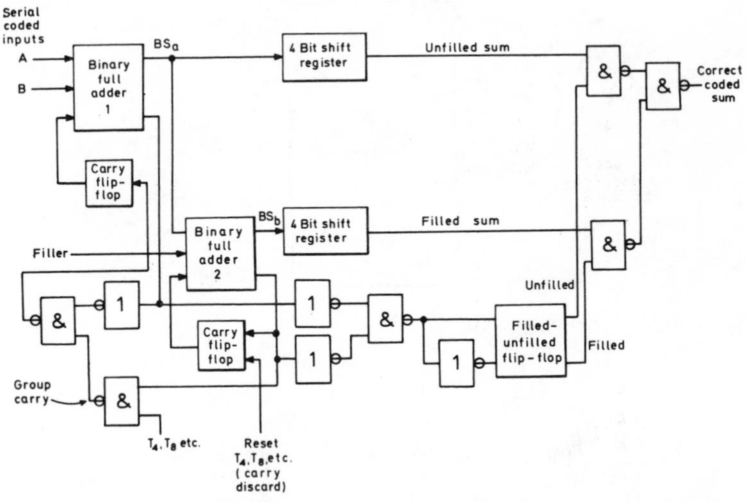

Figure 5.17 Serial variable radix adder

must be arranged that each group carries 1 over into the next group if the sum exceeds the radix for that position, leaving the remainder in the group. This is done by adding $16 - r$, where r is the radix for that group, and $16 - r$ is the 'filler'. The rules for any radix can then be generalised as follows:

$A + B < r$	no filler added
$r \leqslant A + B < 16$	filler added
$16 \leqslant A + B < 32$	filler added.

The filler then becomes a constant which can be stored to convert the adder to any radix, and can be programmed.

Decimal Addition by Look-Up Table

Simple rules can be derived for addition in BCD and 'excess 3' code, and this makes it possible to devise fairly economical logical systems to add in this form. However many decimal codes exist for which no simple rules of addition obtain.

If the addition of 2 parallel binary coded 4 bit numbers is thought of in its most general terms, it can be considered as a code transformation of an 8 bit number to another 4 bit number. A look-up table can be formed with 100 different input combinations and 11 output combinations; This can be easily realised with a read only memory (ROM) which can now be obtained in the form of an integrated circuit

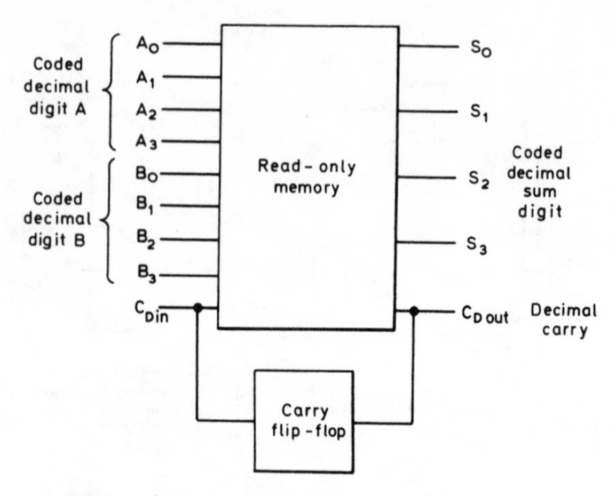

Figure 5.18 Decimal addition by look-up table

which can be programmed to users' requirements. The block diagram of this is shown in Figure 5.18, and will operate for any binary decimal code one cares to invent.

This brute force approach to decimal addition has not been very attractive in the past because of the complicated logic needed to implement it, but modern integrated devices have quite changed the picture and it may be found now that this is the most economical and fastest way of making any type of binary coded adder.

Binary Coded Decimal Subtraction

To perform subtraction in a decimal machine it is usual to add the complement of the subtrahend. Since this is a decimal operation the nine's complement of each of the decimal codes has to be generated, but as this is usually serial by decimal digit it is easier to work in ten's complement, and this is easily taken care of by setting the initial carry in the carry flip-flop to 1 before subtraction and then discarding the final carry.

Generation of the nine's complement of a decimal code is obviously not such a simple proposition as generating the one's complement of a binary number. The 'excess 3' code is particularly simple to complement because the nine's complement code is produced in exactly the same way as in binary code, that is, by inversion, and changing all 1's to 0's and all 0's to 1's which is its chief justification.

To produce the nine's complement of the BCD code it is necessary to insert a code translator, which in the parallel case is merely

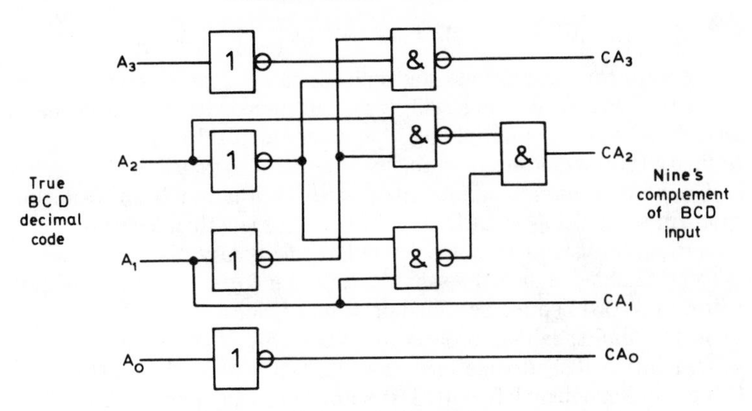

Figure 5.19 BCD nine's complementer

combinational logic as shown in Figure 5.19. In the case of complementing serial BCD code, the simplest method is probably to shift the serial code into a 4 bit shift register, perform a parallel transformation as shown above into a second, or the same, shift register and shift out the nine's complement from the register in serial. Complementing serial 'excess 3' code is simple, as it is only necessary to invert the subtrahend, with a single inverter.

Binary to Decimal Converters

In smaller processors it is not worth while to include a special device to automatically convert binary to decimal numbers and vice versa, and this is usually done by a simple program. However there has been a trend in larger processors to provide hardware dedicated to translation between binary and BCD numbers. Also many new peripheral devices, such as display terminals require their numbers in decimal form, and the advent of large scale integrated logic chips make it feasible to build such special devices, into peripherals. The translation between binary and BCD codes is related to BCD addition and this seems a convenient place to discuss this problem.

A hardware binary to decimal converter has been described by Couleur[15]. This system relies on a conversion method that has been called the 'dibble-dabble' algorithm. The binary integer N can be represented as:

$$N = a_n 2^n + a_{n-1} 2^{n-1} + \dots a_1 2^1 + a_0$$

where $a_n \dots a_0$ can have the values of 1 or 0. This can be rewritten in the form:

$$N - [(....\{[(0 \times 2 + a_n)2 + a_{n-1}]2 + a_{n-2}\}2 + ... + a_1)2 + ap].$$

If we perform the repeated multiplications by 2 as a coded decimal operation, the final result will appear in coded decimal form, in an analogous way to multiplying the binary digits by decimal in the ordinary form would result in the usual decimal conversion.

Doubling a number represented in BCD notation is an analogous problem to addition in BCD. If a BCD digit is less than 5, the doubling operation consists merely in shifting left one binary place. If the digit is to be doubled is $\geqslant 5$ the shifted result is incorrect, and a correction factor of 3 (0011) must be added prior to shifting.

In the 'dibble-dabble' process the bits of the binary number are left shifted into a BCD decade register one bit at a time, the BCD register being simultaneously left shifted. If a number in any decade of the BCD register is $\geqslant 5$, a correction of 3 is added before shifting. The procedure may be more clearly seen in the example in Table 5.4, which shows the conversion of the binary number 111001 (57) into binary coded decimal form 0101, 0111.

The block diagram of a version of this is shown in Figure 5.20. The binary number is first left shifted one bit into the decade 0 of the BCD register. Straightforward combinational code translation circuits then convert the coded contents of the decade register to double its value, correcting accordingly and also generating the carry to the next decade. Then the next binary bit is moved into decade 0 and all BCD decades are left shifted one bit. The process continues until all the bits of the binary number are exhausted. The implementation shown uses separate register decades and separate combinational logic.

Table 5.4 CONVERSION OF 111001 (57) INTO BCD BY THE DIBBLE-DABBLE METHOD

	BCD number		*Binary number*
	Decade 1	*Decade 0*	
Start	0000	0000	111001
Step 1	0000	0001	11001
Step 2	0000	0011	1001
Step 3	0000	0111	001
Correction—add 3		0011	
	0000	1010	001
Step 4	0001	0100	01
Step 5	0010	1000	1
Correction—add 3		0011	
	0010	1011	1
Step 6	0101	0111	
	5	7	

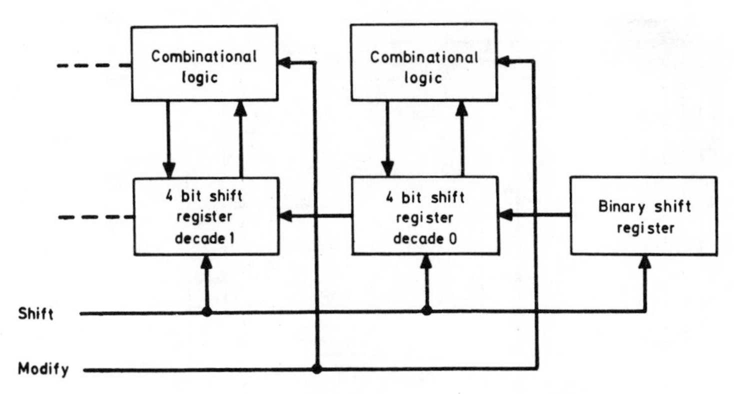

Figure 5.20 Couleur's binary to decimal converter

Binary to decimal code converters can be generalised to any code, by a suitable design of the combinational logic as shown by Rhyne[16], who has also simplified the system to make the shift and translation with a single shift pulse.

Another type of binary to decimal converter has been proposed by Schmookler[17] which relies on the repeated multiplication of a binary fraction by 10 or (1010) in binary.

A serio-parallel converter can be designed which only requires one section of combinational logic, as shown in Figure 5.21, but this is of course, proportionately slower. The sequence of operations in this converter are:

1. Left shift binary shift register and each decade of the serio-parallel register one bit, connecting each decade to the next higher decade.
2. Modify the contents of R_0 and also any carry needed to modify R_1 in the carry flip-flop.
3. Parallel shift all the decades, shifting the next decimal digit into R_0 for correction, and the corrected contents of R_0 in R_n.
4. Repeat 2. and 3. until all decades have been modified, then return to 1. and shift in the next binary bit.
5. Continue until all the binary bits are exhausted.

The procedure can be reversed for converting BCD to binary. In this case the BCD number is placed in the decade registers and right shifted, and 3 (0011) is subtracted from each decade if its contents are 10 (1010). As each right shift takes place the least significant bit of decade 0 is shifted into the binary shift register. When the BCD number is

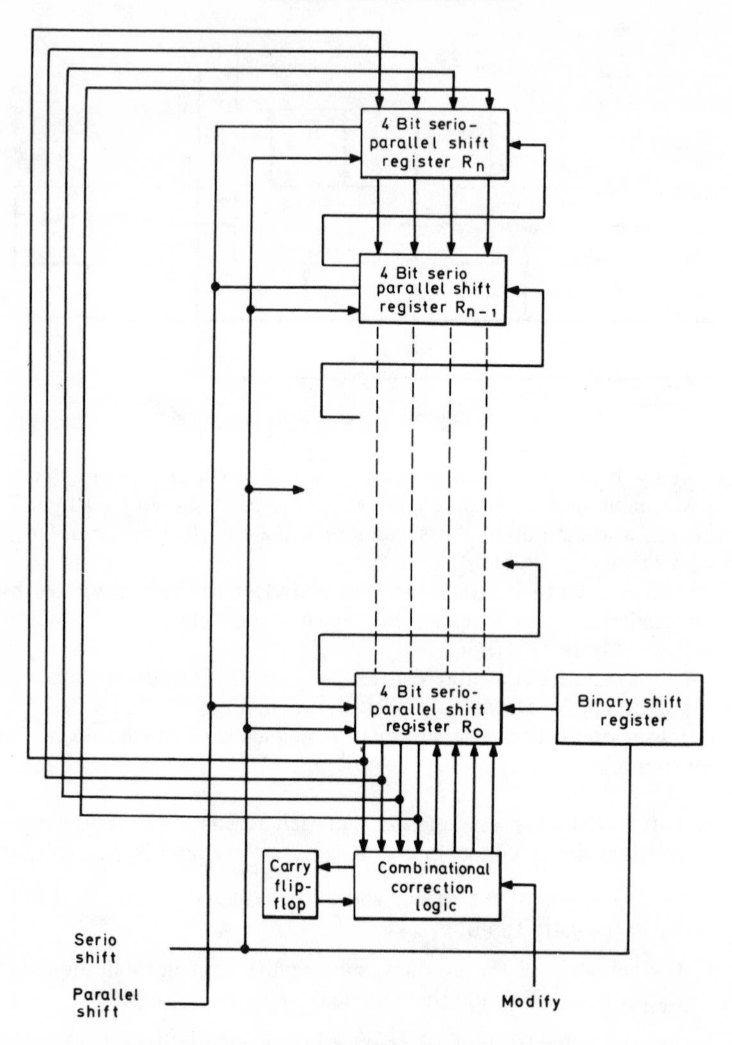

Figure 5.21 Serio-parallel binary to decimal converter

exhausted the binary register contains the binary equivalent of the original BCD number entered into the decade registers.

Problems

1. To minimise the spares necessary for maintenance, a digital device is to be designed using only two input NAND gates. Design a complete

serial adder including the carry delay flip-flop using only two input NAND gates for the device.

2. An adder is needed to add three serial binary number streams in one operation. Design a serial adder, to accept three binary inputs, according to the rules of binary arithmetic. Two separate carries must be developed and accepted, to be added into the next most significant position, and the position two places more significant.
3. The representation of a binary number as *n* serial pairs of two bits in parallel is sometimes called the 'dibit'. (a) Design a conventional adder to add 'dibits' using NAND gates only. (b) Design the same adder using NOR gates only. (c) Design the same adder with look-ahead logic using, generate, and propagate functions to give the maximum speed. Calculate the time for the carry to propagate from input to output with various logic elements and thus calculate the maximum speed for addition of an N bit number. (d) Design the same lookahead adder, treating the adder as a combinational logic circuit with 5 inputs, A_1 B_1 A_2 B_2 and C_{in}. Can the speed be improved from (c).
4. Consider a parallel lookahead adder composed of groups of 4 bit lookahead subsections similar to that shown in Figure 5.13. Design the intergroup lookahead logic by deriving the group generate and propagate functions directly from the adder inputs. Is there any gain in speed and if so what is the cost in additional logic elements.
5. Derive the rules for binary coded decimal subtraction and design a BCD subtractor to work directly from the minuend and subtrahend.
6. Two binary serial numbers A and B of indefinite but equal length are presented to a logical 'black box'. A signal is also provided from control circuits to indicate when the numbers are present at the inputs and there is also a reset signal before the start. The 'black box' must provide 3 output signals at the end of the operation indicating $A > B$, $A < B$, and $A = B$. The problem is simpler if only unsigned numbers are considered, but becomes more interesting with signed numbers.
7. Design the combinational logic for testing for the correction and making the correction in the binary to BCD converter shown as a block diagram in Figure 5.21.
8. Design similar logic for BCD to binary conversion. Can any of the logic be shared, thus producing a more economic design for a dual purpose converter.

REFERENCES

1. BURKS, A.W., GOLDSTINE, H.H., and VON NEUMANN, J.,*Preliminary Discussions of the Logical Design of an Electronic Computing Instrument*

2. REITWIESNER, G.W. *The Determination of Carry Propagation Length for Binary Addition. IRE Trans. Electr. Comp.* 9 No 1 35–38 (1960).
3. BRILEY, B.E. *Some New Results on Average Worst Case Carry. IEE Trans Comp.* 22 No. 5 459–463 (1973)
4. LEHMAN, M. and BURLA, N. *Skip Techniques for High Speed Carry – Propagation in Binary Arithmetic Units IRE Trans. Electr. Comp.* 10 No 4 691–698 (1961)
5. WELLER, C.W. *A High-Speed Carry Circuit for Binary Adders. IEEE Trans Comp* 18 No 8. 728–732 (1969)

Chapter 6

Multiplication and Division

Multiplication is the operation of repeatedly adding the multiplicand to itself a number of times specified by the multiplier. One could of course just count the number of times the multiplicand had been added until one had reached a number equal to the multiplier, and this might be feasible for small numbers, but would be impossibly long winded for large numbers. The usual manual decimal multiplication method is therefore adopted, of multiplying the multiplicand by each multiplier digit separately, and shifting the partial products, i.e. multiplying by ten (10). In simple binary multiplication an analogous process is utilised.

The binary multiplication table is simplicity itself, since $1 \times 1 = 1$, $1 \times 0 = 0$, $0 \times 1 = 0$, and $0 \times 0 = 0$. First consider how one would multiply two unsigned integers manually, by the analogous method to decimal multiplication:

```
   1001       9
   1101      13
-------
   1001
  0000
 1001
1001
-------
1110101     117
```

The multiplier can be inspected from either end and the partial products shifted appropriately. Only right to left inspection of the multiplier will be considered because it can be implemented with a single word length adder in the parallel realisation, and lends itself conveniently to two's complement binary number representation.

It is inconvenient in machine multiplication to have to store each partial product separately and then add them together in a later operation, so that each partial product is accumulated as it is generated. It is also easier to shift the accumulated partial product to the right rather than to shift the multiplicand to the left, saving register capacity as will be seen. Rearranging this multiplication operation to suite the machine, the form is shown in Table 6.1 with signed positive numbers.

Notice that the final product occupies twice the number of places of the original binary words, (a result which is general in all number bases), and also that the accumulated partial product grows by 1 bit

Table 6.1 BINARY MULTIPLICATION TO SUIT A MACHINE

01001	Multiplicand = +9
01101	Multiplier = +13
01001	Add Multiplicand
001001	Shift partial product one place to the right
001001	No multiplicand added, multiplier bit = 0
0001001	Shift right one place
0001001	Add multiplicand
01001	
0101101	
00101101	Shift right one place
00101101	Add multiplicand
01001	
01110101	
001110101	Shift right one place
0001110101	Shift right one place
0001110101	Result +117

at each add and shift cycle, and furthermore that at the same time 1 bit in the multiplier can be discarded. This procedure can be encapsulated simply in the form of a flowchart in Figure 6.1.

Many small computers do not incorporate a multiplier or divider, and the procedure is performed by a simple program. As this is relatively slow it is usual in more powerful machines to incorporate a hardware multiplier or multiplier-divider. Most minicomputers offer this as an optional addition which can be in two forms. A special arithmetic unit embodying the multiplier-divide control logic is designed as an entity and the multiplier, multiplicand and product resid reside in certain specified accumulator registers. Alternatively the hardware multiply-divide option is actually a separate peripheral device connected to the input-output bus. This is slower but causes less disruption to the internal system of the processor if it is added as an option.

The various mutliplier circuits that follow will be described for positive multiplier and multiplicand. The problems concerned with multiplying numbers with negative signs will be discussed later, as they tend to obscure the understanding of the principles of operation.

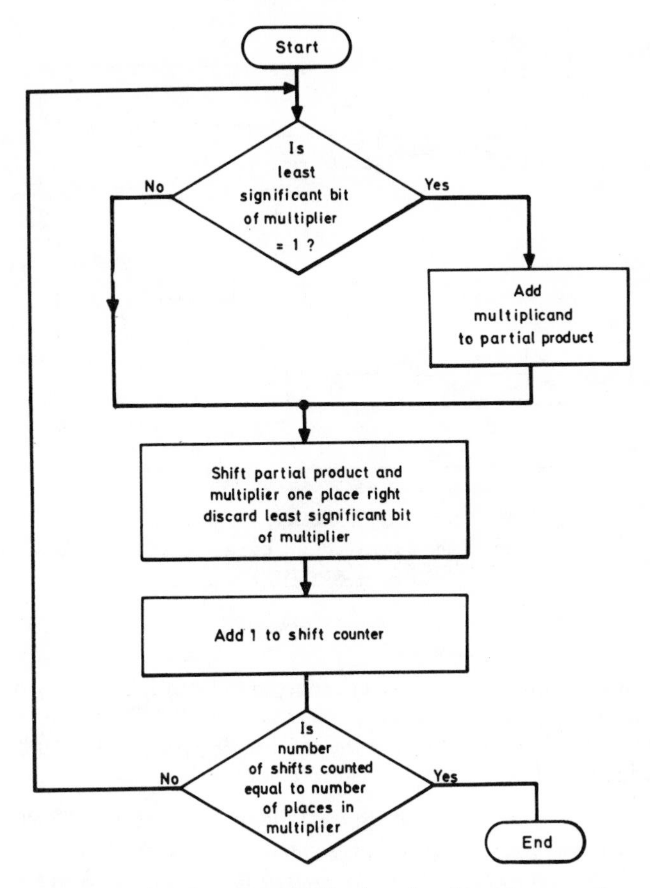

Figure 6.1 Flowchart for multiplication of positive binary numbers

The Serial Binary Multiplier

An implementation of a serial binary multiplier is shown in Figure 6.2 and is composed of three shift registers equal to the word length, and a serial adder. These are called the multiplicand register MD, the multiplier register MR, and the partial product register PP. At the start of the operation the multiplicand is loaded into MD, and the multiplier in MR, and PP is cleared. The least significant bit of MR controls whether the multiplicand is to be added or not in each cycle, and the number of cycles performed is counted in a shift counter, which indicates that the operation is completed when the number of cycles

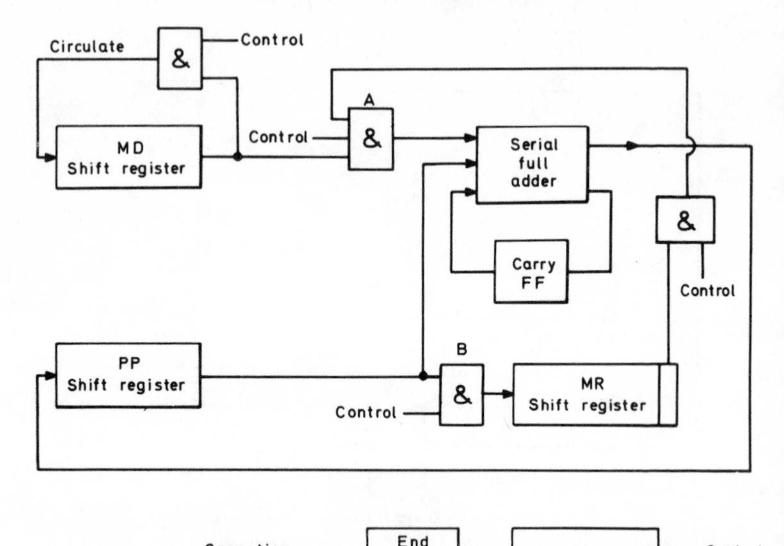

Figure 6.2 Serial binary multiplier

performed is equal to the number of bits in the multiplier. The growing accumulated partial product is shifted 1 bit into the MR register at the end of each addition cycle, and the, no longer needed, least significant bit of the multiplier disappears. The sequence is then:

1. Test the least significant bit of MR. If 1 add MD to PP shifting them simultaneously and returning the sum to PP, and recirculate MD to preserve its contents. Gate B is closed, gate A open. If 0 go to the next step.
2. Open gate B, close gate A, and shift PP and MR one place to the right, losing the least significant bit of the multiplier, and shifting the least significant bit of the partial product into MR. Any final carry overflow remaining in the carry flip-flop is transferred via the adder to the most significant position in PP. Simultaneously add 1 to the contents of the shift counter.
3. These cycles are repeated until every bit in the multiplier has been inspected. At this point the shift counter contains a binary number equal to the number of bits in the multiplier word, and emits a signal to indicate that the operation is complete. The most significant half of the product now rests in PP, and the least significant in MR.

The Parallel Binary Multiplier

Many modern processors operate in the fully parallel binary mode to gain speed, and incorporate a parallel binary multiplier. The same algorithm is used as before but is realised in the parallel form shown in Figure 6.3.

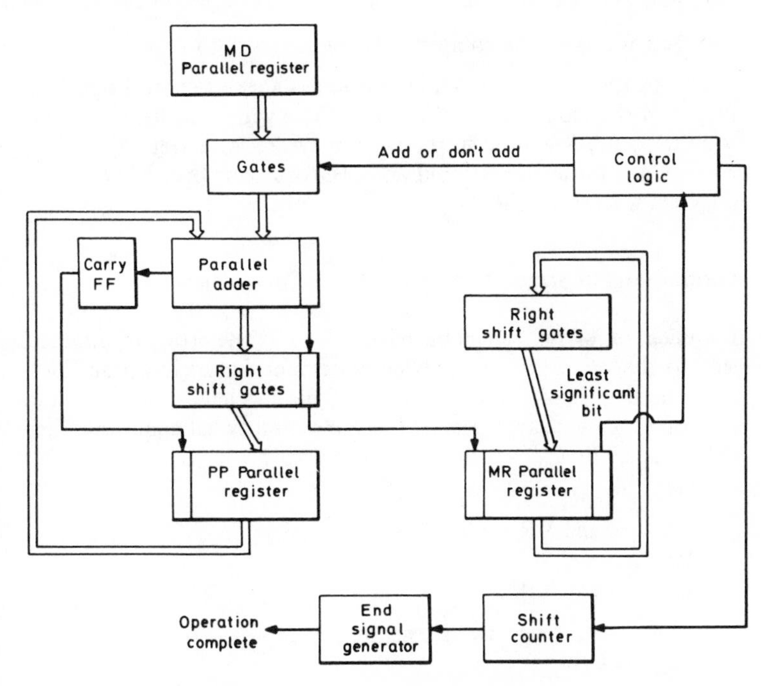

Figure 6.3 Parallel binary multiplier

In this version the MD, PP, and MR are constructed of parallel loading flip-flops. The multiplier MD is added to the partial product in a full-parallel adder, the contents of MD being gated into the adder or not according to whether the least significant bit of MR is 1 or 0. The right shift of one place of PP and MR is obtained by passing the sum of MD and PP through right shift gates whose outputs are connected one place to the right. Similarly MR is gated back into itself via right shift gates connected one place to the right, thus effectively shifting its contents up one place and losing the least significant bit of the multiplier. In the right shift operation the least significant bit of the sum of MD and PP is right shifted or gated into the most significant bit of MR, and any overflow carry from the addition enters the most significant bit of PP. The sequence is:

1. Test the least significant bit of MR. If 1 enable the gates from MD to the adder, if 0 enter zero into the MD adder inputs.
2. Add PP to the controlled output of the gates from MD in the adder and transfer back to PP and MR shifted one place right. Simultaneously shift the contents of MR one place right.
3. Add 1 to the shift counter.
4. Test for operation complete otherwise return to 1.

In both the parallel and serial multipliers various control signals are implicit in the sequence of operations. These will normally be provided by either a sub-operation in the control system or a section of micro-program, and the arithmetic unit and control system become very much enmeshed with each other.

Multiplication of Signed Numbers in Two's Complement

Multiplication of two signed binary numbers by the orthodox approach leads to the necessity for applying correction factors in certain cases. Although they have a theoretical basis, the mechanism of the multiplication process causes these methods to be somewhat empirical. There are four possibilities,

MD = + X and MR = + Y,
MD = –X and MR = + Y,
MD = + X and MR = –Y,
MD = –X and MR = –Y.

Restricting ourselves to two's complement representation we have the following cases:

1. MD = + X and MR = + Y.
   The operation is straightforward and similar to the multiplication of unsigned numbers.

2. MD = –X and MR = + Y.
   In this case the multiplicand is in the complementary form and the sequence is the same as 1, but the sign digit 1 is propagated into the product from the left as shown in Table 6.2. No correction is necessary.

3. MD = + X and MR = –Y.
   The multiplicand is here positive but the multiplier is in the complementary form. In this case the procedure is similar, but a final correction of $(2n - X)2^n$, which is the two's complement of X shifted n places to the left, is added as shown in Table 6.3.

Table 6.2 SIGNED BINARY MULTIPLICATION. MD = −X and MR = +Y

MD = −9 MR = +13

MD	10111	−9
MR	01101	+13
	10111	Add MD
	110111	Shift right propagating sign
	1110111	No addition—shift right
	1011100	Add MD
Discard carry	1010011	
	11010011	Shift right
	10111000	Add MD
Discard carry	10001011	
	110001011	Shift right
Result	1110001011	Shift right

Result is negative, therefore recomplement to find the true value.

0001110100	
1	
0001110101	−117

Table 6.3 SIGNED BINARY MULTIPLICATION. MD = +X and MR = −Y

MD = +9 MR = −13

MD	01001	+9
MR	10011	−13
	01001	Add MD
	001001	Shift right one place
	010010	Add MD
	011011	
	0011011	Shift right one place
	00011011	No addition—shift right one place
	000011011	No addition—shift right one place
	010010000	Add MD
	010101011	
	0010101011	Shift right one place
	0010101011	
	10111	Add correction of two's complement of MD+9 shifted left 5 places
	1110001011	Result is negative, complement to find the true value.
	0001110100	
	1	
	0001110101	−117

Table 6.4 SIGNED BINARY MULTIPLICATION. MD = −X and MR = −Y

MD = −9, MR = −13

MD	10111	−9
MR	10011	−13
	10111	Add MD
	110111	Shift right one place
	10111	Add MD
Discard carry	100101	
	1100101	Shift right one place
	11100101	No addition—shift right one place
	111100101	No addition—shift right one place
	10111	Add MD
Discard carry	101010101	
	1101010101	Shift right one place
	01001	Add correction of two's
Discard carry	0001110101	complement of MD (−9) shifted left 5 places
		= +117

4. MD = −X and MR = −Y.
   Here both the multiplicand and the multiplier are negative and in the complementary form. As for case 3, a final correction of the two's complement of X shifted *n* places to the left is added to the result as shown in Table 6.4.

The difficulty with these methods is that the sign of the multiplier must be tested and the correction added if it is negative, so that the routine is slightly different with a negative multiplier than with a positive multiplier.

Booth's Method

A more elegant method in which the procedure is the same regardless of the signs of either the multiplier or multiplicand was invented by A. D. Booth. With this scheme an extra one bit register is added to the MR register, which stores the discarded least significant bit of the multiplier for an extra cycle. The multiplicand is then added, or subtracted from the accumulating partial product, according to the states of these two bits. The extra one bit register is initially set to zero before starting the process. The rules for multiplication by Booth's method is as follows:

1. If both bits are the same [00 or 11], do nothing and shift the partial product and the multiplier right one place. The least significant bit of the multiplier moves into the extra register.

2. If the least significant bit of MR is 1 and the previous least significant bit is 0, subtract the multiplicand from the accumulated partial product, and right shift one place.
3. If the least significant bit of MR is 0 and the previous least significant bit is 1, add the multiplicand to the accumulated partial product, and right shift one place.

The four different cases are shown in Table 6.5. Notice that when the rule indicates the need for the subtraction of a complementary number the true value is added.

A diagram of a parallel multiplier for signed numbers designed to operate with Booth's method is shown in Figure 6.4.

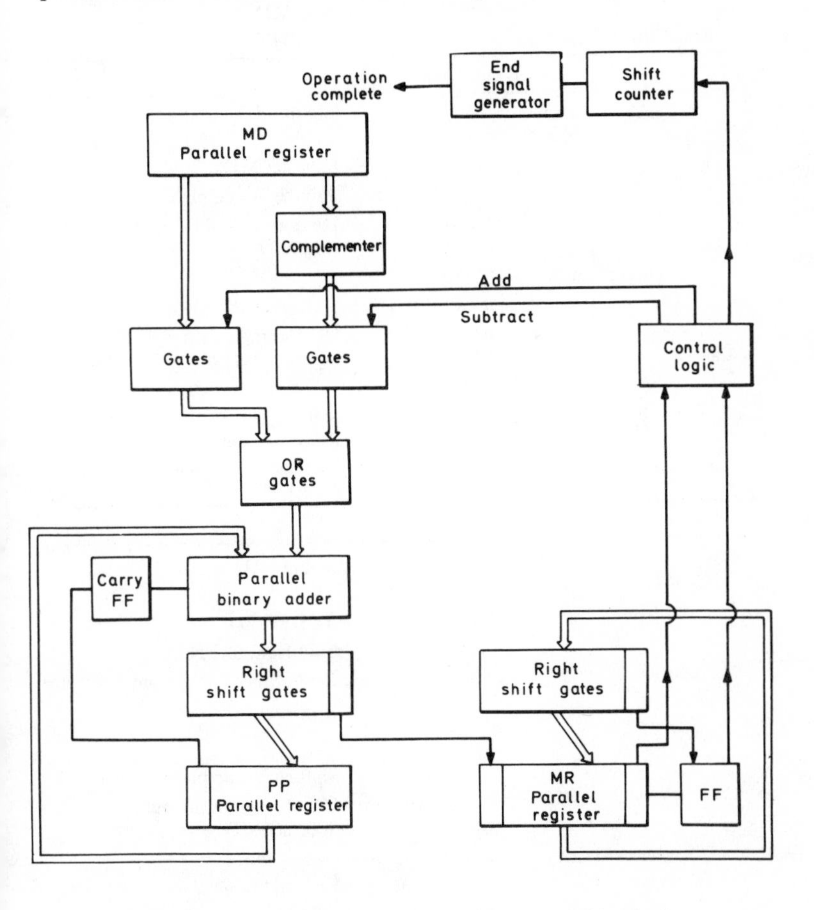

Figure 6.4 Parallel binary multiplier using Booth's method

Table 6.5 BOOTH'S METHOD OF MULTIPLICATION

	MD = +X MR = +Y	
MD	01001 + 9	[comp. MD ≡ 10111]
MR	01101[0]+13	
	10111	Subtract MD
	110111	Shift right one place
	01001	Add MD
Discard carry	001001	
	0001001	Shift right one place
	10111	Subtract MD
	1100101	
	11100101	Shift right one place
	111100101	Do nothing, shift right
	01001	Add MD
Result discard carry	001110101	= +117
	MD = +X MR = −Y	
MD	01001 +9	[comp. MD ≡ 10111]
MR	10011[0]−13	
	10111	Subtract MD
	110111	Shift right one place
	1110111	Do nothing—shift right
	01001	Add MD
Discard carry	0011011	
	00011011	Shift right one place
	000011011	Do nothing—shift right
	10111	Subtract MD
	110001011	
Result	1110001011	Shift right—one place Result is negative
	0001110101	Complement to find the true value = −117
	MD = −X MR = −Y	
MD	10111 −9	[comp. MD ≡ 01001]
MR	10011[0]−13	
	01001	Subtract MD
	001001	Shift right one place
	0001001	Do nothing—shift right one place
	10111	Add MD
	1100101	
	11100101	Shift right one place
	111100101	Do nothing—shift right
	01001	Subtract MD
Discard carry	001110101	
Result	0001110101	Shift right one place = +117

Table 6.5 continued

MD = −X   MR = +Y

MD	10111 −9	[comp. MD ≡ 01001]
MR	01101[0]+13	
	01001	Subtract MD
	001001	Shift right one place
	10111	Add MD
	110111	
	1110111	Shift right one place
	01001	Subtract MD
Discard carry	0011011	
	00011011	Shift right one place
	000011011	Do nothing—shift right
	10111	Add MD
	110001011	
Result	1110001011	Shift right one place Result is negative
	0001110101	Complement to find the true value = −117

Multiplication in Binary Coded Decimal by Count Down

Analogous principles can be applied to the design of BCD multipliers. Figure 6.5 shows a diagram of a parallel BCD multiplier for unsigned numbers, which makes use of parallel 4 bit BCD adders, and the whole system is designed in terms of 4 bit code groups. The least significant 4 bits of the multiplier, which represent the least significant decimal digit, are transferred to a decrementing counter. The multiplicand is added to the PP register in BCD, where it is accumulated, and after each addition the counter is decremented by one. This process is repeated until the contents of the counter are zero. A 4 places right shift is then enabled, the least significant code group of the partial product moves into the most significant position in the multiplier register MR, which has been vacated by a 4 place shift in MR. Simultaneously the next least significant 4 bit code group is transferred to the counter, and the decrementing cycle is repeated. The number of decimal groups is counted in the shift counter which indicates completion of the multiplication operation when all the decimal groups have been shifted out of MR. The decimal product is then left in PP and MR.

This is obviously not the fastest technique since up to nine additions may be necessary for each code group, and the addition process can potentially be speeded considerably.

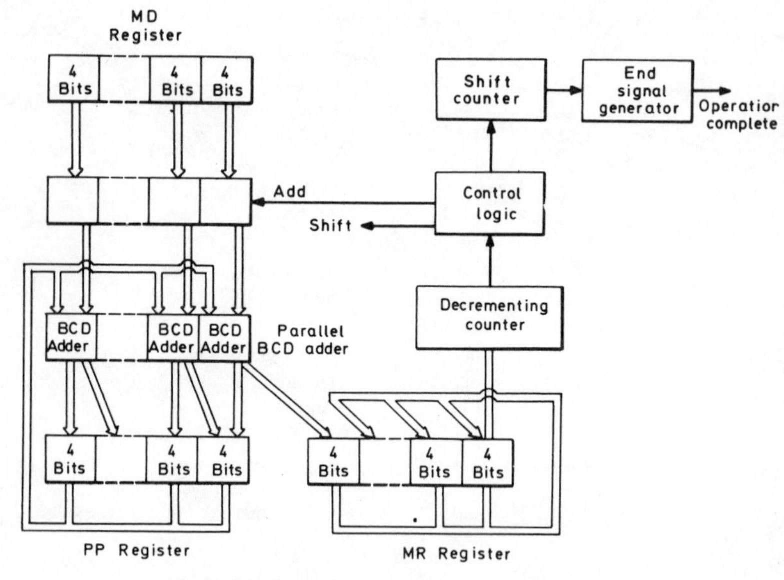

Figure 6.5 Parallel binary coded decimal multiplier

A serio-parallel multiplier can also be designed on this principle, being slower but requiring only a single BCD adder. In this case the slowness of the count down technique does not contrast so much with the addition speed.

Multiplication in Binary Coded Decimal by Halving and Doubling

An interesting method of multiplying binary coded decimal numbers is really a disguised binary multiplication. As such it is theoretically the fastest technique. The multiplier is repeatedly divided modulo 2 or halved and the odd bit discarded, and the least significant binary code group is tested whether it is odd or even. Simultaneously the multiplicand is doubled, which is equivalent to left shifting. After each halving and doubling cycle, the modified multiplicand is added to a BCD accumulator if the least significant digit of the multiplier is odd, and not added if it is even. This is repeated until the multiplier is reduced to zero. The halving and doubling procedure is carried out in a similar way to that described for the binary to decimal and decimal to binary converters described in Chapter 5. An example of multiplying two decimal numbers by halving and doubling is shown in Table 6.6.

Table 6.6 DECIMAL MULTIPLICATION BY HALVING AND DOUBLING ($17 \times 13 = 221$)

MD		MR		*Partial product*		*Accumulated partial product*
17	0000 0001 0111	13	0001 0011	+	0001 0111	17
34	0000 0011 0100	6	0000 0110	do nothing	0001 0111	17
68	0000 0110 1000	3	0000 0011	+	1000 0001	85
136	0001 0011 0110	1	0000 0001	+	Result =	221

The principle has some interesting aspects. It works equally well on non-uniform numbers systems, and was the basis of an early electronic multiplier for sterling. It could also be applied to non-weighted decimal codes by suitable design of the halving and doubling logic.

High Speed Binary Multiplication

The speed of multiplication is an important factor in the overall speed with which a program can be executed. The speed of mathematical computation in particular appears to be strongly dependent on how fast the processor can multiply. In the simplest machines multiplication can be handled by a small program, but this is a slow method, and in general it is an operation that cannot be avoided. Division on the other hand can be circumvented, by multiplying by reciprocals, or using iterative formulae which convert the division operation into a series of iterations containing multiplication.

For these reasons much attention has been given to increasing multiplication speed especially in large processors. Some of the techniques are now described.

Reduction of the Average Time by the Carry Save Method

In the conventional parallel multiplication systems it is necessary to allow time for the carry to propagate for the full length of a parallel adder every time the multiplicand is added to the accumulated partial product. However, the multiplication process is different to an addition or subtraction in which the result must be complete at the end of each addition operation.

As it is known in multiplication that there are to be a series of additions before the final result, it is possible to arrest the carry propagation after traversing one binary adder stage, and the state of the

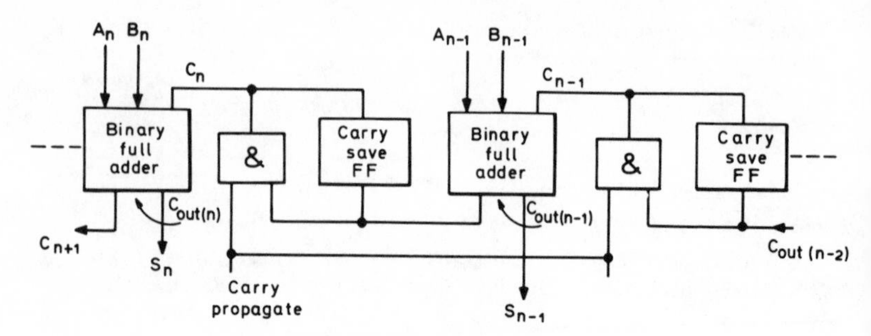

Figure 6.6 Carry save adder

carry is stored in an intermediate carry flip-flop. In this way the addition time need only provide for the time for carry propagation through one stage. The carriers are allowed to propagate one stage at a time until the final addition. At this point the remaining stored carries must be eliminated from the system, so that only the final addition cycle must have sufficient time allowed for the complete carry propagation. This carry save adder system is implemented by the introduction of double rank flip-flops to store the carry between stages. For the final addition cycle the carry stores can just be by-passed, allowing the carries to propagate in the usual way. Two binary stages of a carry save adder with an intermediate carry store are shown in Figure 6.6.

Multiplier Recoding with Uniform Shifts

Instead of making one addition cycle for every bit position in the multiplier, the speed can be increased by accepting the multiplier 2, 3, or more bits at a time. This involves the storage of prefabricated multiples of the multiplicand in different registers, the correct multiple being chosen to be added according to the code with the group of bits.

The method works out particularly neatly in the case where the multiplier is accepted in pairs, because all the prefabricated multiples are present if the device is capable of shifts of both one and two places and subtraction. This has also been called ternary multiplication because examination of the pairs of multiplier bits may require one of three decisions: add, subtract, or shift and add.

If a pair of multiplier bits are considered, they can represent the binary numbers 00 to 11 or (0 to 3). In the case 00, the multiplicand is not added, and for 01 it is added normally as in the simple one bit multiplier system. In the case of 10 or (2), we need to add 2 times the multiplicand, and this is easily accomplished by a shift of one place left with respect to the accumulator.

The case 11 or (3) is interesting because it would appear to be necessary to make two additions, one direct and one multiplied by 2 by left shifting. But 3 can be represented, or recoded, to be 4–1. In the present cycle one can then subtract the multiplicand and remember to add 4. But in shifting the partial product two places to accept the next pair multiplier bits, the multiplicand has effectively been multiplied by 4 with respect to the partial product and it is only necessary to add the multiplicand. But this modifies the rules for multiplicand addition for each multiplier pair. The necessity to add the multiplicand an extra time in the following cycle is stored in a carry flip-flop, and the contents of this in combination with the code of the multiplier bit pair determines the action taken.

Table 6.7 CONDITIONS FOR MULTIPLYING POSITIVE NUMBERS IN THE TERNARY METHOD

Carry in	*MR bit pair*	*Add MD*	*Carry out*
A. No demand for 4 times MD was made in the preceding cycle.			
0	00	0	0
0	01	1	0
0	10	2	0
0	11	−1	1
B. A demand was made in the previous cycle for the addition of 4 times MD.			
1	00	1	0
1	01	2	0
1	10	−1	1
1	11	0	1

These conditions can be best summarised in Table 6.7, and the control logic can be implemented by a simple sequential circuit with a single carry flip-flop.

It may be noticed that if the first pair of multiplier bits is 11 there will be a request for a subtraction of MD on the first cycle. This will result in a negative accumulated partial product. Furthermore, if the following pair of multiplier bits are 10 or 11, there will be another subtraction and the accumulated partial product will become even more negative. This can continue throughout the inspection of most of the multiplier MR, but it is eventually compensated by the addition of a positive number larger than the accumulated partial product, resulting in a final positive product.

This technique can be applied to the multiplication of signed numbers in two's complement representation with additional complication.

Following the same principles, rules can be evolved for the multiplier to be accepted in groups of 3 bits. It is then necessary to be able to add 1, 2 and 4 times the multiplicand, that is shifted none, one or two places, and it is also necessary to generate and store the prefabricated multiple of 3 times the multiplicand.

Multiplication with Variable Shifting

Multiplication with variable shifting depends for its speed on the presence in the multiplier of strings of 1's and 0's. Each string of 1's requires one subtraction and one addition with this method. Only shifting is needed for a string of 0's. A string of 0's must always be interspersed with a string of 1's, so that in effect one subtraction or addition is required for each string in the multiplier, whether 1 or 0.

Even with a purely random binary sequence of 1's and 0's it can be shown that the number of addition or subtraction cycles is reduced. But since in most practical cases the capacity of a word is not fully utilised, the more significant part of the word will consist of a string of 1's or 0's leading to greater saving.

To implement this system, it must be possible to perform a variable number of shifts. In a parallel system this means that multiple gating is necessary. The saving in time is greater if more shifts are possible, but this increases the cost. The method also lends itself conveniently to serial multiplication, where extra shift pulses are all that is necessary to give a variable shift.

Consider a string of 1's separated by 0's

$$\begin{array}{l} f \qquad\qquad\qquad\quad g \\ 0111.........1110 \end{array}$$

Where $f-1$ is the most significant bit in the string and g the least significant bit. This number can be expanded as the binary polynomial

$$2^{f-1}+2^{f-2}.....2^{g}$$

If we add 1 at the gth place a carry will be propagated and the result becomes 2^f therefore we can also represent the string by 2^f-2^g. Or if g happens to be the least significant bit in the whole number, then $g=0$, and the expression becomes 2^f-1.

So it can be seen that 1 times the multiplicand can be subtracted in position g and 1 times the multiplicand added in position f. Therefore instead of performing an addition for each 1 in the string, the equivalent result can be realised by performing one addition and one subtraction in the correct positions.

This can be generalised by considering a number n consisting of two strings of 1's and two strings of 0's, having the least significant bits of each string at p, q, r, and s.

$$\begin{matrix} & p & & q & & r & & s & \\ n = 0 & 111 & \ldots\ldots & 111\ 000 & \ldots\ldots & 000\ 111 & \ldots\ldots & 111\ 00 & \ldots\ldots 00 \end{matrix}$$

The most significant string of 1's can then be expressed as $2^p - 2^q$, and the next string as $2^r - 2^s$.

Therefore the number n can be represented as

$$2^p - 2^q + 2^r - 2^s$$

So that the string of 1's in the multiplier in which each requires an addition of the multiplicand can be substituted with a subtraction for the least significant 1 in the string and an addition one position to the left of the most significant 1 in the string. An example of this is shown in Table 6.8.

Straightforward binary multiplication would have required 11 additions, which has become in this case 4 additions and 4 subtractions.

Table 6.8 VARIABLE SHIFT MULTIPLICATION—ADDITIONS AND SUBTRACTIONS

Multiplier	0	1	1	1	1	1	0	0	1	1	0	1	0	0	0	1	1	1
Addition of MD	1	0	0	0	0	0	0	1	0	0	1	0	0	0	1	0	0	0
Subtraction of MD	0	0	0	0	0	1	0	0	0	1	0	1	0	0	0	0	0	1

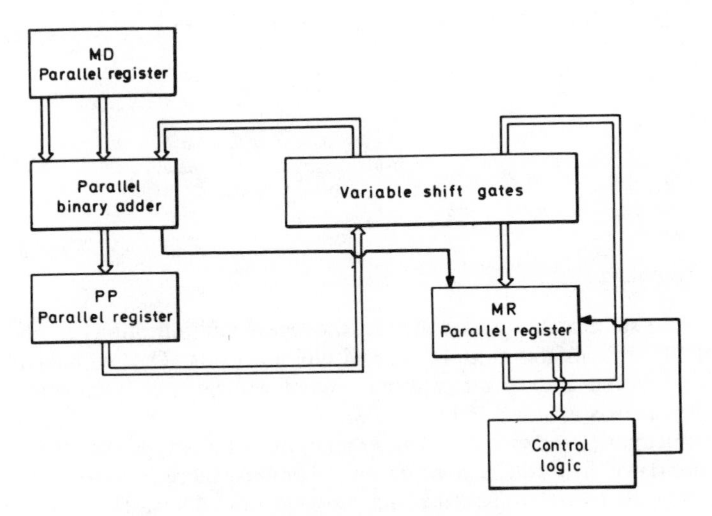

Figure 6.7 Variable shift multiplier

It will be noticed that an isolated 1 in a string of 0's or an isolated 0 in a string of 1's results in either a subtraction followed by an addition or vice versa. This somewhat detracts from the beauty of the method and can even cause there to be more operations than in the normal method in certain cases. This can be overcome by a look-ahead circuit which detects the isolated 1 or 0 and replaces the subtraction of MD followed by the addition of 2 MD by the single addition of MD, or vice versa. A block diagram of this type of multiplier is shown in Figure 6.7.

Array Multipliers

In the simple carry save system described earlier, the multiplicand is added after shifting in repeated cycles, but the carries are not allowed to propagate by more than one stage. The same idea can be implemented with a cascade of carry save adders in which the carries are allowed to propagate up in significance through an array of adders. In the final level of addition the remaining carries must be expelled by propagation, either through ripple carry addition, or a lookahead adder may be used here to increase speed[5].

Consider the multiplication of two 4 bit binary numbers $a_0 \ldots a_3$, $b_0 \ldots b_3$ as shown in Table 6.9. The 16 summands must be formed, and then added in columns, propagating the carries to fabricate the product $P_0 P_1 \ldots P_7$; P_7 being due to the final carry.

Table 6.9 4 × 4 MATRIX OF SUMMANDS FOR AN ARRAY MULTIPLIER

				a_3	a_2	a_1	a_0
				b_3	b_2	b_1	b_0
				a_3b_0	a_2b_0	a_1b_0	a_0b_0
			a_3b_1	a_2b_1	a_1b_1	a_0b_1	
		a_3b_2	a_2b_2	a_1b_2	a_0b_2		
	a_3b_3	a_2b_3	a_1b_3	a_0b_3			
P_7	P_6	P_5	P_4	P_3	P_2	P_1	P_0

The summands are generated by the logical multiplication (or AND), of the appropriate multiplicand and multiplier bits. Thus with an n bit multiplicand and m bit multiplier there will be n m summands. A 4 × 4 matrix is shown in Figure 6.8.

Figure 6.9 shows a 4 × 4 array multiplier of this type. The first row consists of half adders needing only 2 inputs, successive rows receive carries that are propagating and must be full adders. The remaining carries in the last level must ripple through the final row of adders. The speed can be increased by making this row a parallel carry lookahead adder.

In an $n \times n$ multiplier with this scheme the first row contains $n - 1$ half adders, and each successive row holds $n - 1$ full adders, except the last row which only needs a half adder in the least significant position. The whole multiplier then requires n half adders and $n^2 - 2n$ full adders. The diagram in Figure 6.9 can be expanded progressively to the size required.

Dadda[11] has regarded the problem from a slightly different point of view and suggests a multiple input adder for each vertical column in the array of Figure 6.5. This can also be implemented by an array of half and full adders with a different connection pattern. This array multiplier requires the same number of adders as the carry save arrangement of Figure 6.6 and is faster for large numbers of bits. But it is less systematic and does not lend itself so well to large scale integrated circuits. Multiple input adders can be constructed from a chain of full adders, but the interest in array multipliers is stimulating interest in faster types of multiple input adders[3].

The multiplier described is designed for unsigned positive binary numbers, and it is of course always possible to convert complementary numbers to positive numbers before the multiplication. But array multipliers can also be designed for handling signed numbers. Multiplier arrays need not be constructed from 1 bit binary adders and can also be built from 2 bit or 4 bit adders[4].

Until recently array multipliers were only considered in applications where cost was of low importance, but recent developments in microcircuits have changed the picture, and renewed interest is being taken in this type of multiplier.

Division – The Restoring Method

Division is the converse of multiplication and is performed by repeated subtraction of the divisor from the dividend to find the quotient, and is mechanised by the subtraction and the shifting of the divisor downwards in significance. A problem exists in division, which is not present in multiplication, in that it is not known whether the dividend is larger than the divisor. In decimal manual division, an educated guess is made as to how many times the divisor will go into the dividend, or partial remainder. This is then verified, and if wrong a new estimate is made. This is difficult to instrument by machine, and instead the divisor is substracted and the result tested to see if it is negative. In binary division only two possibilities exist during each subtraction step. If both numbers are positive, and the divisor is smaller than the dividend

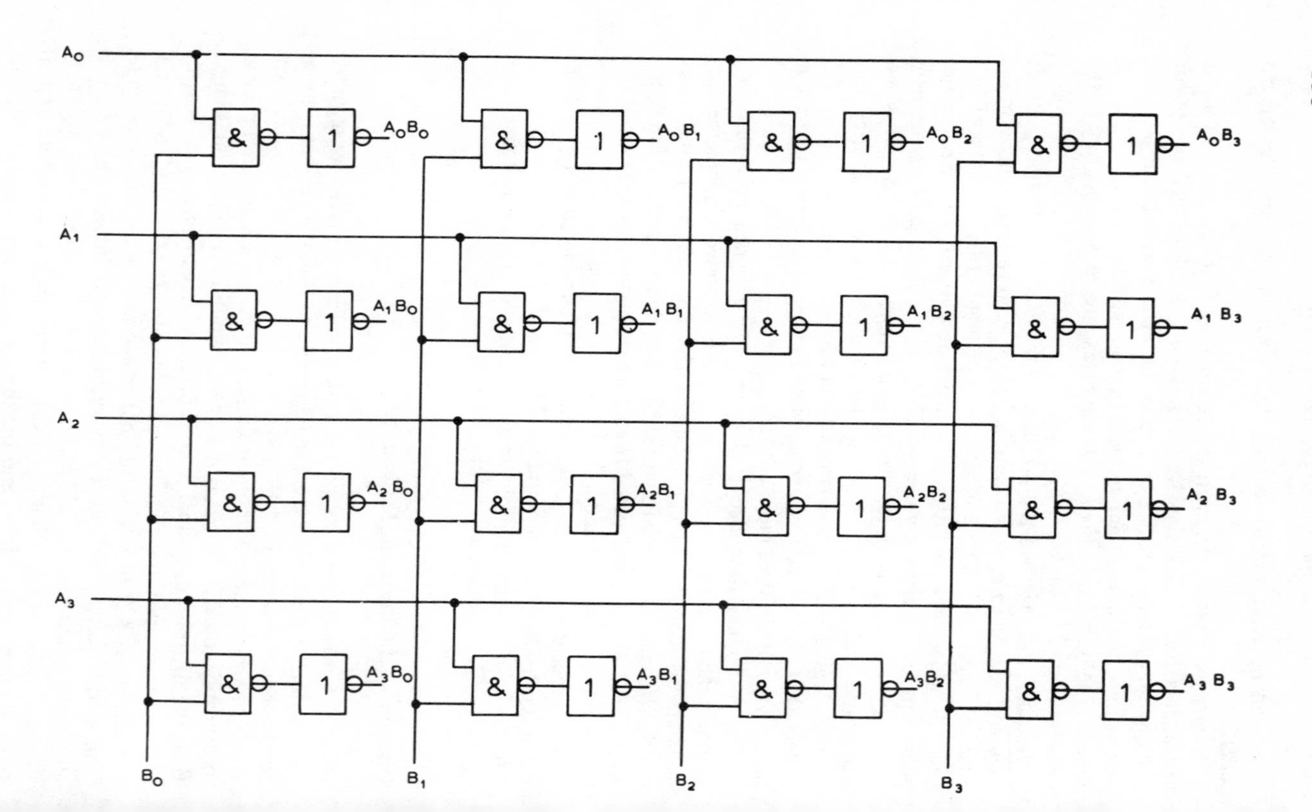

A0
A1
A2
A3
B0
B1
B2
B3
A0B0
A0B1
A0B2
A0B3
A1B0
A1B1
A1B2
A1B3
A2B0
A2B1
A2B2
A2B3
A3B0
A3B1
A3B2
A3B3
&
1

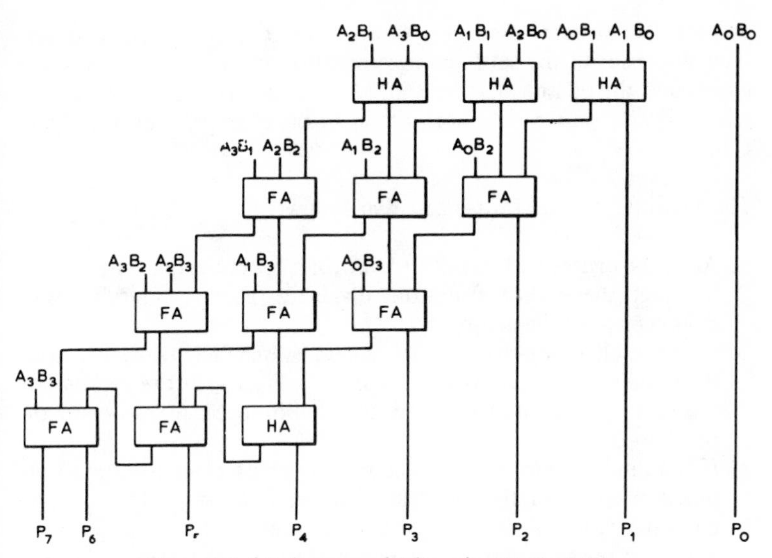

Figure 6.9 4 × 4 array multiplier of carry save type

Table 6.10 RESTORING METHOD OF BINARY DIVISION
(+145 ÷ +13 = +11 and +2 remainder)

	001011	= 11
13 = 01101	0010010001	= 145
2's complement of 13 = 10011	10011	Subtract
	1011110001	Result negative. Shift divisor right and repeat. with the same dividend Put 0 in quotient
	0010010001	
	110011	Result still negative repeat as before
	1111000001	
	0010010001	
	1110011	Result positive, put 1 in quotient and shift divisor right and subtract
Discard carry	0000101001	
	11110011	
	1111110101	Result negative. Put 0 in quotient, replace the previous partial remainder shift the divisor and subtract
	0000101001	
	111110011	Result positive. Put 1 in quotient. Shift divisor and subtract
Discard carry	0000001111	
	1111110011	
Discard carry	0000000010 = 2	
	Remainder = 2	

or partial remainder, there is a positive result. If the divisor is larger, then the result of the subtraction is negative. In this case the guess was wrong and the divisor must be shifted right one place, and another test made. The process can be seen better in the example shown in Table 6.10.

The algorithm for this simple case is as follows:

1. Align the divisor with the most significant bit in the dividend.
2. Subtract the divisor from the dividend. That is, add the two's complement of the divisor.
3. If the result is negative (1 in the sign position), the divisor was larger than the divident (or partial remainder). Place 0 in the appropriate position of the quotient. Add the divisor back to return to the previous result.
4. If the result is positive (0 in the sign position), place 1 in the appropriate position of the quotient. For the following subtraction we continue with this result as partial remainder.
5. Shift the divisor complement one place right propagating the sign. Repeat 2., 3. and 4.
6. The process terminates when the least significant bits of the divisor and the partial remainder are aligned. This is found by counting shifts in a similar way to that used in multiplication. The final result is the remainder.

Notice that if the result of a subtraction produces a negative answer, the divisor must be added to this answer to restore it to the original value. Hence this is known as the restoring method of division. A flowchart of this method is shown in Figure 6.10 and a diagram of a parallel divider with the restoring method is shown in Figure 6.11.

Initially the dividend, which is twice the length of the divisor or quotient, is placed in register DD and Q. After each subtraction the result is tested in DD and 1 or 0 is entered at the least significant end of Q. If the result is negative the divisor is added to restore the previous result. Both the dividend and the quotient are then left shifted one position by transferring back to the DD and Q registers through left shifting gates. The dividend decreases by one bit at each step making room for the quotient bit to be entered at the least significant position of the quotient register.

The close similarity between this diagram and the parallel binary multiplier in Figure 6.3 can be seen, and it is common practice to combine these two devices in one section of hardware. Since one process is the converse of the other an algorithm can be easily devised which combines both operations.

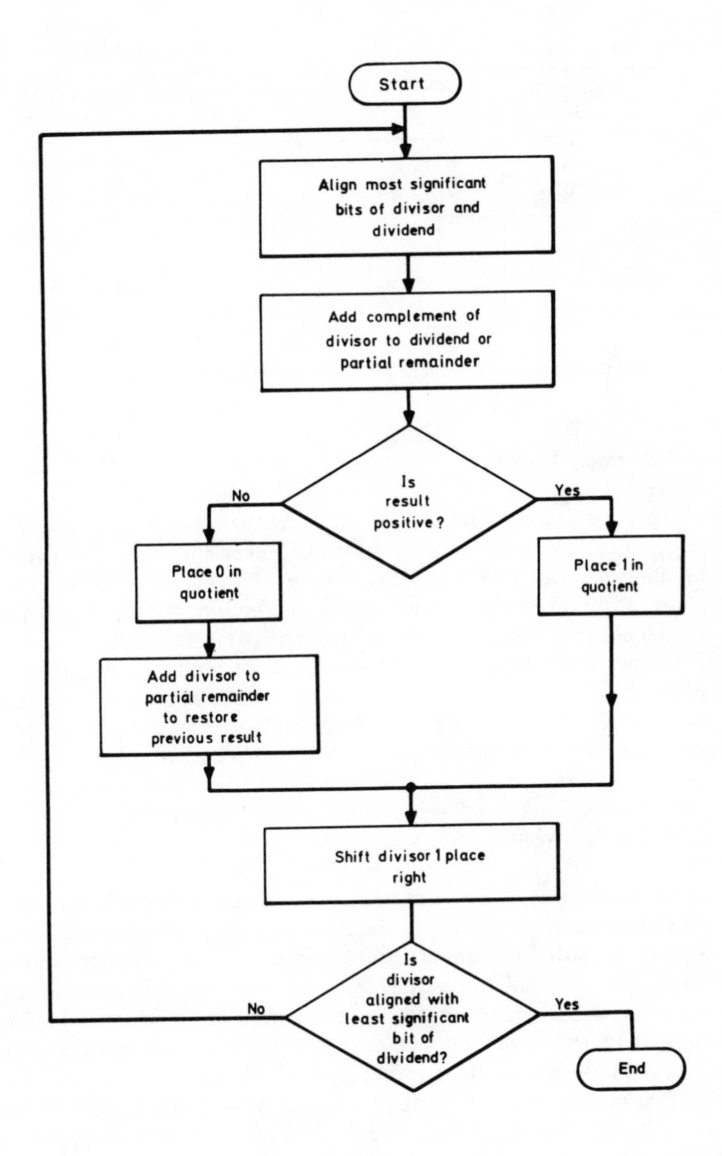

Figure 6.10 Flowchart for restoring method of division

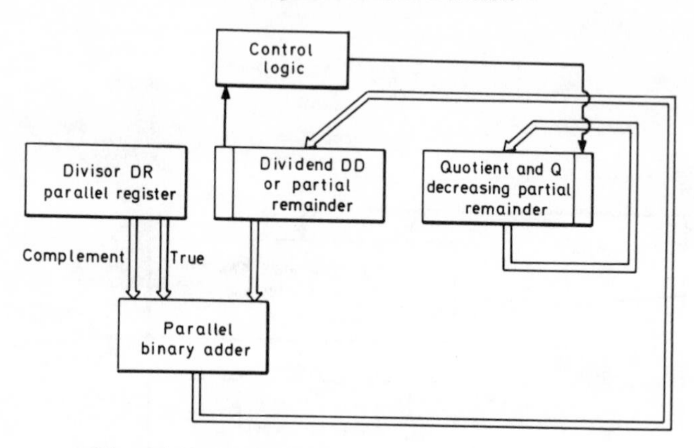

Figure 6.11 Parallel divider using the restoring method

Non-Performing Division

The process of subtracting, discovering that the result is negative, and then restoring the original value by adding back the divisor, is a time consuming process. In the parallel system, the change of sign can be detected at the adder before transferring the result to the register. If the sign changes, the original partial remainder is transferred into the DD and Q registers with a left shift of one place immediately, and the quotient bit is entered into the Q register at the same time. In serial division this is not possible since it is not until the subtraction and transfer are complete that the sign of the result is known.

Non-Restoring Division

A more elegant way of avoiding the necessity for adding the divisor to restore the partial remainder is the non-restoring method. Instead of restoring the partial remainder, or retaining it as in the non-performing method, the fact that the partial remainder has changed sign can be accepted, and the following operation changed accordingly. The sign change is remembered and the next operation is performed in the complementary mode, the divisor being added instead of subtracted. The rule for entering the quotient when dividing positive numbers is: enter 1 if the result is positive, and 0 if the result is negative regardless of the signs of the dividend and divisor. The same problem as that demonstrated in Table 6.10, is shown in Table 6.11, using the non-restoring method. The block diagram looks essentially the same as

Table 6.11 NON-RESTORING METHOD OF BINARY DIVISION
(+145 ÷ +13 = +11 and +2 remainder)

	00101	= +11
+13 01101	0010010001	= +145
−13 10011	10011	Subtract divisor (add
	1011110001	complement)
	001101	Add divisor (true value)
	1111000001	shifted right 1 place
	0001101	Add divisor (true value)
Discard carry	0000101001	shifted right 1 place
	11110011	Subtract divisor (add
	1111110101	complement) shifted right
		1 place
	000001101	Add divisor (true value)
	0000001111	shifted right 1 place
	1111110011	Subtract divisor
Discard carry	0000000010	
	Remainder = +2	

Figure 6.11, the difference between the two systems being in the design of the control logic.

Division by an Iterative Method

The designers of a recent very fast machine, the IBM System/360 Model 91, have chosen a quite different approach. Statistical studies of programs have shown that multiplication is a more frequent operation than division, so that there is less overall speed to be gained by adding cost to the machine in the form of a divider than the multiplier. The machine was therefore designed with a very fast multiplier and an iterative technique of dividing is employed using the fast multiplier.

The divider described is part of a floating point arithmetic unit and operates on bit-normalised binary fractions which represent the mantissa portion of a binary floating point number.

The algorithm applied in this instance appears to have been originally employed in a program for division in Edsac. It converges quadratically, in other words the 'number of correct significant figures is approximately doubled for each repetition of the iterative process. The number of iterations required is then proportional to $\log_2$ of the fraction length.

The dividend and divisor are treated as the numerator and denominator of a fraction. Both the numerator and denominator are then multiplied by a factor K_m so that the new denominator converges quadratically towards 1, and the new numerator converges quadratically towards the final quotient. Thus in dividing A by B we have:

$$\frac{A}{B} \times \frac{K_0}{K_0} \times \frac{K_1}{K_1} \times \frac{K_2}{K_2} \times \ldots . \times \frac{K_n}{K_n} \to AK_0K_1K_2 \ldots K_n = \text{Quotient}$$

and $$B K_0K_1K_2 \ldots . K_n \to 1$$

The important point in the algorithm is the derivation of the K_m, B is a bit normalised fraction thus

0.1XXXX. . . . .

Therefore B can be expressed as

$$B = 1 - y \quad \text{where } y \leqslant \tfrac{1}{2}$$

Now if K is given the value $(1 + y)$ and the denominator B is multiplied by K then

$$B_1 = BK = (1 - y)(1 + y) = 1 - y^2$$

where $y^2 \leqslant \frac{1}{4}$ because $y \leqslant \frac{1}{2}$.
The new denominator must therefore be in the form

0.11XXXX. . . . .

In the next iterative cycle K_1 is chosen to be equal to $1 + y^2$, giving

$$B_2 = B_1K_1 = (1 - y^2)(1 + y^2) = 1 - y^4$$
$$= 0.1111\text{XXXX}. \ldots .$$

and thus doubling the number of leading 1's in the fraction. The process is repeated until a denominator of 0.11111. . . . . 111 is obtained which is equivalent to 1 within the accuracy obtainable in the machine.

Since the numerator has also been multiplied by K_0, K_1, K_2, K_3, ... K_n it has converged quadratically to the quotient.

The factor K is simply derived, as it is the two's complement of the denominator. Thus

$$K_{m+1} = 2 - B_m = 2 - (1 - y_n) = 1 + y_n$$

So the multiplier constant for each iteration is found by taking the two's complement of the resultant denominator of the previous iteration.

Large Scale Integrated Arithmetic Units

With the development of very large scale integrated circuits it has become possible to form complete high speed arithmetic units on a single silicon chip. These are discussed at the end of Chapter 9.

Problems

1. Design the control system for a parallel multiplier for signed numbers using Booth's method.
2. Design a serial binary multiplier using Booth's method.
3. Evolve a logic design of a fully serial binary coded decimal multiplier using the doubling and halving technique.
4. Investigate the alternative methods of designing a multiplier for decimal numbers coded in 'excess 3' code, and decide which method(s) are best on the grounds of speed and economy.
5. Design a combined parallel multiplier-divider for two's complement numbers making use of the non-restoring method of division and choosing whichever type of multiplication principle is most suitable to combine with this.
6. Design a serial binary divider using the restoring method of division.
7. Plan the system for a ternary multiplier for unsigned positive numbers, and design the sequential logic control system to generate the add MD, add 2 × MD, and subtract MD signals.
8. Produce a paper design of an array multiplier using standard integrated circuits, and calculate the time taken to complete the formation of the product, this can be tried with individual gates and complete integrated circuit full adders.

REFERENCES

1. FLORES I, *The Logic of Computer Arithmetic.* Prentice-Hall (1960)
2. HWANG, K, *Computer Arithmetic,* John Wiley
3. McSORLEY, O.L., *High Speed Arithmetic in Binary Computers. Proc IRE.* 49 No. 1 67–91 (1961)
4. TOCHER, K.D., 'Techniques of Multiplication and Division for Automatic Binary Computers.' *Quart. J. Mech. App. Math 11.* Pt 3 364–384 (1958)
5. ROBERTSON, J.E., 'A New Class of Digital Division Methods IRE *Trans Electr. Comp.* 7 218–222 (1958)
6. DADDA, L., *Some Schemes for Parallel Multipliers, Alta Frequenza* 34 349–356 (1965)
7. FERRARI, D, and STEFANELLI. R. *Some New Schemes for Parallel Multipliers. Alta Frequenza* 38, 843–852 (1969)
8. DADDA, L. and FERRARI, D. *Digital Multipliers: A Unified Approach. Alta Frequenza* 37 1079–86 (1968)
9. SWARTZLANDER, E.E., *The Quasi – Serial Multiplier. IEEE. Trans. Comp.,* C–22. 317–321 (1973)
10. WALLACE, C.S., *A Suggestion for a Fast Multiplier. IEEE. Trans. Electr. Comp.* EC–13 14–17 (1964)

Chapter 7

Computer Memories

It is impracticable to give more than a review of the field of memories, because of the very rapid rate of technological change, and the range and complexity of the subject. The aim can only be to give an introduction to the various types of memories in use at present or perhaps in the near future. The only way to keep up-to-date in this area is by continuously reading trade literature to know what is available and in which direction developments are leading. Semiconductor memories are now sold as chips with their performance specifications, but little detailed information can be found about the way they are designed, which is highly specialised, and is the private know-how of manufacturers.

The memory might well be regarded as the most important component of a computer. As a consequence of improvements in microcircuitry the cost of the central processing logic is being progressively reduced, so that the aim is to cram as much memory capacity into the smallest space, and with the shortest access time to stored data, and also at the lowest cost per bit. The needs of memory users have applied continual pressure to development, which leads to continuing revolutionary changes in technology. Out of the welter of different types of memories, several successful technologies have emerged.

The speed and organisation of a memory can profoundly affect the fundamental arrangement of the processor, and therefore the way in which it is fitted into the rest of the processor organisation. It is therefore essential to have a conceptual understanding of the various types and properties of memories.

The subject is suffused with jargon and acronyms which are constantly changing with new developments. The following terminology may elucidate some of the language.

Terminology

Word A group of bits. These may represent a binary or coded decimal number, binary coded symbols for letters or other data which has been received or is to be sent to an input-output device, or to mass storage. Or it may represent a machine instruction which will be interpreted as part of the program.

Word Length The number of bits in the word.

Byte A smaller group of bits, usually 4 or 8, representing a character or decimal number, and forming part of a word.

Address A location within a memory which can store a word, analogous to a card in a file.

Access Time The time required to obtain a word from the memory after having previously entered the address and given a 'read' signal.

Read The operation of obtaining or 'reading' some data from the memory.

Write The operation of writing some data into an address in the memory

Volatility This refers to the property of some memories such that their contents are lost when the power is removed. Non-volatile memories retain their contents indefinitely without any power.

Destructive Read-Out Memories have destructive read-out when the contents of a word are obliterated by the reading operation. This should be distinguished from volatility, since the rest of the memory contents are unaffected, and may be retained when the power is removed.

Non-destructive Read-Out An operation in which the contents of a memory location may be read without being destroyed.

Latency This refers to the time necessary to wait with a drum, or disc memory, for the desired information to rotate to the reading head. This is a variable time depending on the position of the disc or drum at the time the data is requested.

RAM Random access memory. This refers to the fact that any word can be accessed, (i.e. read or written) at random with the same access time.

ROM Read only memory. A type of memory in which data is permanent or semi-permanent, and can only be read by the processor and not written.

PROM Programmable read only memory. A type of read only memory in which the contents can be entered on a separate instrument, usually at a much slower rate. This is sometimes referred to as 'blowing' a PROM. The PROM can also be erased for reuse.

EAROM A type of PROM in which the contents are erased electrically.

Hierarchy of Memories

If an overall view of all types of memories is taken it is found that there is a trade-off between the capacity of the memory, its speed, and the cost per bit of storage. In larger computers both fast and slow memories may be incorporated in a hierarchy of several speeds and capacities, and data is transferred to and from the slower high capacity memory in blocks to the fast memory for high speed processing and then returned to the slower memory for long term storage. This attempts to make the optimum use of the high speed of the smaller fast memory and the lower cost of the slower memory.

Table 7.1 AREA OF MEMORY CAPACITY AND SPEED.

Type of Memory	*Technology Used.*	*Access Time.*	*Capacity*
Scratchpad Memory (high speed) (a)	Semiconductor MOS Technology	down to 35ns	16 Kilobits
(b)	Semiconductor bipolar technology	down to 20 ns	16 Kilobits
Main Memory (a)	Semiconductor MOS Technology Static RAM	down to 35ns	16 Kilobits per chip
(b)	Semiconductor MOS Technology Dynamic RAM	100ns to	64 Kilobits 256 Kilobits per chip
Special Purpose Memories	Semiconductor MOS Shift Registers		
Mass Memory (a)	Magnetic Discs (fixed-rigid)	0.02 s	up to 300 megabytes
(b)	Magnetic Discs (floppy)	0.16 s	10 megabytes
(c)	Magnetic Bubbles	1 2 ms	256 Kilobits per chip
Archival Storage. (a)	Magnetic Tape reels.	Treated as input-output	Unlimited "
(b)	Magnetic Tape Cassettes.	"	"
(c)	Punched Cards	"	"
(d)	Paper Tape	"	"

The areas of speeds and capacities are shown in Table 7.1. The limits of these areas are not exact and are changing as technologies develop, and in some areas more than one technology may be in competition, and cost and reliability may be the determining factor in the choice of memory in a particular application.

Semiconductor Memories

Before describing semiconductor memories in detail it will be useful to classify the various types of memories available at present in terms of function and technology. A block diagram of these is shown in Figure 7.1.

Random Access Memories or RAMs form the general purpose main memories, and are also used for scratchpad memories when they have very fast circuits. They are volatile and the contents are lost when the power is removed. If it is necessary to retain the contents of the memory after switching off, or during a power failure, a standby battery supply can be designed to maintain the power to the memories. This is usually a very small power in the case of MOS memories.

Metal Oxide Semiconductor (MOS) memories have emerged as the most successful types at present. Those interested in the principles of the various semiconductor technologies used for memories should

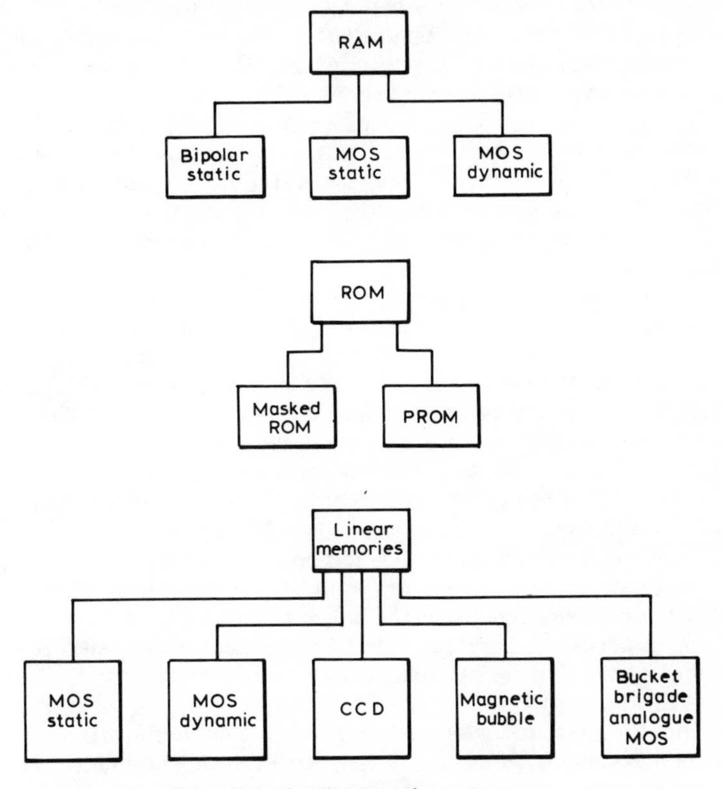

Figure 7.1 Classification of memory types

consult books and journals on semiconductor theory. The following technologies have been or are being used in memories. NMOS – negative channel metal oxide semiconductor, PMOS – positive channel metal oxide semiconductor, CMOS – complementary metal oxide semiconductor, MNOS – metal nitride oxide semiconductor. Each of these covers more detailed variations. There are two types of MOS RAMs, the static RAM and dynamic RAM. The bipolar technology only uses the static principle.

Read Only Memories or ROMs also use a variety of technologies. They are found in two types. The masked ROM has the patterns permanently impressed, and cannot be changed, once made. The EPROM – or Electronically Programmed Read Only Memory – can have programs or patterns of bits entered electrically, but once entered they are not normally changed. However the chip is provided with a window, and the contents of the EPROM can be wiped by irradiation by Ultra Violet light for a period of several minutes. New data can then be re-entered so the EPROM can be re-programmed and used again.

Each bit location in a RAM or ROM must be individually addressable, so that data can be entered or retrieved on a random basis. This requires that a binary number representing the address must be directly entered via pins on the chip. RAMs may therefore need a large number of pins, with the attendant problems of cost and reliability. For instance a 4096×1 bit RAM has 2^{12} locations, and if directly addressed would need 12 address pins in addition to power and input and output pins. This can be somewhat mitigated by addressing the RAM in two steps of six bits. This saves pins at the expense of a small loss in time.

If the memory is arranged in a linear fashion in the form of a long shift register similar in principle to that described in Chapter 3, the only pins needed are input, output and a shift pulse, apart from power pins. Any bit can be located by counting the number of shifts from a start time, which can be done on a separate counter. The price paid is the inability to sample a particular bit until it has been circulated to the end of the shift register. But in many applications speed of access can be sacrificed to obtain lower cost, and also this form is suitable for other technologies.

Shift registers made with MOS technology have been available with a moderate number of bits (up to 1024) for some time. Their cost advantage has been eroded by the low cost of dynamic RAMs which are being produced in large quantities. Another technology which is well suited to the shift register configuration is the Charge Coupled Device or CCD.

But the most interesting technology which lends itself particularly to long shift register type storage is Magnetic Bubbles. These various types of semiconductor memories will now be described in more detail.

The Static RAM

In the continual struggle to increase both speed and memory capacity, the static RAM fills the niche for memories of very fast access times, but only with limited capacity. The speeds are continually being increased, and now approach access times of 10 nanoseconds.

The capacity of the memory is limited by the need for several transistors in a memory cell, requiring more area on the silicon chip. Static RAMs are made with both bipolar and MOS technology.

Basically the Static RAM consists of an array of cross-coupled flip-flops on a silicon chip, similar in principle to that shown in Figure 3.2. As well as the array of flip-flops, the chip also contains decoders, write

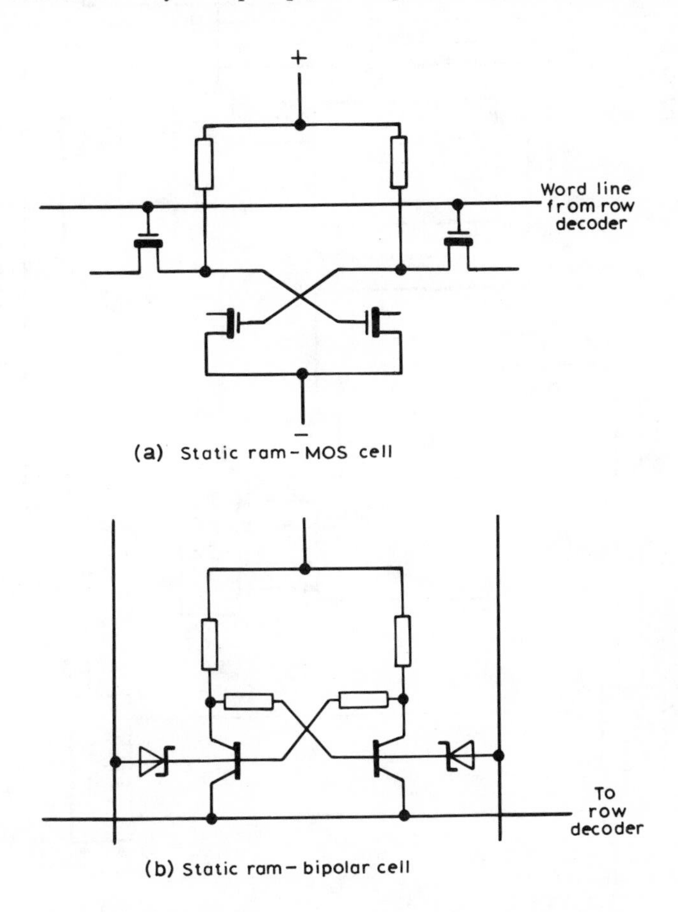

Figure 7.2(a) Static RAM, MOS cell (b) Static RAM, bipolar cell

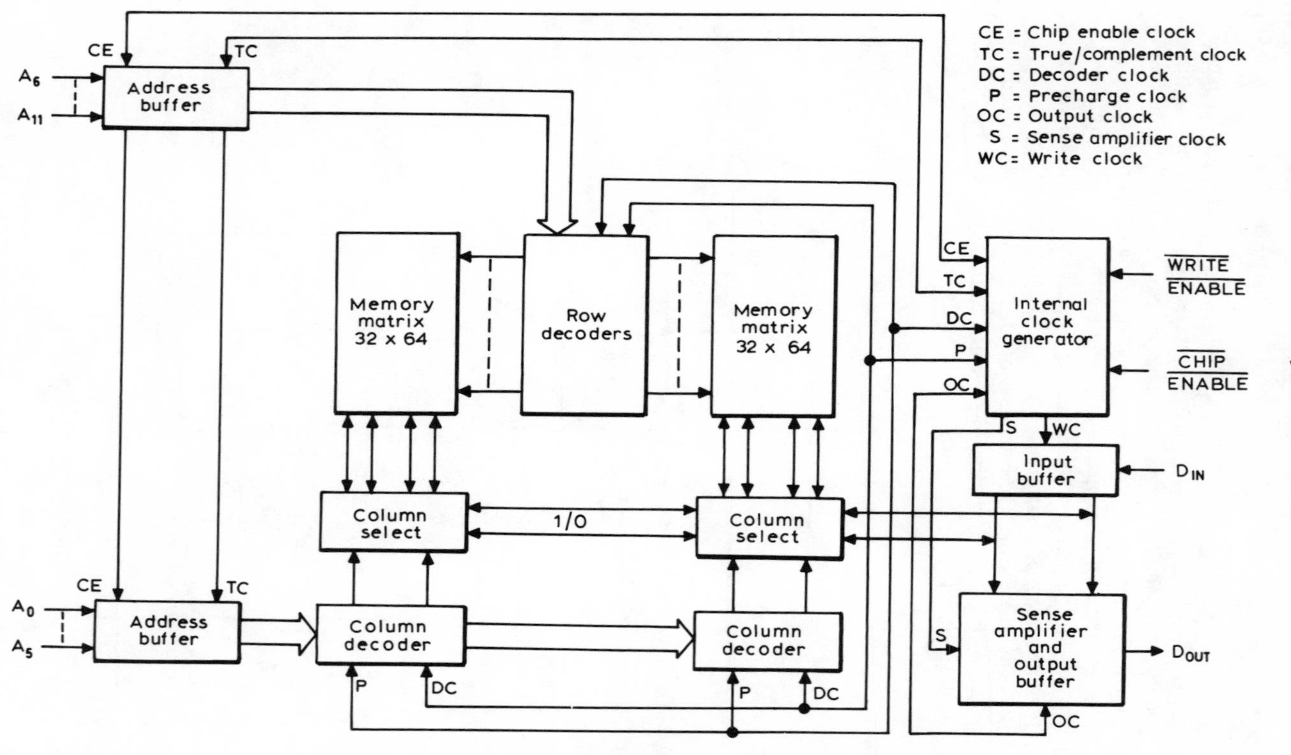

Figure 7.3 Block diagram of 4K MOS static RAM (Mostek MK4104)

and sense amplifiers and buffers. The circuits of typical cells are shown in Figure 7.2., (a) being an MOS cell and (b) a bipolar cell. The MOS cell is a very high resistance device, the resistors shown being as high as 5000 megohms, with a cell current of less than a nanoampere. To make the memory change state fast, the circuit capacitances must therefore also be kept very small, in order to achieve the small time constants required.

The bipolar cell uses low impedance bipolar transistors in contrast to the very high impedance FET transistors of the MOS cell. The lower impedances make it easier to obtain short time constants and high speeds, but at the expense of taking more current, with the attendant problems of heat dissipation.

Since the cells are flip-flops, either one side or the other will be conducting, and therefore all cells draw current whether set to 1 or 0. Unless the supply is removed the cell flip-flops remain set, retaining their data indefinitely. Switching off of course, destroys the memory contents.

A block diagram of a 4K MOS Static RAM is shown in Figure 7.3. Although the storage uses static flip-flop cells, the sense amplifiers are clocked to reduce power and current consumption.

The Dynamic RAM

Although the Static RAM still retains a place as a very fast memory of moderate size, the major storage system for the main processor memory is being taken over by the Dynamic RAM. Instead of storing the data on an array of flip-flop circuits, the dynamic storage principle makes use of the inherent circuit capacitance as a memory.

Consider the circuit shown in Figure 7.4.

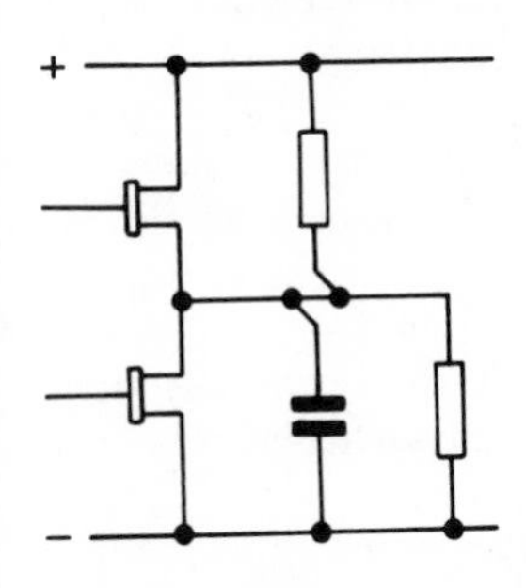

Figure 7.4 Capacitor storage

If the upper transistor is turned on by a pulse, and the lower one turned off, the capacitor is charged to the positive potential. Conversely, if the bottom transistor is turned on and the upper one off, the capacitor is discharged to the ground level. If the leakage were zero, the voltage to which the capacitor had been set, would be retained indefinitely. Unfortunately due to leakage resistance from the capacitor, the charge immediately begins to drain away. In a typical dynamic storage cell, the charge set into the capacitor leaks away in the order of a millisecond. How, then, can such a device be used for long term storage?

The answer is to read out the contents of each cell periodically, sampling to see whether it has been set to 1 or 0. This must of course be done before the time in which the contents have decayed beyond recovery. The cell is then set back to its original state of 1 or 0 again, and this is done repeatedly. This process is called 'refreshing' the contents of the memory. As long as this is carried out continuously the data stored in the memory is retained dynamically. The refreshing operation must be interleaved with reading or writing the memory and it is arranged that whenever a cell is read, it is refreshed, and of course no cell must go unrefreshed for longer than the maximum time allowed. Switching off, of course, loses the contents.

Much effort has gone into simplifying the circuit, and reducing the area of silicon used for a storage cell to the minimum. Originally it was necessary to use 3 transistors per cell, but this has now been reduced to 1 transistor per cell.

A typical arrangement of memory cells and sense amplifier is shown in Figure 7.5. The circuit shown is a one transistor per cell scheme with a dynamic sense amplifier. To get the maximum signal into the sense amplifier the cell capacitance is made as large as possible, and the capacitance of the digit/sense line to the sense amplifiers is minimized. The digit/sense line shares a large number of cells – 128 in the case of a 16K memory – so that the stray capacity can easily become relatively large compared with each cell. The sense amplifier is set in the middle of a digit/sense line, so that it senses the differential voltage between two halves of the line.

There are two types of sense amplifiers, static and dynamic. The dynamic amplifier shown in Figure 7.5 has no load resistors, and therefore uses less current. When a row is selected, the charge from the cell capacitance is transferred by the selected transistor to the digit/sense line. This occurs on all columns. The column selection, from the column decoder, enables the digit/sense for that particular column to the sense amplifier.

The dynamic sense amplifier, consists merely of cross coupled transistors, without any load resistors, which are set in one sense or the other by the voltage on the digit/sense line. When reading, this is determined by the charge on the cell capacitance, and since the row selected transistor remains conducting the amplified output from the

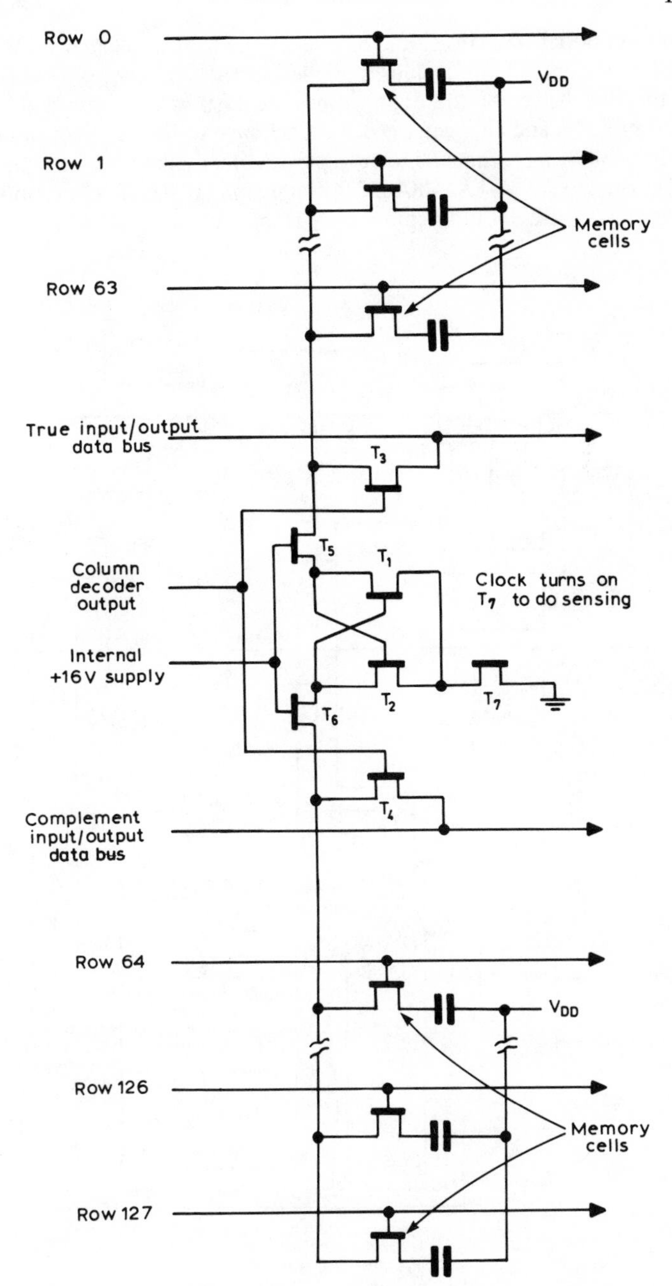

Figure 7.5 Memory cells and dynamic sense amplifier (Mostek)

sense amplifier recharges, or refreshes, the cell capacitance. When writing, the input/output data is applied in true and complement form to the two halves of the digit/sense lines, setting the sense amplifier appropriately, and charging the cell capacitance to the new input value.

The following comments refer to a particular dynamic semiconductor memory, the MOSTEK MK4027 4K dynamic RAM. This memory is arranged as a 4K × 1 bit memory on a 16 pin chip.

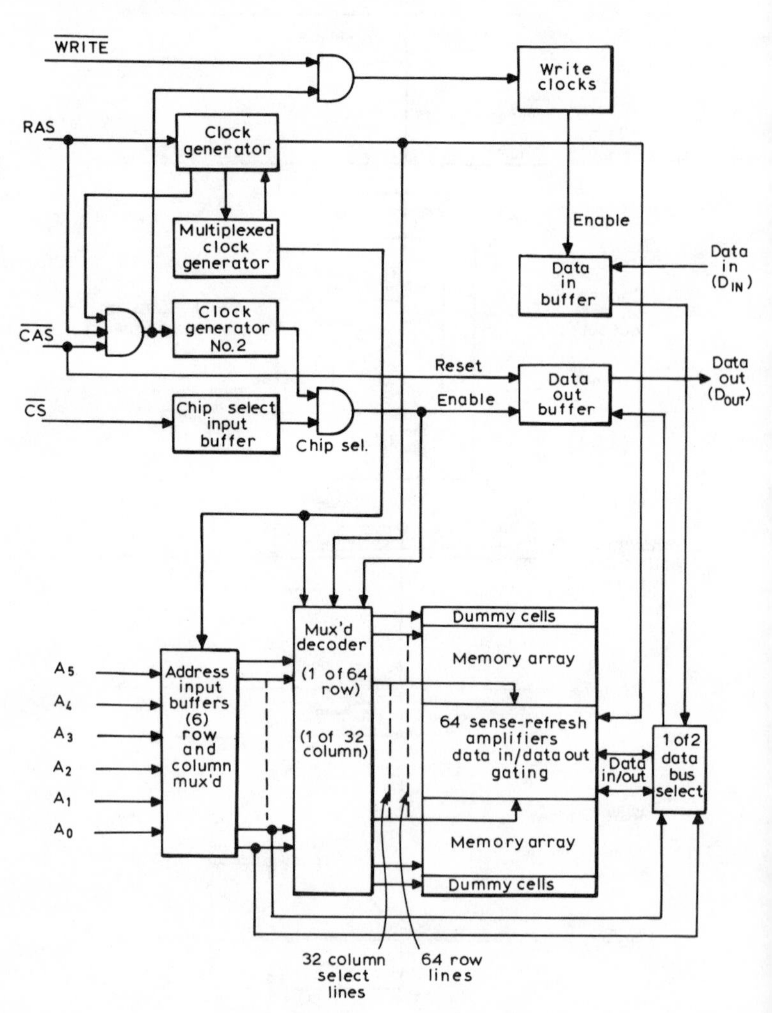

Figure 7.6 Block diagram of dynamic RAM (Mostek MK4027)

Internally it has a 4096 (2^{12}) array with 64 rows and 64 columns. To reduce the number of pins the rows and columns are multiplexed. The rows are selected first, followed by the columns. In this way 6 pins only are needed for 4096 addresses, i.e. 64 (2^6) plus 64, or 6 bits for row and column successively. The remaining pins are needed for Data Input (DIN) and Data Output (D OUT), Row Address Strobe (RAS) Column Address Strobe (CAS), Chip Select (CS), Write Enable (Write), and Power Supplies. (+12v, +5v, –5v and 0v). A functional block diagram is shown in Figure 7.6.

To create, for example, a 16 bit X 4096 memory, 16–1 bit memories are wired in parallel and selected simultaneously. Larger capacities can be obtained by using the chip select input to select different banks of chips.

In order to continually refresh the memory, it is normally cycled repeatedly through a Read-Write-Modify cycle, for each address sequentially, and the timing is arranged so that the data is always read and

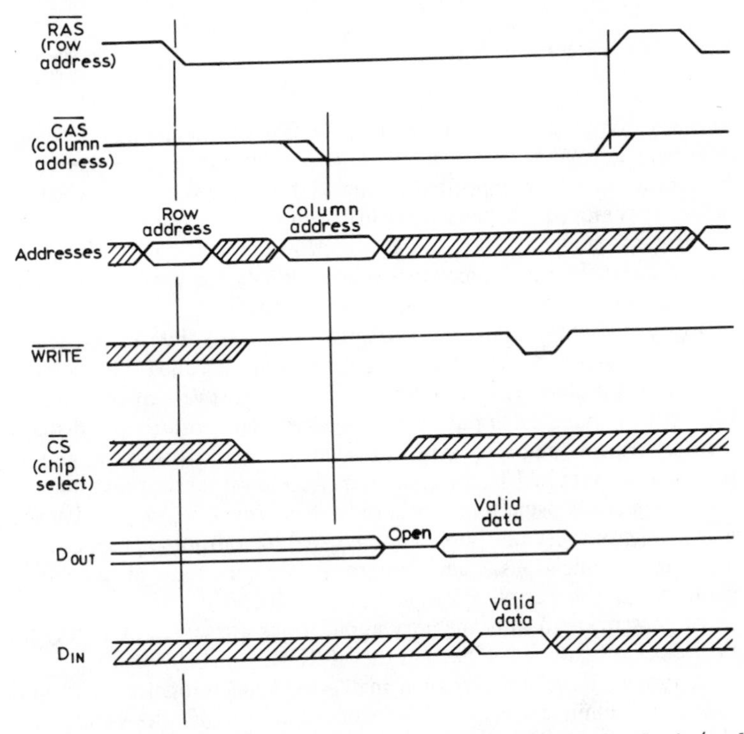

Figure 7.7 Timing diagram, dynamic RAM (Mostek MK4027) Read-write/read, modify, write cycle

refreshed within the maximum 2 milliseconds allowed. Reading and refreshing occur in the same cycle. The contents of a particular bit are first sensed by the Sense Amplifiers and stored temporarily. If the contents of the cell do not need to be changed, the same data is then written back into the same address. This proceeds continuously.

When new data is to be written into a cell, the last read address in the sequence is stored in external registers, and the write address is entered in row and column order. The contents of the cell are read, destructively, and the new data bit is entered into the cell. The read refresh cycle then resumes where it left off, and only a single cycle is lost, which introduces a negligible delay in refreshing. Of course care must be taken in the system design to ensure that the introduction of too many write cycles does not delay the read-refresh operation too long.

The timing diagram of the Read-Write-Modify cycle is shown in Figure 7.7.

Read Only Memory

In many computer applications a large section of the memory never has new data written into it, and is only read, during normal operation. Furthermore, it is an important advantage that data is not lost when the power is removed. In particular this occurs where the main memory consists of semiconductor RAMs which are volatile. The solution to loss of data when designing with volatile RAMs has been to introduce sections of memory with permanent data in ROMs.

Every computer must contain some permanent data to put it into operation when it is switched on. This program is called the Bootstrap in small computers. Larger computers contain software of considerable size which handles input-output devices, and priorities, manages memory space, and performs other duties, and this must also be permanently retained in the computer. At a lower level of program, the microprogram is usually in a read only store, (see Chapter 10). Because many microprocessors are used as special purpose processors in dedicated applications, they require a large amount of permanent memory. All these applications are filled by ROMs.

At present, read only memory applications are served by two types, the mask programmed ROM, and the EPROM.

A typical ROM consists of a matrix of MOS transistors with both row and column drivers, and decoders, deposited on the same silicon chip, as shown in Figure 7.8. of the Mostek MK 34000. This memory holds 16 Kilobits in the form of 2K × 8 bit words. Thus each bit has an

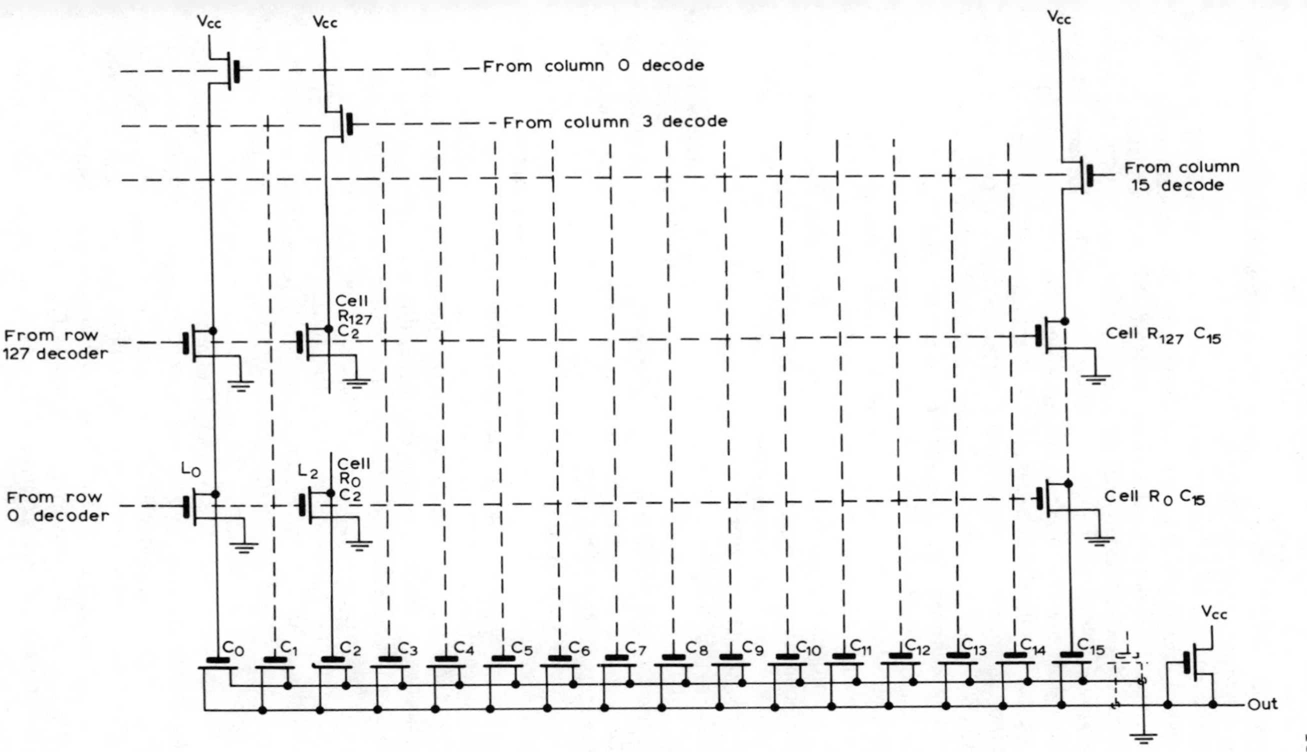

Figure 7.8 ROM matrix and output circuitry (Mostek MK34000)

array of 2K cells, using a common decoder to select the equivalent bit in each array.

The pattern of bits held in the mask programmed ROM is superimposed during the fabrication of the chip by the application of a mask which allows or omits the connection of the cell transistors to the output lines. Consider the case where the cell Ro C2 has been addressed. When the binary addresses are decoded Ro and C2 are selected. If the drain contact of cell Ro C2 is connected to bit line L2, then L2 is pulled down, turning 'off' transistor C2, thus raising the output line to Vcc giving a logical 1 output. Notice that the lines Co, C1 and C3 through C15 are not addressed and are therefore also 'off'.

Now consider the case when C2 is masked and there is no drain contact to bit line L2. When this cell is addressed, the transistor does not hold down L2, which rises to Vcc. This turns on transistor C2 which causes a logical 0 to be put on the output line.

To program a pattern of bits into the ROM the drain contact is either connected or omitted, so that the output is either a 1 or 0. This is of course permanently fixed in the ROM.

The PROM or EPROM is a programmable read only memory. A similar matrix of cells, and selecting and decoding circuits are used, but the design of the cell is different. The EPROM is programmed electrically, and the data is erased by exposing the chip to ultra-violet light which is allowed to fall on the chip through a plastic window in the chip package.

Each cell has a floating silicon gate which is placed within a silicon dioxide layer and controls the flow of current between the source and drain of the cell. During programming, when a logical 1 is entered a high voltage is applied to the source and gate of the cell transistor. This causes the injection of electrons into the floating silicon gate. This gate is effectively insulated within the silicon dioxide layer, and when the setting voltage is removed the charge on the gate is retained indefinitely.

The presence, or absence, of the charge on the gate controls the conduction in a channel between the source and the drain of the particular cell. This determines whether a 1 or 0 is stored. The conduction or not of the cell acts in a similar way to the presence or absence of the connection in the mask programmed ROM.

The contents of all the cells together are erased by flooding the chip with ultra-violet light. This sets up photocurrents in the floating silicon gates, allowing the charge to dissipate into the substrate of the chip.

Both the setting and erasing operations are comparatively slow. Entering a bit requires a fraction of a millisecond, and erasure of all the contents may take a quarter of an hour. This is not important, since once the data has been entered it can be read out in under a microsecond.

Linear Memories and Shift Registers

The term 'linear memories' is used to describe charge coupled device and magnetic bubble memories, since shift register seems inappropriate in these cases. The term shift register is retained for the smaller capacity MOS shift registers.

Memories such as RAMs and ROMs which have to be randomly accessed, must have sufficient pins to enter an address to select a particular bit or word. As the size of memories grows, this becomes a problem which can only be partly assuaged by sequencing the entry of row and column addresses as in some dynamic RAMs. In many cases it is acceptable to sacrifice access time for simplicity and reduced number of pins. This can be done by organising the data in a line, which is continually being shifted through the device, somewhat in the way data travels down a delay or transmission line, except that the speed is

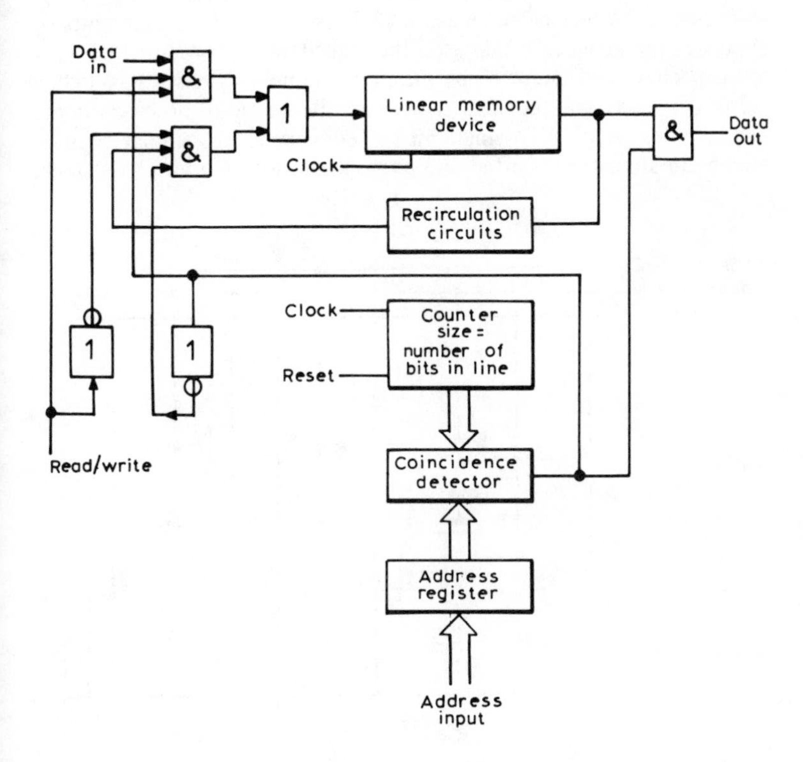

Figure 7.9 Addressing system for linear memory

controlled by the clock rate. Only the input and output of the device need to be accessible, and a particular bit of data is found by counting, which can be performed by separate logic. The logic for locating a particular address for writing or reading is shown in Figure 7.9.

MOS shift registers can be briefly mentioned, although they are now largely relegated to special circuit applications. The principle of the shift register has been covered in Chapter 3. As in MOS RAMs, both static and dynamic circuits are in use. Dynamic shift registers store the data on the small capacitance associated with each cell. A two phase clock signal is taken to alternate circuits, and this continually moves data from one cell to the next. New data is fed in at the beginning of the shift register, and the old data is shifted out of the end. If it is necessary to preserve the contents it must be recirculated as shown in Figure 7.9.

Because the charge on the cell capacitance can only be held for about 20 microseconds the data must be shifted along at least at this speed. Figure 7.10 shows a typical circuit of a 1 bit cell of a dynamic shift register. When clock phase 1 ($\emptyset$ 1) is on it transfers contents of circuit 1, preserved as a charge on the capacitance (shown dotted), into the capacitance of circuit 2, by means of a coupling transistor. $\emptyset$ 1 then turns off, and $\emptyset$ 2 transfers data from the previous circuit into the capacitor of circuit 1. A single bit cell consists of two similar circuits, which are alternately shifted and immobilised by the two phase clock,

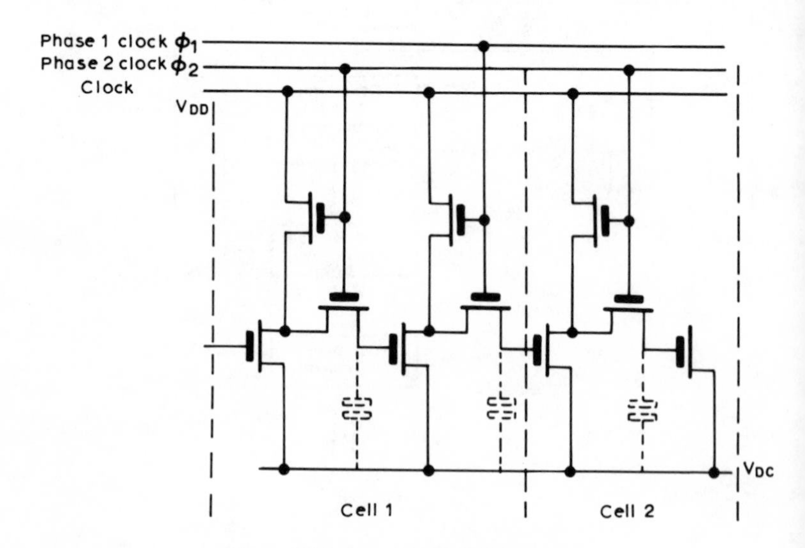

Figure 7.10 Dynamic MOS shift register

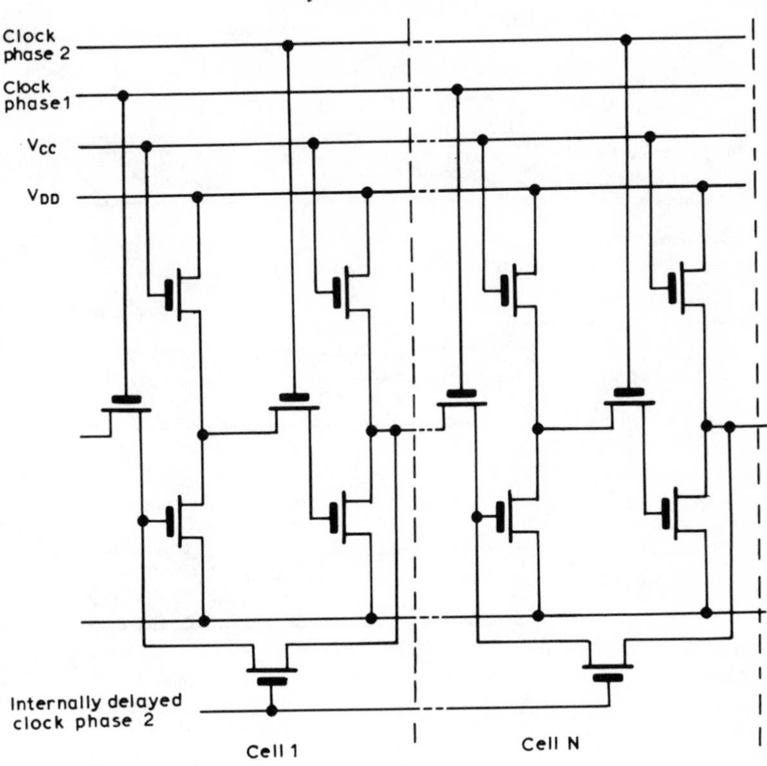

Figure 7.11 Static MOS shift register

and up to 1024 bit cells are connected in series. A development of this named a 'Bucket Brigade Device' is used for delaying and shifting analog samples. The analog potential on the storage capacitors is preserved from cell to cell, so that a delayed sample analog signal is delivered at the output.

A static shift register consists of MOS flip-flops with coupling transistors to hand on the data from one to the next. As before, there are two similar circuits per bit cell, and the data is shifted alternately into the flip-flops by a two phase clock. An internally delayed clock clears each flip-flop before the new data is entered. A circuit of a 1 bit cell is shown in 7.11.

Charge Coupled Devices

Two quite different technologies are contending for the territory of memory capacities beyond the present range of MOS RAMs. These are

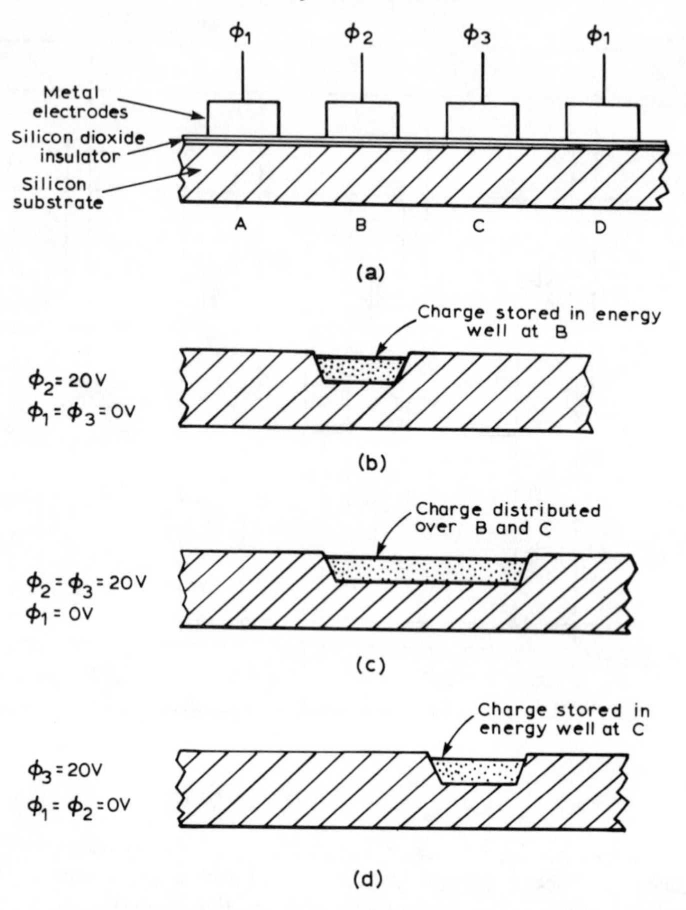

Figure 7.12 Charge transfer in charge coupled device

Charge Coupled Devices (CCD) and Magnetic Bubble Memories. This field has been dominated by surface magnetic recording devices, mainly magnetic discs, in which the recorded data is mechanically moved past a read-write head. But no true electronic engineer really feels happy with a mechanically moving device, and great efforts are being expended to find a cheaper and more reliable replacement, at least at the lower capacity end of the range.

Charge Coupled Devices use silicon technology and can therefore draw on the accumulated expertise from microcircuitry. The principle is based on the transfer of a buried charge along a layer of silicon by a series of electrodes. A section of a simple type of charge coupled device is shown in Figure 7.12. This consists of a silicon substrate, with a silicon dioxide layer, and a series of identical metal electrodes deposited on top. Every third electrode is joined together, and these three sets are taken out to a three phase driving circuit.

It is assumed that a charge has been introduced to the surface between the silicon oxide and silicon beneath the second electrode. Its position is maintained by holding the potential of the second electrode at 20v and the electrodes (A and C) on each side at 0v. This creates a potential 'well' where the mobile charge rests, Figure 7.12.b.

In the next step, phase 2(Ø 2) and phase 3 (Ø 3) are set to 20v and Ø 1 remains at 0v. The potential 'well' now extends across electrodes B and C spreading the charge. Now Ø 1 and Ø 2 are set at 0v and Ø 3 at 20v, and the potential 'well' is under electrode C, and the charge has been transferred from electrode B to electrode C. By repeating this sequence of pulses on the electrodes a pattern of charge or no charge can be moved from electrode to electrode.

Three sets of electrodes are needed to determine that there is no ambiguity, and the charges move in one direction.

Various more advanced electrode structures have been evolved to overcome problems connected with leakage and photo lithography. At present 64 Kilobit sizes have been made, and sizes of 4 megabit are anticipated, with a minimum geometry of one micrometer. These memories have the advantage of using the well understood technology of silicon, but they are being pressed by the remarkable achievements in dynamic RAMs.

Magnetic Bubble Memories

Thin films of orthoferrites or garnets can be formed in single crystals in which the magnetic domains are oriented in a direction normal to the film. When no magnetic field is applied perpendicular to the film, the magnetic domains orient themselves in random patterns, with some pointing one way and the others oppositely. When a perpendicular magnetic field is applied, the patterns first reduce, and then leave small cylindrical areas of magnetization directed in the opposite sense to the surrounding film, as shown in Figure 7.13. These are called magnetic bubbles, and can be used to represent a bit of stored information. The preferred materials at present are synthetic garnets such as europium-yttrium-thulium (EuYTm) garnet, which is grown epitaxially on a gadolinium gallium garnet substrate.

In order to use this effect for the storage of data it is necessary to devise a method of controlled movement of the bubbles. This is done by depositing a shaped magnetic structure of Permalloy on top of a

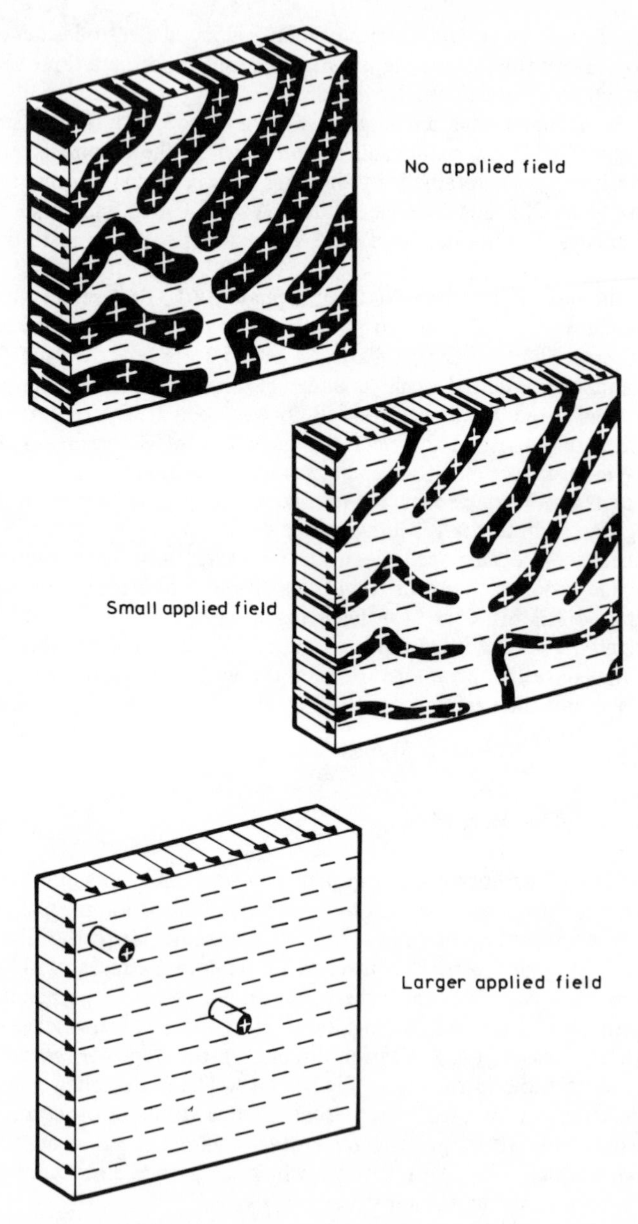

Figure 7.13 Formation of bubbles in thin crystal of garnet. As the external field increases, the domains that oppose the external field decrease in area so that they form cylindrical domains or bubbles

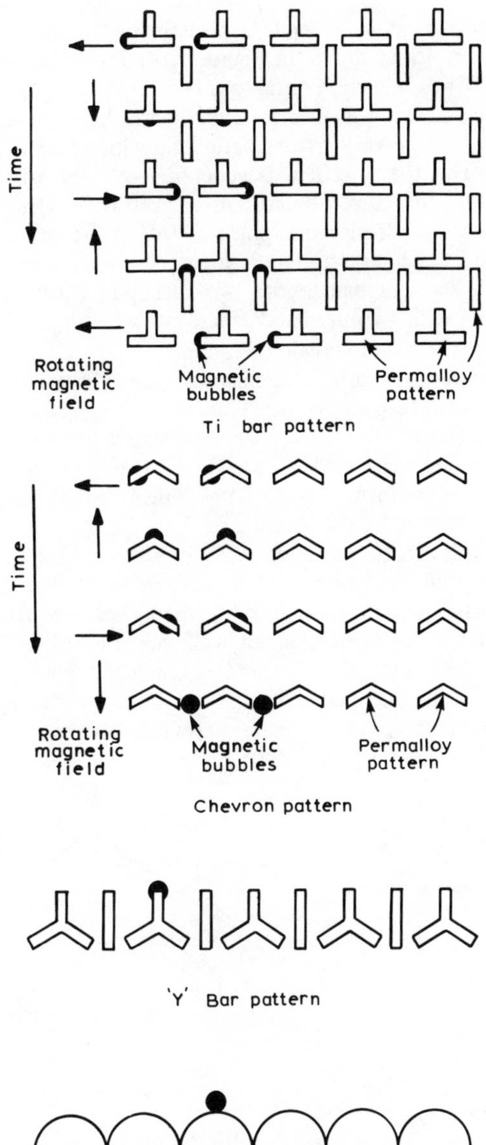

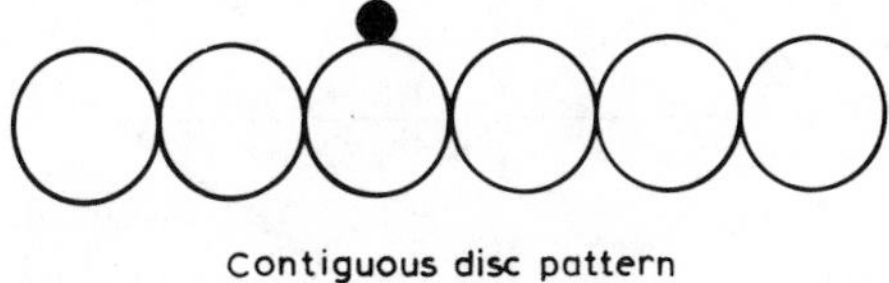

Figure 7.14 Permalloy patterns for bubble memories

silicon dioxide spacing layer. A variety of patterned Permalloy structures are in use as shown in Figure 7.14. These are the Ti bar, the Chevron, the Y bar, and the Contiguous Disc.

The bubbles position themselves underneath the Permalloy structure and are moved as shown by a magnetic field which rotates in the plane of the film. The rotating field is generated by two orthogonal coils wrapped around the chip. The coils are driven with triangular current waveforms which are displaced in phase by 90° as shown in Figure 7.15. The structure of a complete bubble memory is shown in Figure 7.16. The memory slice wrapped in the two orthogonal drive coils is then sandwiched between two permanent magnets which provide the steady field normal to the slice to create the bubbles.

The structure of the actual slice is shown in Figure 7.17. The epitaxial magnetic film is deposited on the non-magnetic gadolinium-gallium-garnet substrate. The Permalloy pattern is formed on top of the magnetic film and separated by a silicon dioxide spacing layer. The magnetic bubbles are formed in the layer beneath the Permalloy pattern where they are moved by the rotating field.

With this structure bubble sizes of 2 micrometers have been achieved with a capacity of 256 Kilobits. Data rates of more than 250 Kilobits per second with power dissipation of less than a watt are attainable.

In a recent development charged walls are created by ion implantation in the magnetic layer around a deposited gold pattern. The bubbles stick to the charged walls and can be moved as before with a rotating field. This technique enables smaller structures and bubble sizes to be realised with the possibility of storage densities of 16 Mb/cm^2.

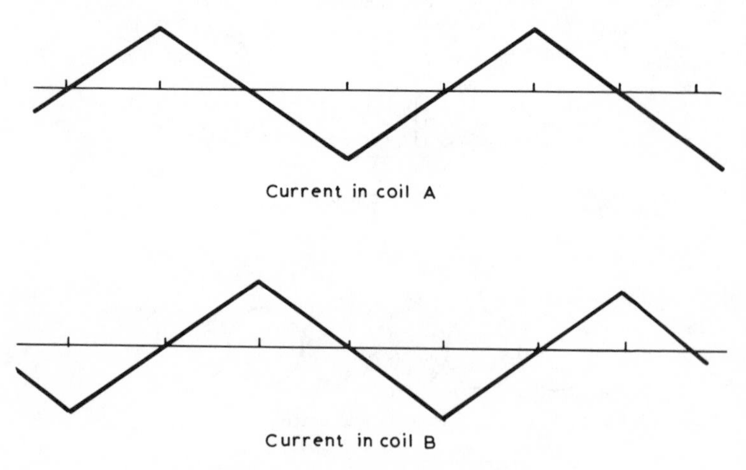

Figure 7.15 Bubble memory. Rotating field currents

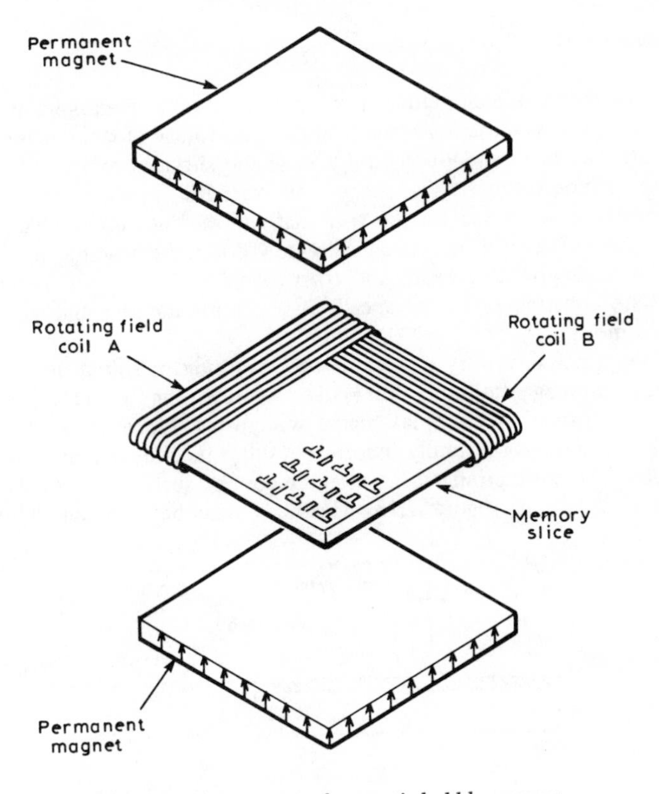

Figure 7.16 Structure of magnetic bubble memory

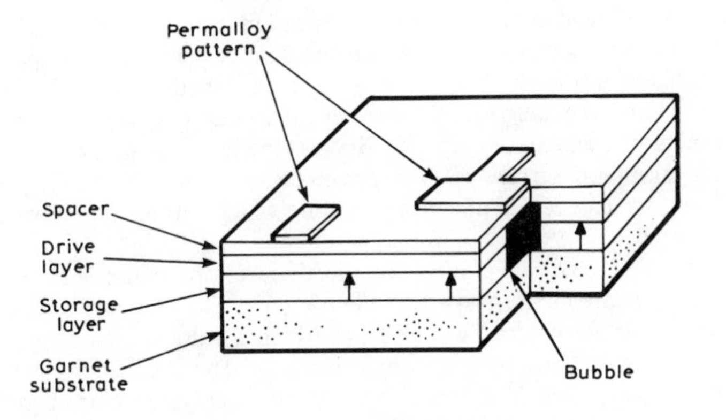

Figure 7.17 Section of bubble memory

Magnetic Surface Storage Systems

Just as the semiconductor memory has become predominant for the main processor memory, the field of mass storage of large quantities of data has been monopolised by magnetic surface storage systems. These include magnetic disc stores and magnetic tape systems. Their performance is limited by the fact that the medium upon which the data is recorded must be mechanically moved in some way into position at the reading/writing head, and then passed under it, and therefore they are constrained by the speeds at which mechanisms and surfaces can be moved.

The principle is very similar to the recording of sound and video signals on magnetic tape, but pulses representing binary data are recorded instead of complex signal waveforms. Since an error in a single bit may give a totally incorrect result, much greater precision is needed. The basic arrangement of the recording surface and read/write head is shown in Figure 7.18. The head may be in actual rubbing

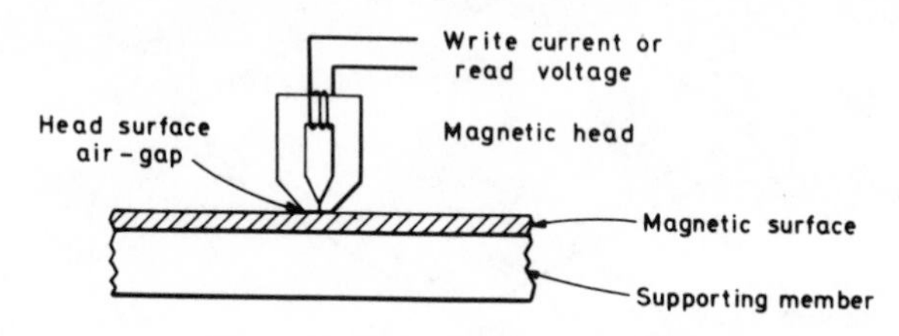

Figure 7.18 Magnetic read-write head

contact with the magnetic surface as in magnetic tape recording, or spaced a very small distance above the surface and not touching it, as in magnetic disc and drum systems. The medium is passed under the head at a constant velocity, and when writing data current pulses are passed through the read/write head. The fringing field at the gap in the head extends into the magnetic surface and magnetises it, and causes the recording of elementary magnetic dipoles longitudinally in the medium. If the magnetic surface is now passed again under the head, small voltages are induced in the head winding which can be amplified and interpreted.

Write and read waveforms for the three of the commonest pulse recording methods are shown in Figure 7.19. The simplest recording system is the Return to Zero (RZ), in which a pulse is passed through the head for a '1' reading, and none for a '0'. The idealised signal read from this recording is shown above. As the voltage developed in the head, when the magnetised medium is passed under it, is proportional to $d\phi/dt$, the signal that is read is approximately a differential of the

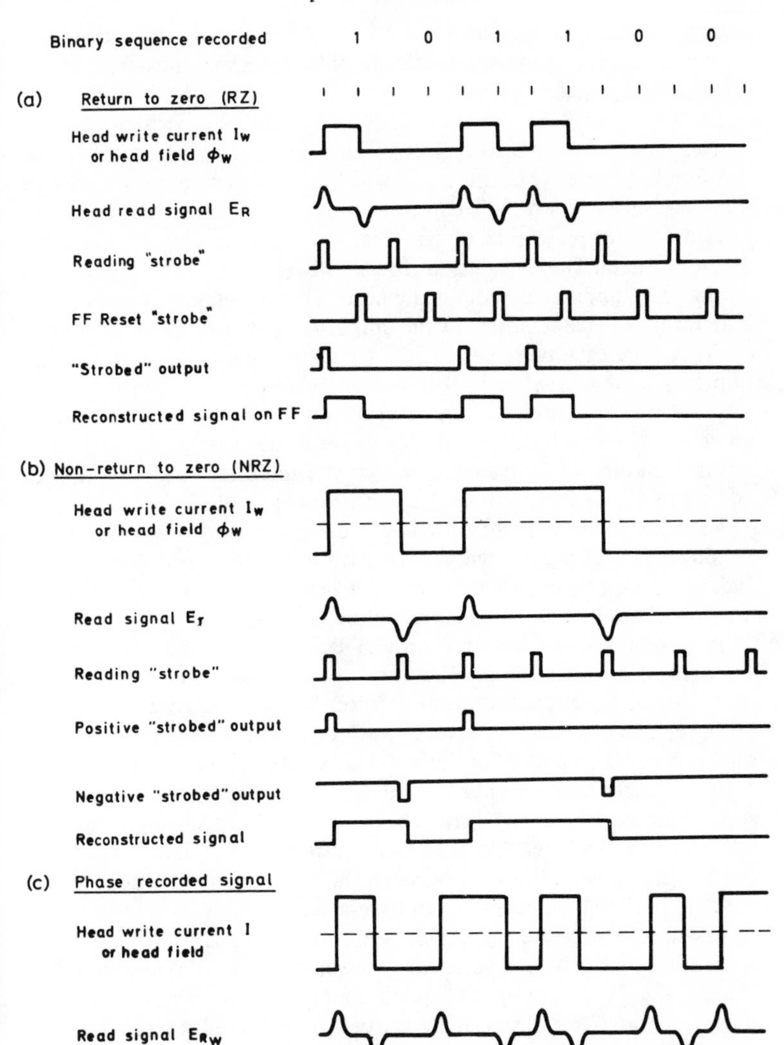

Figure 7.19 Pulse recording methods

original signal deformed by the characteristics of the head and the medium. The signal is recovered by 'sampling' the output of the read amplifier at the start of each pulse period, the resulting output setting a flip-flop, which is then reset at the middle of the next pulse period.

A modification of the RZ system is the return to saturation or RS system. In this case a dc bias current is superimposed on the write current causing the medium to be negatively saturated, unless there is a '1' signal which positively saturates it, thus increasing the amplitude of the recorded signal.

In the Non-Return-to-Zero (NRZ) system the writing current remains continuously in the positive direction during a series of '1's or continuously negative during a series of '0's. As a maximum of only one flux reversal occurs per bit compared with two in other methods, this gives a reading pulse rate of half that for RZ recording for the same density of data. The difficulty is that a long series of '1's or '0's requires a long pulse approaching dc in the head. This imposes the necessity for a dc response characteristic in the amplifier. The read signal is sampled at the start of each pulse period, and a positive signal sets an output flip-flop to 1, and a negative to 0 thus reconstructing the original signal. It may be arranged that a flux reversal always occurs after a certain number of pulse periods, by so designing the code to be recorded, thus setting a minimum frequency to which the amplifier must respond. An odd parity bit in every word achieves this for example.

With the phase recording method a pulse is recorded at every pulse period, but a '1' is recorded as a positive followed by a negative pulse, and an '0' vice versa. When the signal is read it can be seen that the '0's are shifted in phase by half a pulse period from the '1's.

A 'strobing' signal has to be generated for reading, and two methods exist for this. In the simple case a continuous clock signal is recorded on a special track on the drum or disc. This can be read and is used both to synchronise the writing waveform and to generate 'strobe' signals, and is acceptable for fairly low density drum or disc systems.

In modern high density recording, the packing density may be several thousands of bits per inch, and a minute mechanical displacement of the clock reading head with respect to the data head would cause a large phase difference between the clock signal and the recorded data. It is therefore necessary to have a self clocking system in which the clock and 'strobe' signal are derived from the signal itself. The phase recorded signal is well adapted to this, since it can be seen that a flux change always occurs at the middle of every pulse period. The read pulse generated by this can be extracted and used to generate the various sampling signals.

Magnetic Disc Storage

The physical arrangement of a large disc store is shown in Figure 7.20. A stack of metal discs are assembled on a vertical shaft and rotated by an electric motor. The discs are coated on both upper and lower sides with a magnetic surface, usually nowadays a magnetic oxide with an

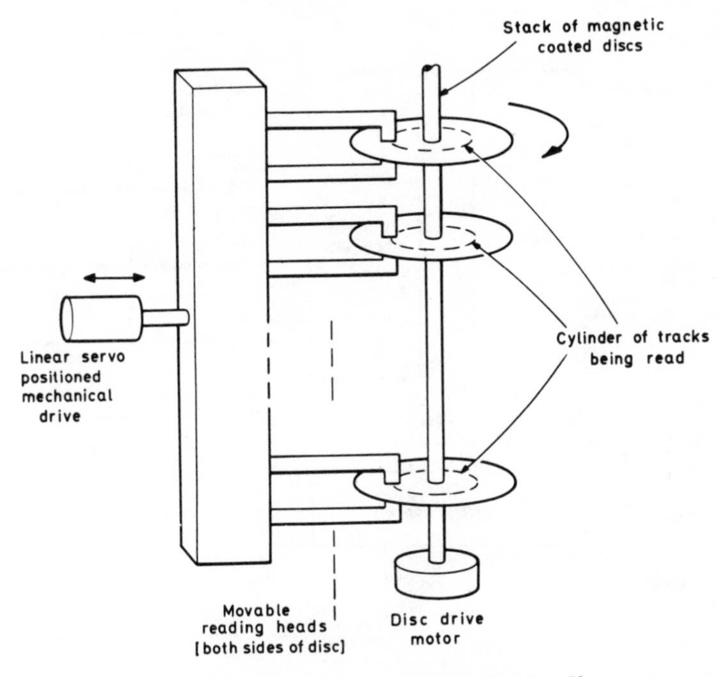

Figure 7.20 Physical arrangement of large disc file

epoxy plastic binder. The discs must be very flat and are polished to a mirror finish. In the past, high quality nickel plating has been in vogue, but this has now been superseded by magnetic oxide surfaces. The surface must be highly homogeneous and without pinholes or dead spots.

The read/write heads for both sides of the discs are supported by a comb-like structure, and can be moved radially across the discs from the periphery towards the centre. The head structure is driven in and out by a linear motor on a precision rail system. The position of the heads is located by an electro-optical transducer, and the drive is servo controlled to the desired position. In some cases the head structure is driven by a fast analogue servo to within one or two tracks of the correct position, and the final positioning is controlled by a fine positioning digital servo. The read/write heads are maintained at a very small separation from the surface of the disc by an air bearing, in which the head actually planes on the thin viscous film of air at the disc surface. The heads are withdrawn from the surface when the discs stop rotating and are carefully lowered at speed in order to prevent damage to the disc surface.

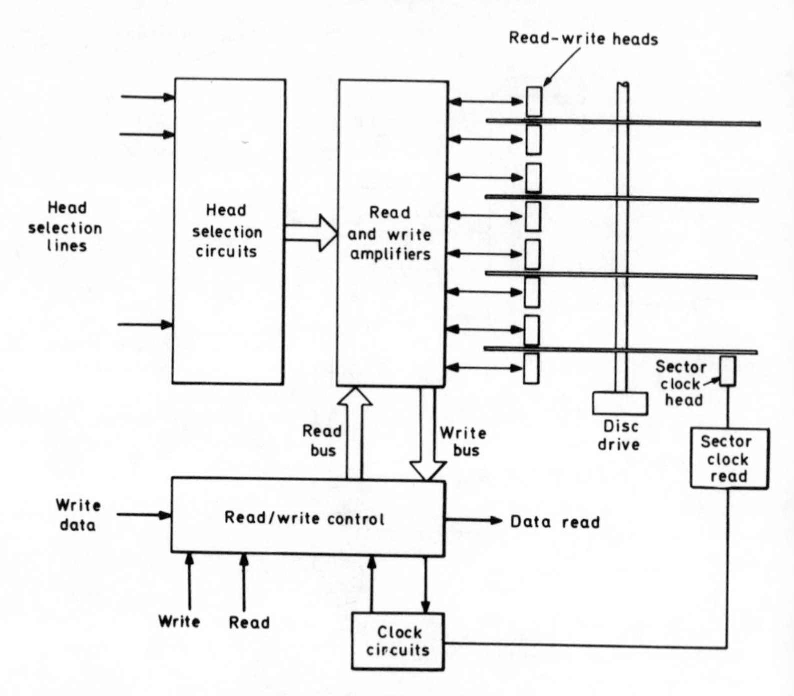

Figure 7.21 Disc memory system

Disc stores are available in a wide range of sizes from single disc memories storing about 1 million 16 bit words on one disc, to the large mass memory multiple disc stores holding up to 10^9 bits. External mass storage with removable disc packs occupies a niche somewhere between large random access disc memories and magnetic tape storage. A block diagram of a disc memory system is shown in Figure 7.21.

Magnetic Tape Storage

For archival storage of data which may not be required very rapidly, magnetic tape is the most successful medium. The fundamental problem with all tape systems is that any particular desired piece of data may be located at a point on the tape which is distant from that being served at the time. This then requires winding for a long distance, to retrieve the required information.

This can be overcome by storing large blocks of data, which may be required at any one time, and transferring this in a block to the main memory for processing. Alternatively the data is sorted in sequence, so that a block of data can be retrieved at the same time as an associated block on another tape. This requires continually resorting of the tape data which either needs the use of a large disc file, or else a number of separate tape drives.

Tape drives are made in a wide range of sizes, from the large servo controlled drives on the expensive computer systems to the inexpensive cassette type drives for attachment to minicomputers. There does not appear to be any obvious challenger to magnetic tape for low cost unlimited capacity storage in the near future.

Floppy Discs

Floppy discs are a type of storage which fills a niche between rigid discs and magnetic tape. They consist of a magnetic coated Mylar disc which is carried in a thin cardboard sleeve. When the sleeve and disc are inserted into the drive unit, the coated disc is engaged and driven around inside its sleeve. A slot in the sleeve allows a movable head to make contact with the disc. Because of less accurate alignment, and dust from the surroundings, it is not possible to achieve such high recording densities.

Standard floppy discs have a diameter of 8 inches and store up to 10 megabytes on 80 tracks. In comparison, high performance rigid discs can store 100 to 300 megabytes. Rigid discs also revolve faster at 3000 r.p.m. compared with 360 r.p.m. fór floppy discs.

REFERENCES

General

1. ALTMAN, L. *Memory Design. Microcomputers to Mainframes.* McGraw-Hill (1978).
2. MAJUNDER, D.D. *Digital Computers, Memory Technology.* Wiley, New Delhi.
3. MILLER, S.W. *Memory and Storage Technology,* AFIPS Press (1977)
4. Special Issue on Large Capacity Digital Storage Systems. *Proc IEEE Vol 63 63 No 8* 1089–1264.

Surface Storage.

5. WILLIAMS, F.C., KILBURN, T., and THOMAS, G.E. *Universal High Speed Digital Computers: A Magnetic Store.* Proc IEE Pt 11 94–106 1952.
6. HOBBS, L.C. *A Review of Electromechanical Mass Storage.* Datamation 12. 22, 1966.
7. STEIN, L. *Generalised Pulse Recording IRE.* Int. Conv. Recording, 36–52 1962.

Semiconductor Memories.

8. HNATEK, E.R. *A User's Handbook of Semiconductor Memories.*
9. MOSTEK. *Memory Data Book and Designers Guide.*

Charge Coupled Devices.

10. *Technology and Applications of Charge Coupled Devices.* International Conference Proceedings. University of Edinburgh 1974.

Magnetic Bubble Memories.

11. ESCHENFELDER, A.H. *Magnetic Bubble Technology.* Springer-Verlag 1980.
12. O'DELL, T.H. *Magnetic Bubbles.* Macmillan London.
13. CHANG, H. Ed. *Magnetic Bubble Technology: Integrated Circuit Magnetics for Digital Storage and Processing.* IEEE Press 1975.
14. CHANG, H. *Magnetic Bubble Memory Technology.* Marcel Dekker Inc.

Chapter 8

Functional Description of a Small Processor

Before any decisions can be made about the system and logical organisation and physical design of the central processor, a specification has to be provided which describes in detail the operations for each instruction, and the addressing systems to be used. The functions of each bit in the instruction must be defined so that the programmer can understand the operation, and also the logical designer can implement the specification in a hardware form. This aspect of computer design is sometimes referred to as the architecture of the system, although this often applies to the design of the specification for a whole range of compatible processors of different sizes and speeds, upon which the same programs can be performed.

In theory it is intended that the architecture of the processor should be completely independent of the physical implementation, but this is a difficult ideal to achieve since inevitably the number of accumulators must for example be specified, and sometimes even small and unsuspected details of the architectural specification may have unforeseen effects on the logical design of the processor. In fact processor architecture has evolved and continues to evolve by a continual interaction between the needs of programmers and computer users, and the feasibility and cost of producing this in a physical form.

In particular the architecture of minicomputers has reached a state of comparative uniformity in performance, although they may differ considerably in detail, and therefore it is not generally possible to run a machine language program from one machine on any other. The modern minicomputer embodies many of the functions to be found on larger machines, albeit in a restricted form, and therefore may be conveniently used to illustrate the functioning and design of the central processor.

At this point one is faced with the problem of designing the architecture for a special processor as an exemplar, and then to design the system around this architecture. If this is done the student will learn a unique and possibly eccentric machine, which in all likelihood will never be realised in hardware form. Having familiarised him or herself with the instructions it will be necessary for the student to relearn the instructions on some real computer on which he may have to work.

Alternatively one may describe the hardware of some existing small computer. But understandably there is much know-how and neat tricks which manufacturers prefer to regard as confidential and would rather not publish freely.

The course adopted here is a compromise solution in which the functional specification of a known commercial processor – the NOVA – has been adopted as an example of a small computer with a modern architectural concept. In this way the knowledge of the functional specification acquired by the student may be of use in application to the NOVA machines.

It is not intended here to attempt to reproduce a system reference manual for programmers, but merely to use the system and instruction formats as a basis for the design of a hypothetical machine. Those needing to know full details are referred to the programming instructional manual.

Memory Features

In the current state of computer design the main memory is usually of the semiconductor type with destructive read-out. This type of memory lends itself naturally to a parallel organisation in which words of a fixed number of bits are read-out and written in parallel in a cycle time of 1–2 μsec.

In respect to the system design of the processor the memory may be regarded as a separate system or black box having N parallel input-output lines through which the data must flow into and out of the memory, M address lines to select the address of the word to be read or written, and the control signal lines read and write to cause the memory to perform one of the operations. The memory is frequently designed to be modular in capacity so that the number of words of storage can be tailored to the users requirements. But having decided on the size of the word, this becomes a rather fundamental parameter, as it is more difficult to make the processor modular in this respect. In the case where a range of compatible machines is being designed it is however common for the larger machines to have memories with multiples of the basic word length.

The cycle time of the memory has the greatest influence on the speed of the machine. Since the memory represents the largest single cost component in the machine it is important that it is in used as continuously as possible, and time in which the memory is idle means that the most costly part of the machine is not in use.

Both operands and instructions are of the same word length and are indistinguishable from each other within the memory. The determination of whether a word is interpreted as an operand or an instruction depends purely on the control system.

Word Size

The determination of the word size depends on considerations of both instructions and operands. A sufficient number of bits are needed in the instruction to provide a suitably flexible and rich instruction set and also to address a large enough portion of the memory. From the operand point of view a word length should be large enough to contain numbers to a size and accuracy sufficient for most needs. Where greater accuracy is required it is possible to resort to multiple length arithmetic although this represents a loss in speed. For our processor a word length of 16 bits is chosen.

It is also decided that the arithmetic unit of this processor should have 4 accumulator registers. The possession of 4 accumulators allows fast arithmetic operations between accumulators without the necessity of reference to the memory, as will be seen in the description of the Arithmetic Instructions.

Number Formats

Numbers are represented in Two's complement convention and the bits in the word are numbered 0 to 15 from the leftmost end of the word. Thus a single precision number appears as in Figure 8.1a, and a double precision number as in Figure 8.1(b). As an example $+117_{10}$ and -117_{10} are shown in (c).

In a single precision number the bit 0 represents the sign of the number, 0 indicating a positive number and 1 a negative number. When multiple precision is used, the less significant words are treated as unsigned numbers. In two's complement, arithmetic operations on signed numbers are identical to operations on unsigned numbers. For example if a memory location or register contains the binary word shown in Figure 8.2 then as an unsigned number this would be equivalent to 32881_{10} but as a signed number in two's complement notation it would be -32655_{10}.

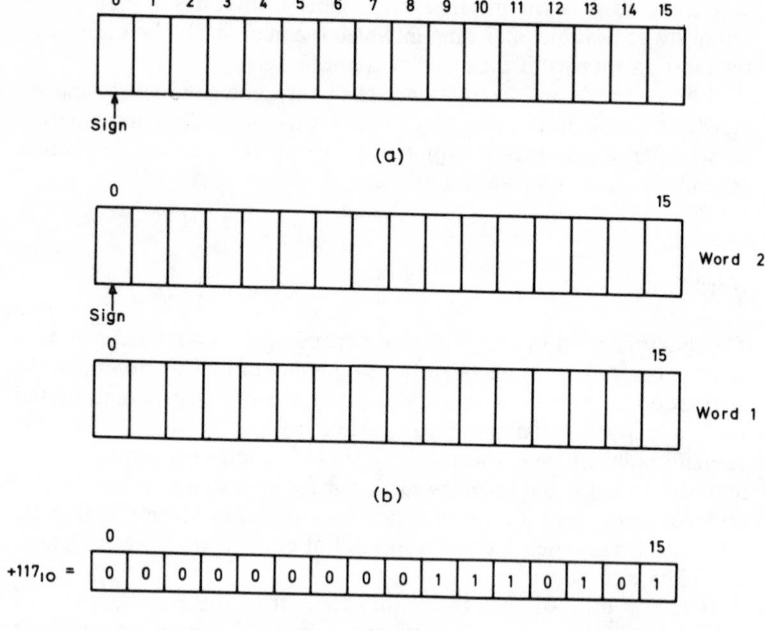

Figure 8.1

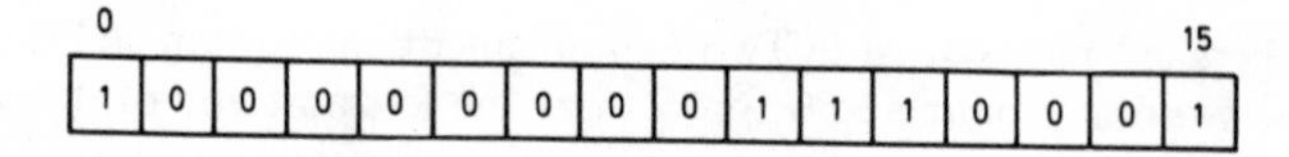

Figure 8.2

Octal Numbering

Up to this point we have given the decimal equivalents of these binary numbers but as will be seen the word does not necessarily have any numerical significance and is merely an array of bits, and it is also a tedious process to convert the binary number into decimal. So we need a convenient means of writing a binary word in a more concise and easily readable form. A commonly accepted method is to convert the

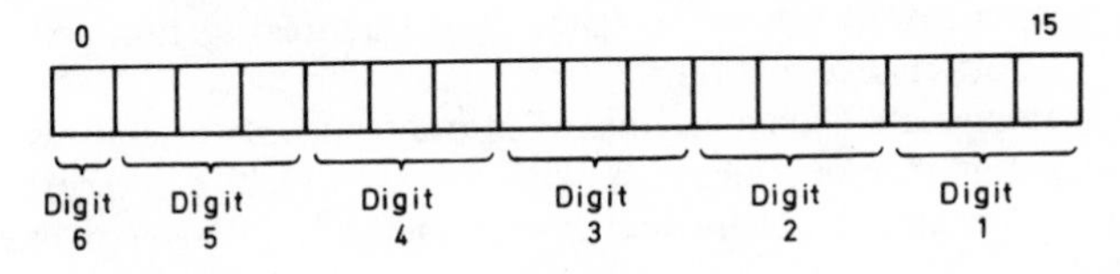

Figure 8.3

word into an octal number. This is a simple process which merely requires that the word is divided into groups of 3 bits from the right hand or least significant end, and each group of 3 bits written as its decimal equivalent, Figure 8.3. The numbers shown in Figure 8.1(c) then become:

$$+117_{10} = +000\,165_8$$
$$-117_{10} = -000\,165_8$$

where the subscripts 10 and 8 refer to the base of notation.

Logical Word Formats

In cases where a logical word is used, the word is only a string of 16 bits and each bit has no arithmetical significance.

Instruction Word Formats

Instructions may be assigned to three different classes:

1. Memory Reference Instructions
2. Arithmetic and Logical Instructions
3. Input-Output Instructions

Classes 1. and 2. are now described in more detail and Class 3. is described in Chapter 11.

Memory Reference Instructions

In this class all the instructions which refer to data stored in the memory are included. As these instructions refer to the memory, part of the instruction must contain a binary number, which can be interpreted as an address of the operand within the memory. The remaining part of the instruction must be reserved for a binary number which can be decoded to indicate the operation to be performed and also indicating that it falls in the class of memory reference instructions.

Thus in this case 8 bits are assigned to the address section and 8 bits to the operation code section.

It is immediately obvious that it is only possible to address 2^8 or 256 different memory locations with 8 bits, which is a very limited amount of memory. There are several methods for overcoming this problem.

Before describing the various ways of addressing the operand in the memory, it is necessary to digress into an explanation of the generally accepted method of finding the next instruction in the memory. The processor alternates between obtaining an instruction from the memory, and then obeying this instruction. In the simple case the instructions in the machine program are obeyed in direct sequence and the address of the next instruction is found by adding 1 to the address of the present instruction. It is also possible to jump to another instruction or to skip the next instruction and advance by 2 steps instead of 1. For the present purpose it is merely necessary to realise that the machine always has the address of the present instruction stored in a register. The hardware processes involved will be expanded in following chapters.

Direct Addressing

In the simplest case the 8 bit number in bits 8 to 15 shown in Figure 8.4 which is referred to as the 'Displacement D', can address the first 256 words in the memory starting at word 0 and ending at word 255, this method is called Direct Addressing.

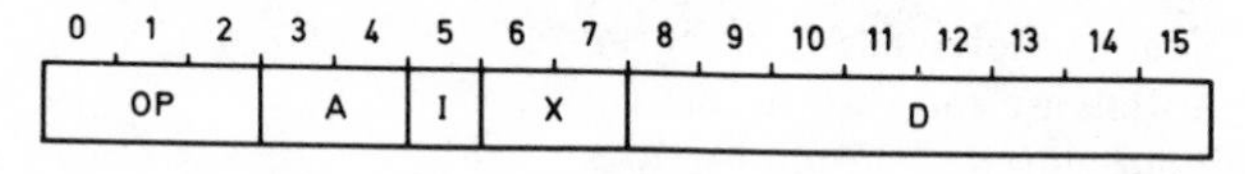

Figure 8.4

The 256 words addressed by the displacement are referred to as a 'page' in the memory and in the case of direct addressing this refers to page zero.

Indirect Addressing

Instead of having the displacement refer to the address of an operand, one can interpret the number in this address as another address. This makes it possible to obtain a 15 bit address for the next access to the memory (1 bit is used to indicate that there is a further indirect address, so that multiple indirect addressing can occur).

Relative Addressing

The Displacement D can be added to the address of the instruction that the processor has just accessed in the memory. This makes it possible to address locations between -128_{10} and $+127_{10}$ relative to the instruction address.

Indexing or Base Register Addressing

The Displacement can be added to a number that has been previously placed in one of the arithmetic registers thus creating a 16 bit address word.

The operand address which is found by these various means is referred to as the 'Effective Address', and the different methods have advantages depending on the programming techniques used.

Format of Memory Reference Instructions

It is now possible to go into the detail of the general memory reference instruction which is shown in Figure 8.4. As stated bits 8 to 15 represent the displacement address D to be used in computing the effective address E. Calculation of the effective address E depends on I and X, bits 5, 6 and 7. X is a code allowing 4 possibilities as shown in Table 8.1.

I or bit 5 is the indirect bit. If I is 0 addressing is direct and the address found from X and D is the effective address E. If I is 1, then addressing is indirect, the word found from X and D represents another

Table 8.1

X	*Address defined*
00	Page zero address. (Direct Addressing) D represents an address between 00000_8, and 00377_8.
01	Relative Address. D represents a signed displacement (-200_8 to $+177_8$) that is added to the address of the present instruction.
10	Indexing. D is a signed displacement (-200_8 to $+177_8$) which is added to the number in Accumulator Register 2 (AC_2).
11	Indexing. D is a signed displacement (-200_8 to $+177_8$) which is added to the number in Accumulator Register 3 (AC_3).

Figure 8.5

address and *not* an operand. This indirect address word has bit 0 reserved as another indirect bit I, as shown in Figure 8.5 so that a chain of indirect addresses may be linked together.

In memory reference instructions which refer to an accumulator register, A (bits 3, 4) can represent one of four registers, so that it is arranged that the machine will have 4 accumulator registers. Bits 0, 1, 2 define the operation code of this type of memory reference instruction.

There is one final ingenious trick used in the NOVA, in which, if at any point in calculation of the effective address a word is fetched from locations 00020_8 to 00037_8 it is automatically incremented or decremented by 1, and the new value is written back in memory and used either as the effective address or an operand depending on whether bit 0 is 0 or 1. Addresses taken from 00020_8 to 00027_8 are incremented and those taken from locations 00030_8 to 00037_8 are decremented.

The set of all addresses is cyclic with respect to the operations performed in the calculation of the effective address. Thus the next address beyond 77777_8 is 00000_8 and the next below 00000_8 is 77777_8.

Memory reference instructions can be further subdivided as follows.

Data Transfer Instructions

This type of instruction is concerned with the transfer of data between the accumulator registers and the memory, and bits 3 and 4 select the one of four accumulators involved in the transfer. In this case there are only two instructions.

LDA Load Accumulator (Figure 8.6(a)): The contents of the accumulator specified by A is replaced by the contents of the effective address E.

STA Store Accumulator (Figure 8.6(b)): The contents of the effective address E is replaced by the contents of the Accumulator specified by A.

Since the following instructions do not involve the accumulators, the field A–bits 3 and 4 no longer refers to the accumulators, but now becomes part of the operation code.

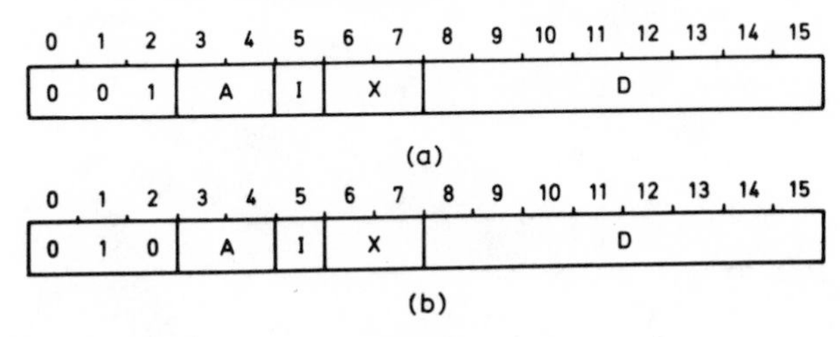

Figure 8.6

Memory Modification Instructions

These two instructions add or subtract 1 from the contents of a memory location, and test the contents for zero, in which case the next instruction is skipped. They are useful mainly in counting loop iterations.

ISZ Increment and Skip if Zero (Figure 8.7(a)): The contents of the effective address E is incremented by 1, and if the resulting value is 0 the next instruction in sequence is skipped. If the contents is not 0 then the next sequential instruction is obeyed.

DSZ Decrement and Skip if Zero (Figure 8.7(b)): The contents of the effective address E is decremented by 1 and if the resulting value is 0 the next instruction is skipped. If the content is not 0 then the next sequential instruction is obeyed.

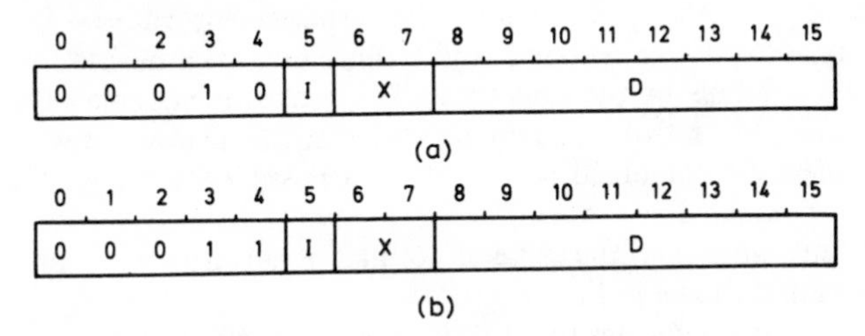

Figure 8.7

Jump Instructions

These instructions allow the program to branch from the direct sequence by jumping to an arbitrary address. They are necessary for calling and returning from subroutines and for looping.

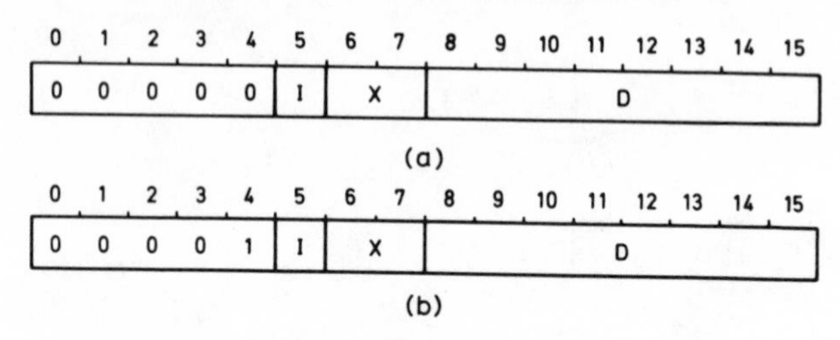

Figure 8.8

JMP Jump (Figure 8.8(a)): The next instruction is taken from the effective address E and sequential operation is continued from there.

JSR Jump to Subroutine (Figure 8.8(b)): 1 is added to the address of the present instruction and this is loaded into Accumulator 3 (AC_3). The next instruction is taken from the effective address E and sequential operation is continued from there.

This instruction is used for returning from a subroutine. At the end of the subroutine a Jump instruction is given with Base Address Indexing on AC_3 and D is made zero. This has the effect of transferring control back to the next instruction in the main program.

Arithmetic and Logical Instructions

Since it has been decided to have 4 Accumulator Registers it is possible to perform all the arithmetic and logical operations of the processor by transfers between Accumulators via the Arithmetic Unit. Because no reference to memory is needed, the displacement address D to the memory is no longer required, and 8 more bits are available for use in describing details of the operation. This makes it possible to accommodate a wide set of different functions in the instruction word, and when these are combined in the different possible ways a very flexible system is obtained.

In this processor the general format of an arithmetic or logical instruction is shown in Figure 8.9.

A 1 in bit 0 indicates that this is an arithmetic or logical instruction. Since there are 4 accumulators and in many cases two accumulators will

0	1 2	3 4	5 6 7	8 9	10 11	12	13 14 15
1	A.C. source address	A.C destination address	Function	Shift	Carry	No load	Skip

Figure 8.9

be involved in an arithmetic operation, both a source and a destination accumulator must be specified, each requiring 2 bits, in positions 1, 2, 3, and 4. Bits 5, 6 and 7 indicate one out of eight different functions to be described. The adder contains a 1 bit register called Carry and the instruction also sets the carry bit and bits 10 and 11 specify the carry setting condition Table 8.2.

In the case of arithmetic functions a carry out may be generated from bit 0, and if this occurs the original state of the carry bit is complemented. The primary use of the carry bit is as a carry out in unsigned numbers, when performing multiple precision arithmetic. It

Table 8.2

Bits 10–11	*Setting of carry input bit*
00	Current State of Carry (ie. no change in existing state).
01	Zero (0)
10	One (1)
11	Complement current state of carry, i.e. if carry state is 1 change to 0, and if 0 change to 1.

Table 8.3

Bits 8–9	*Shift operation*
00	No shift.
01	Rotate left one position. The carry bit is shifted into bit 15 and bit 0 is shifted into the carry position. 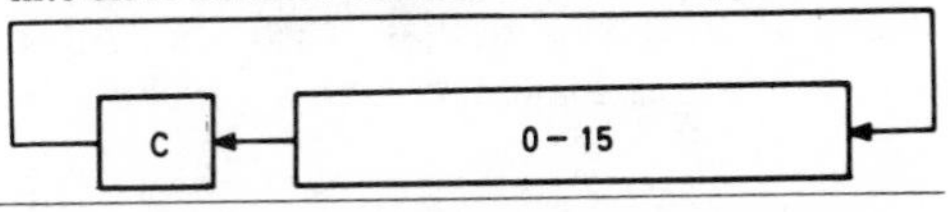
10	Rotate right one position. The carry bit is shifted into bit 0, and bit 15 is shifted into the carry bit. 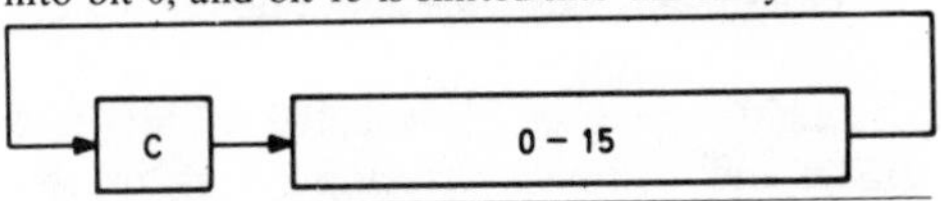
11	Swap over the halves of the 16 bit result. The carry bit is not changed. 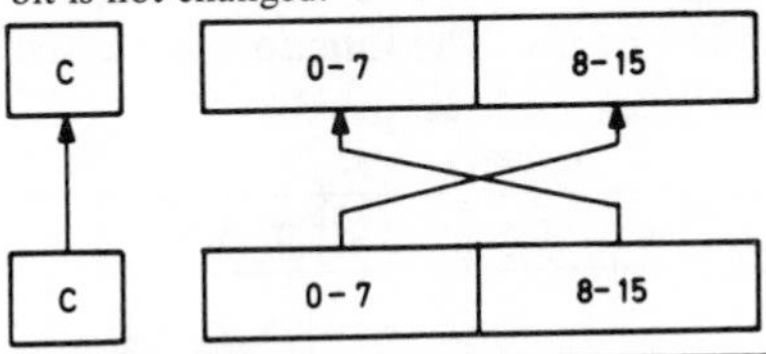

can also be used in combination with the sign of the result to detect overflow.

It is also possible in this machine to combine a shift operation with some other arithmetic function, and this is specified by the shift field in bits 8 and 9, and again there are four conditions which operate on the result of the arithmetic operation (Table 8.3).

The result of the foregoing operations is loaded into the carry and the destination accumulator determined by bit 3, 4, if bit 12 is 0. If bit 12 is 1, loading is inhibited, and the carry and accumulator are unchanged. This is useful in making tests on the result of arithmetic operations where the result can be discarded.

Table 8.4

Bits 13, 14, 15	*Skip test condition*
000	No skip.
001	Unconditional skip (always skip).
010	Skip on zero carry.
011	Skip on non zero carry
100	Skip on zero result.
101	Skip on non zero result.
110	Skip if either carry or result is zero.
111	Skip if both carry and result are non zero.

Finally the result of these operations can be tested and the following instruction skipped on the outcome of the test determined by the skip field bits 13, 14, 15, as shown in Table 8.4.

As the test is made on the shifted result, the sign of the result can be tested if it is shifted left. Also the test can be made whether the accumulator is loaded or not by making bit 12 in the instruction 0.

Arithmetic and Logical Functions

The eight functions are selected by bits 5, 6, 7 of the instruction. The source and destination accumulators are selected by S and D bits 1, 2, and 3, 4, and are referred to as ACS and ACD. In every case the next instruction is skipped if the shifted result satisfies the condition specified by SK. The functions are listed below:

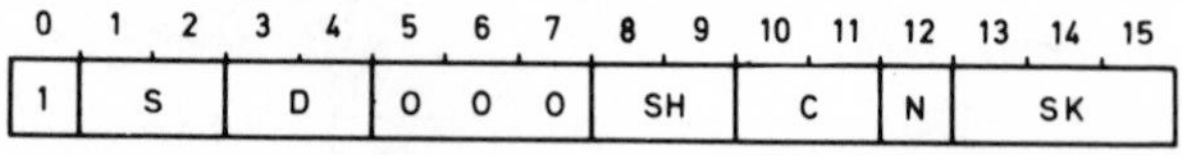

0	1 2	3 4	5	6	7	8 9	10 11	12	13 14 15
1	S	D	0	0	0	SH	C	N	SK

Figure 8.10

COM Complement (Figure 8.10): Form the (logical) complement of the word from ACS and the carry bit specified by C. Perform the shift operation specified by SH and load the shifted output into Carry and ACD unless N is 1.

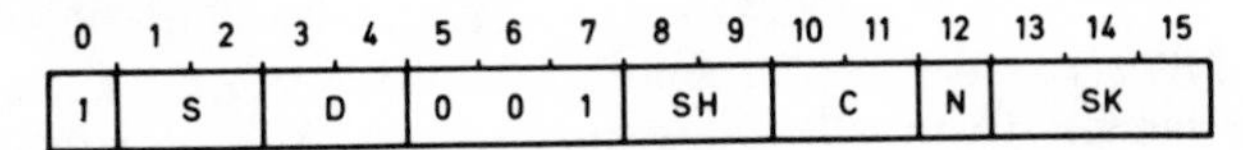

Figure 8.11

NEG Negate (Figure 8.11): Form the two's complement of the number in ACS. If ACS contains zero, supply the complement of the value specified by C as the carry bit, otherwise supply the specified value. Perform the shift operation specified by SH and load the shifted output into carry and ACD unless N is 1.

0	1 2	3 4	5 6 7	8 9	10 11	12	13 14 15
1	S	D	0 1 0	SH	C	N	SK

Figure 8.12

MOV Move (Figure 8.12): Take the contents of ACS and the carry bit specified by C, perform the shift operation specified by SH and load the shifted output into carry and ACD unless N is 1.

0	1 2	3 4	5 6 7	8 9	10 11	12	13 14 15
1	S	D	0 1 1	SH	C	N	SK

Figure 8.13

INC Increment (Figure 8.13): Add 1 to the number from ACS. If ACS contains $2^{16} - 1$ (signed -1) supply the complement of the value specified by C as the carry bit; otherwise supply the specified value. Perform the shift operation specified by SH and load the shifted output into carry and ACD unless N is 1.

0	1 2	3 4	5 6 7	8 9	10 11	12	13 14 15
1	S	D	1 0 0	SH	C	N	SK

Figure 8.14

ADC Add Complement (Figure 8.14): Add the (logical) complement of the number from ACS to the number from ACD, perform the shift operation specified by SH and load the shifted output into Carry and ACD unless N is 1.

0	1–2	3–4	5	6	7	8–9	10–11	12	13–15
1	S	D	1	0	1	SH	C	N	SK

Figure 8.15

SUB Subtract (Figure 8.15): Subtract by adding the two's complent of the number from ACS to the number from ACD. If ACD $\geqslant$ ACS (unsigned) supply the complement of the value specified by C as the carry bit, otherwise supply the specified value. Perform the shift operation specified by SH and load the shifted output into carry and ACD unless N is 1.

0	1–2	3–4	5	6	7	8–9	10–11	12	13–15
1	S	D	1	1	0	SH	C	N	SK

Figure 8.16

ADD Add (Figure 8.16): Add the number from ACS to the number from ACD. If the unsigned sum is $\geqslant 2^{16}$, supply the complement of the value specified by C as the carry bit, otherwise supply the specified value. Perform the shift operation specified by SH and load the shifted output into Carry and ACD unless N is 1.

0	1–2	3–4	5	6	7	8–9	10–11	12	13–15
1	S	D	1	1	1	SH	C	N	SK

Figure 8.17

AND And (Figure 8.17): Form the logical AND function of the word from ACS and the word from ACD in the shifter, and supply the value specified by C as the carry bit. Perform the shift operation specified by SH and load the shifted output into Carry and ACD unless N is 1.

Multiplication and Division

In common with many minicomputers, the basic NOVA machine does not have hardware Multiply and Divide instructions, and these are performed by program subroutines, which are slower than specially adapted circuits. These instructions can be added to the NOVA as an extra option and this is done by making a separate Multiplier, Divider, which is treated as an input-output device. The operands are transferred to this device by an input-output instruction, and also the result is read into the processor when the operation is complete. So that effectively the Multiplier-Divider is an external 'black box' and the multiply and divide instructions are a form of input-output instruction.

A faster machine – the SUPERNOVA – which is compatible with the NOVA does have a hardware multiply–divide which can be incorporated directly into the arithmetic unit of the processor. In this case three of the accumulators are concerned in the operations.

In the case of the 'multiply' instructions the multiplier is placed in AC_1 and the multiplicand in AC_2 and the double length product appears in AC_0 and AC_1 added to the contents of AC_0.

In the 'divide' instruction the double length dividend is placed in AC_0 and AC_1 and the divisor in AC_2 and the single length quotient appears in AC_1 with the remainder in AC_0.

Some Instructions Found on Other Machines

It may be of interest to mention some instructions which are found on other small processors. Some additional memory reference instructions are Add and Subtract from memory which allows the contents of a memory location to be added to or subtracted from the contents of one of the accumulators in a single instruction, and only requiring one accumulator.

Multiple store and load instructions can be very useful during input-output programs when it is necessary to clear all the addressable registers and store the data at some location in the memory, so that the accumulators are wholly available for the input-output process. At the end of this process the register contents are retrieved from the memory by a single multiple load instruction so that the main program can proceed from where it was stopped by the input-output interruption.

Immediate instructions are sometimes incorporated and have the benefit of saving both program steps and storage capacity. In this type of instruction, the operand is incorporated directly into the instruction itself, typically in the same position, as the Displacement Address in bits 8–15. Clearly only small numbers, e.g. up to $2^8 = 256$ can be stored in this position but the method can be useful in handling small constants such as Teletype characters.

With the specification of memory reference and arithmetic and logical instructions described here it is now possible to proceed to the discussion of the data flow system of a processor to perform these instructions.

Problems

1. Study the possibility of reorganising the meaning of bits 0 to 4 in the instruction. Bits 0, 1 and 2 can represent eight different combinations. Let five of these represent operations involving both a

memory reference and register definition, instead of just load and store. Add from memory and subtract from memory can now be accommodated. Of the remaining codes, one combination of 0, 1 and 2 can refer to an IO instruction, and one combination of 0, 1, 2, 3 and 4 must be reserved for arithmetic operations.

2. Consider introducing load multiple and store multiple instructions to handle all four accumulators.
3. Consider the introduction of an immediate add instruction in which bits 8–15 represent an 8 bit operand.
4. If a simpler machine is designed having only two accumulators, only one bit is needed for the A field to define the accumulators. This releases another bit for use in the function section. Experiment with different instruction combinations in this case.
5. Suppose the shift operations are not combined with the other arithmetic operations in the same instruction. More complicated shifting operations can now be arranged, but add and shift requires two instructions. Consider the advantages and disadvantages of this.

Chapter 9

The Data Flow System of the Processor

Having now defined the memory reference and arithmetic instructions of our processor, it is possible to proceed to illustrate the design of a hypothetical machine to perform the specified operations.

The electrical signals travelling throughout a processor can be separated roughly into two types:

1. The data signals consist of information being transferred to and from the memory, and between arithmetic and other registers. These signals may consist of actual numbers or symbols which are being operated on by the processor, or they may consist of numbers to be used as addresses at a later time. Alternatively the data may be instrution words which are transferred from the memory to registers from which they are to be interpreted to define the processor operation.

2. To control the complex flow of this data within the processor another layer of signals, so to speak, has to exist: which opens and closes register input and output gates; controls the flow of data in the data bus, signals the memory when and whether to read or write data to or from its buffer register; sets various control flip-flops, and so forth. These are the control signals.

Before attempting to visualise the control system one must first know what devices one wishes to control. The usual procedure for designing a processor is therefore to first lay out the data flow organisation of the machine. Having decided on this it is then possible to proceed to the more complicated act of designing the control system to make the data flow perform the operations defined by the architectural specification. The complexity of the control system is undoubtedly dependent on the organisation of the data flow system which is chosen, as well as on the requirements of instructions. It is therefore easy, apparently, to simplify the data flow system with the intention of reducing the total complexity of the machine, only to find later that this has engendered a more than proportionate increase in the cost and intricacy of the control system. This can only be avoided by experience and always keeping in mind both aspects of the design.

First Requirements of the Data Flow System

The architectural specification has already determined in some respects the necessary registers which are needed in a processor to fulfil it, these are as follows:

The word size of the machine: 16 bits.
Accumulators: AC_0, AC_1, AC_2, AC_3.
Arithmetic Unit: This unit must be capable of performing the various functions defined by the arithmetic and logical instructions including left and right shifting of numbers, testing of results of calculations and appropriate setting of the carry register C.
Memory: The size of the memory will be assumed to be made of modules having a capacity of 1024, 2048, or 4096 words. These modules may be assembled into a larger memory which can be increased to a maximum size in this machine of 2^{15} or 32 767 words, which is the largest address which can be accommodated by the chosen size of the instruction word.

As the memory is a separate system which includes its own timing circuits, it is asynchronous with the rest of the processor, in which all the flip-flops are timed by a master clock generator. A 16 bit buffer register is therefore incorporated which also acts as a synchronising device between the synchronous world of the processor logic circuits and the internally timed memory circuits.

A Single Data Bus Data Flow System

When designing a processor or explaining its mode of operation it is best to start somewhere in the centre of the system and work outwards towards the periphery. There may be various preferences for starting points, but the worst is to try to start at the beginning and proceed to the end since it is difficult to see which point is the beginning or end. One of the best places to start is at the memory, and then to follow the data flow and operation from there.

A block diagram of a simple processor with a single data bus is shown in Figure 9.1. The data flow system consists of the memory, the arithmetic unit or adder, a number of registers whose function will be described, and in our case providing temporary storage for 16 bit words, and a bussing system for transferring data in parallel from register to register and to and from the memory.

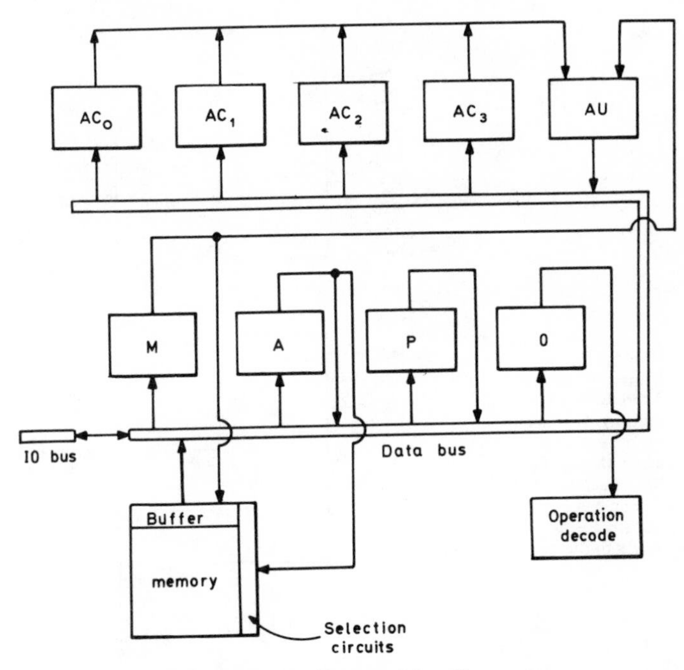

Figure 9.1 Block diagram of data flow system

The *Data Bus.* This is a 16 bit parallel gating system for transferring data between registers, the memory and the arithmetic unit. Only a single word may be on the data bus at any one time although one or several registers may have data simultaneously gated into them.

As shown on Figure 9.1 the data bus may receive inputs from six places and the bus can also be used for entering two fixed constants which will be needed in the system. The Inputs to the data bus are:

Memory Buffer
M register
A register
P register
Arithmetic unit
Input-output (IO) bus
Two-possible fixed constants.

It is of course necessary to transfer the contents of the memory via the memory buffer to the data bus to transfer it to various registers. The address in the A register has to be transferred to the P register and in certain cases the M register, and it is also necessary to transfer words

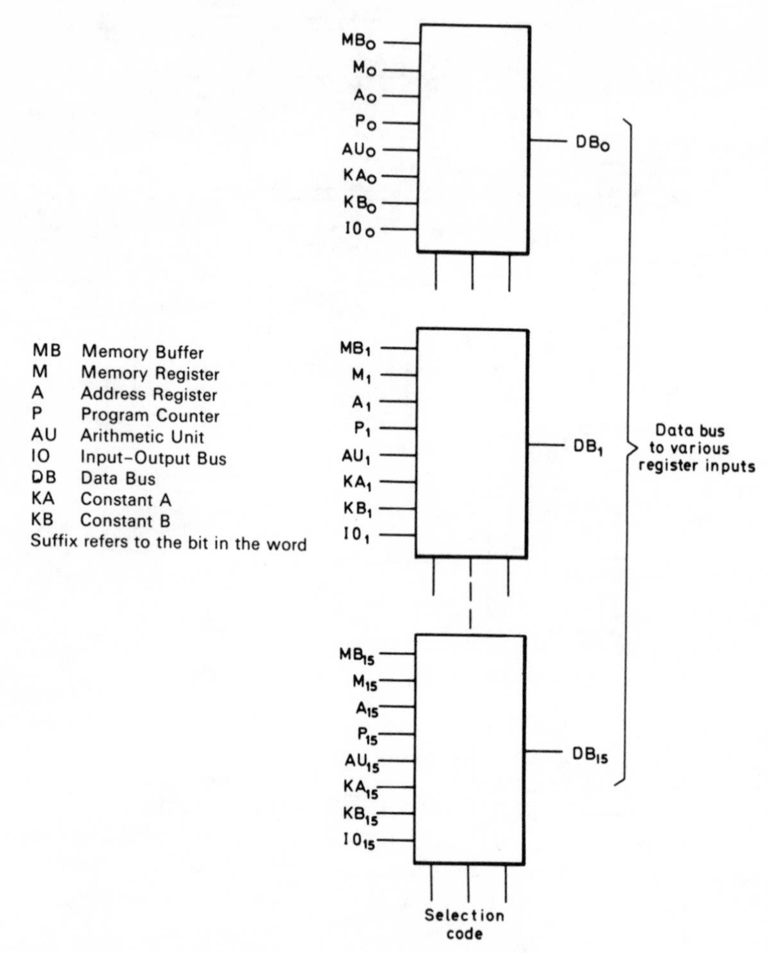

Figure 9.2 Data bus block diagram

or parts of words held in the M register to the A register during effective address derivation.

The next instruction address which is generated by incrementing the present instruction must be transferred to the A register at the end of an instruction, so that P also must have an input to the data bus. The results of arithmetic operations must be transferred to the accumulators for temporary storage or via the data bus to the M register from which they may be transferred to the Memory Buffer in the store operation.

Information is transfered in and out of the machine via the Input-Output (IO) bus which is effectively an extension of the data bus which

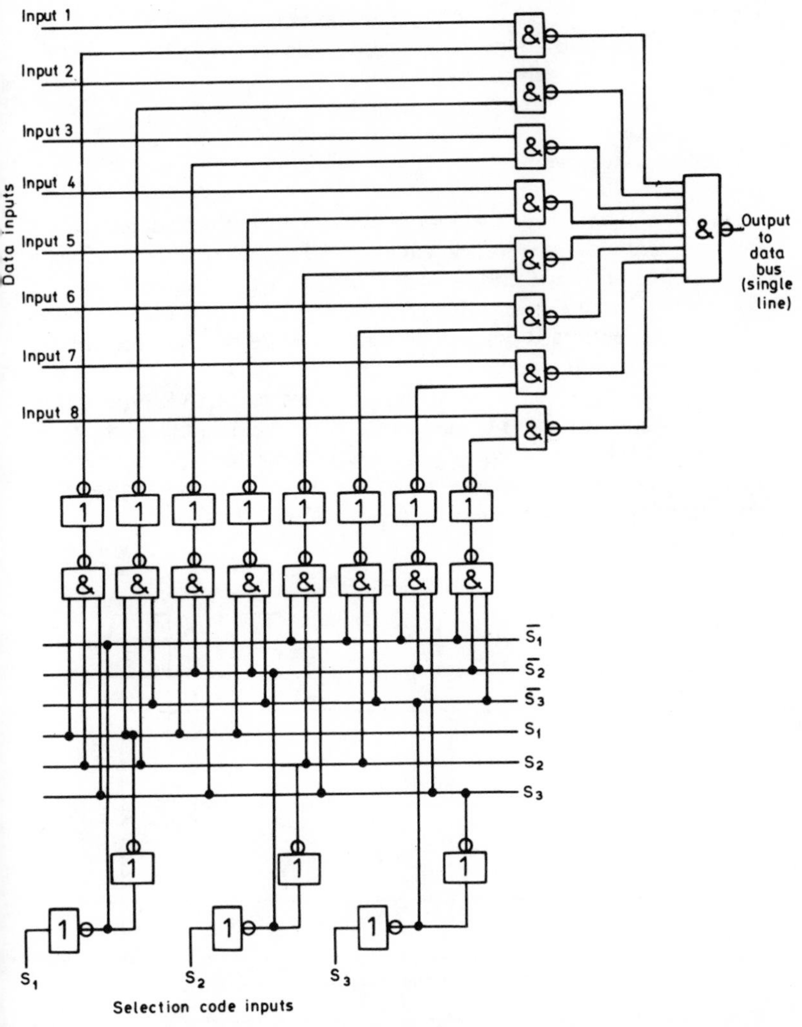

Figure 9.3 Logic diagram of multiplexer – single bit cell

is gated to it at the appropriate times. Information thus placed on the data bus can be transferred to or from the selected accumulator register.

It is more economical to design the multiplexer for the data bus for a binary size, so an 8 input multiplexer fits well here and at the same time allows two spare inputs which can be used for inputs of fixed constants. A block diagram of the data bus selection logic is shown in

Figure 9.2. Each block consists of a multiplexer circuit which is usually constructed on a single integrated circuit chip and the gating structure inside one of these is shown in Figure 9.3.

The Address Register

In order to operate the memory it is essential that the address of the location from or into which data will be transferred be held in a register. The output of this is taken to the memory selection circuits. If our system design is reasonably efficient the memory should be in use as much of the time as possible, therefore it is not possible to share this register for any other purpose.

The A register consists of a straightforward set of 16 D type double rank flip-flops with gates to their input from the data bus as shown in Figure 9.4. The output from the A register is connected directly to the inputs to the memory selection logic. It is also connected to an input of the multiplexer, to be gated on to the data bus.

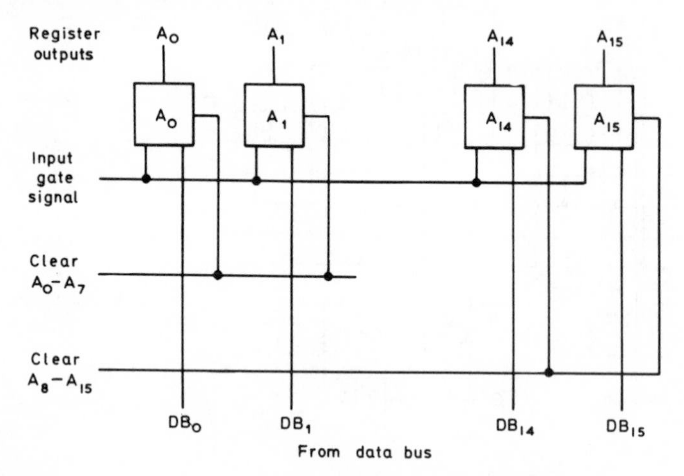

Figure 9.4 Block diagram of address register. The operation register and the accumulator register are similar

During address calculation it is necessary to be able to separate the displacement address section from an instruction, so that one can address the zero page in the memory, by placing binary zeros in bits A_0 to A_7. In the case of relative addressing or indexing it is required to add the displacement D (i.e. bits 8 to 15 of the instruction word) to either the address stored in the Program Counter or to a number stored in an accumulator. For these reasons an input is provided to clear A_0 to A_7, which leaves only the displacement address in the A register, then removing the unwanted upper 8 bits.

The M Register

Although the memory is provided with its own memory buffer, this is usually interconnected with the memory reading, writing and control circuitry in such a way as to make it inconvenient to use for other than its assigned purpose, and it also acts as an asynchronous to synchronous converter. It is usual then to provide a general purpose data transfer register in which numbers can be stored to be added or subtracted from other numbers in the accumulator registers.

This register is a straightforward parallel storage similar to the A register, with the ability to clear either the least or most significant 8 bits.

The Program Counter

Some means is needed by which the processor can proceed through the program from one instruction to the next. The memory contains both instruction words and operands, so that the Address register sometimes contains the address of an instruction and sometimes the address of an operand. Except in the case of jump instructions, the next instruction is found by incrementing the address of the previous instruction by 1, or if there is a skip condition by 2. The address of the present instruction must therefore be preserved so that it can be incremented appropriately, while the address register is in use for other purposes. This is done in the program counter into which the present instruction is transferred

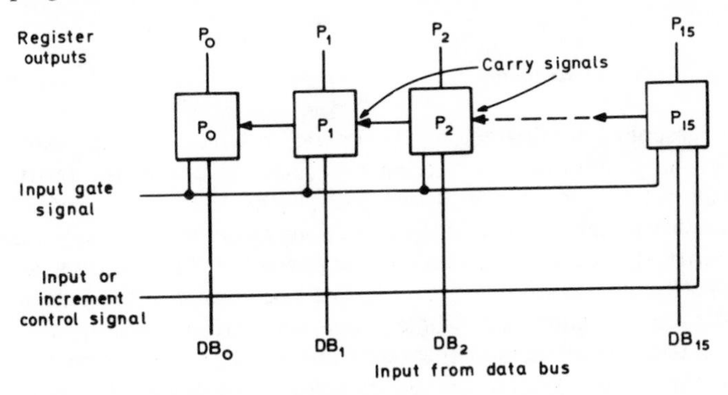

Figure 9.5 Block diagram of a program counter

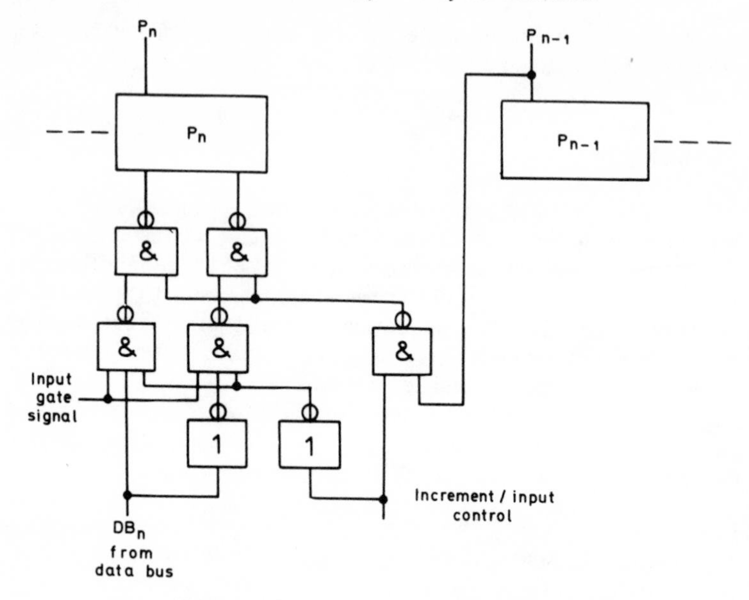

Figure 9.6 Program counter – individual cell

before it is destroyed in the address register. The program counter is designed to be able to count in binary so that incrementing can occur within the register. There are thus two control inputs to the program counter. One gates the data from the data bus into the register and the other causes the register to behave as a binary counter so that the address it contains can be incremented. The diagram of the program counter is shown in Figure 9.5, and an individual cell is shown in Figure 9.6.

The Operation Register

As described in Chapter 8, the operation which the processor is to perform during each instruction is defined by bits in the instruction code whose meaning is designated by the functional specification. The instruction is stored in the operation register where it is decoded to control the sequence of small operations within the processor and the selection of appropriate registers. The operation register contains the instruction during the whole operation until it receives the next instruction word. It is at this point that the data flow system impinges on the control system of the processor. The operation register is a straightforward parallel register of 16 bits as for the address register and the block diagram is similar to that in Figure 9.4. The output from the register is taken to the operation decoding logic and also to the device address lines for the input-output system.

The Accumulator Registers

These registers are all similar to each other and consists merely of temporary storage for numbers or other words upon which arithmetic or logical operations are to be performed. No special functions are incorporated, and although certain accumulators may be involved in special operations such as indexing for base addressing in memory reference operations, or as temporary storage for the next instruction in the main program during a 'jump to subroutine' instruction, these functions are determined by the operation code and control system. The programmer must of course remember what is stored in each accumulator or that its contents may be destroyed in the 'jump to subroutine' instruction. In some ways these registers may be looked on as a high speed extension of the memory. They are all simple parallel registers similar to the A register shown in Figure 9.4.

The Arithmetic Unit

This consists basically of a 16 bit parallel adder. Subtraction is performed by negation of the subtrahend, and logical operations occur via separate logic circuits.

Following the adding and logical function circuits sets of gates may be selected to transfer the number direct to the data bus, or shifted one place to the left or right.

A carry register (C–1 bit) is set by conditions determined by the instruction at the start of the operation and receives the final carry at the end of the arithmetic operation. The various skip conditions are determined on the result of the operation and the state of the carry flip-flop. As there is considerable detail to be explored in the arithmetic unit a block diagram is shown first in Figure 9.7 and some of the individual blocks will then be expanded in other diagrams. To simplify the diagram certain AND gates for steering the data, and OR gates for merging data from different blocks are omitted.

The output bus from one of the four accumulators defined by bits 1, 2 in the instruction is selected by a multiplexer (not shown) and connects to the parallel adder and the logical AND gates, providing one input for the arithmetic operation. The other input is taken from the memory register and is connected to the logical AND gates and via

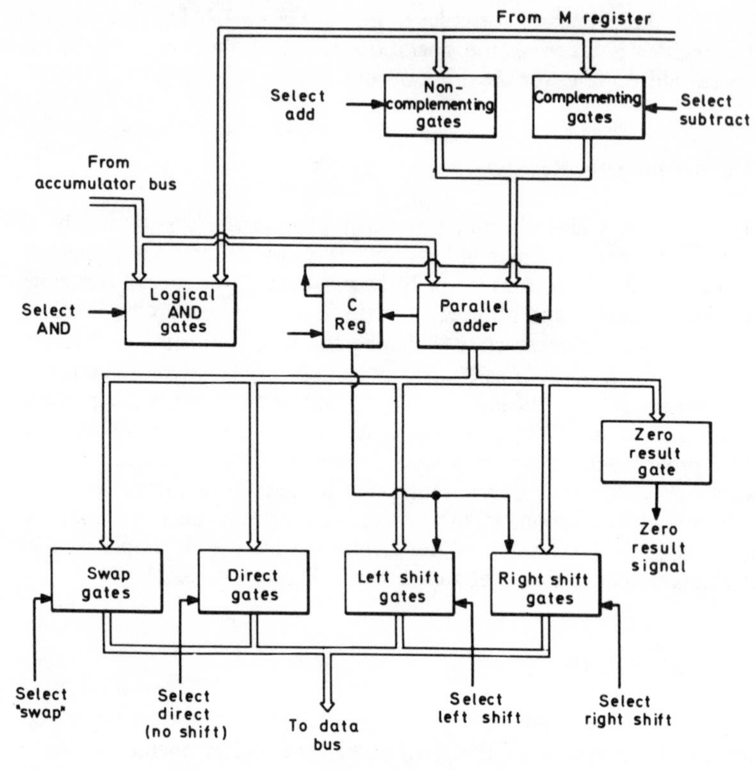

Figure 9.7 Block diagram of the arithmetic unit

inverting and non-inverting gates to the other adder inputs. By choosing the non-inverted – and therefore complemented – inputs to the adder, the number residing in the M register can be added or subtracted from the number selected from the accumulators. The C register which provides the carry input at the least significant bit is set to 0 or 1 accordingly before the start of the operation. At the end of the adding operation the carry from the most significant bit of the adder sets the final output carry condition into the C register.

The outputs from the logical AND gates and the adder are merged via OR gates (not shown) and go to the direct (no shift), left and right shift, and swap gates. These gates are all selected by the appropriate shift condition in the instruction defined by bits 8–9. In the case of left and right shift the C register may be shifted into the least or most significant bit, so that this is also taken to the appropriate shift gates.

This basic arrangement provides all the elements necessary to perform the various operations specified in the arithmetic and logical instructions. In a separate step before the arithmetic operation the source accumulator is selected and its data is transferred through the adder and no shift gates to the data bus, whence it is transferred to the M register. Data is transferred unchanged through the adder by not selecting either the non-inverting or inverting gates and therefore adding zero the number from the source accumulator. The stage is now set for the intended arithmetic operation as follows, the required destination accumulator having been selected.

Complement: The output from M (now containing contents of ACS) is gated through the inverting gates, creating the logical complement to the adder, and at the same time no output from the accumulators is gated to the other adder input, so that the logical complement is gated to the shift circuits. The C register is previously set to 0.
Negate: The two's complement is formed in a very similar way, the C register being set to 1 in this case.
Move: The output from M is gated through the non-inverting gates to the adder, and again no output from the accumulators is gated to the other adder inputs. The C register is set to 0.
Increment: This operation is very similar to the move operation but C register is set to 1.
Add Complement: The number from the destination accumulator is gated to one adder input and the number in M is complemented and gated via the inverting gates to the other adder input. The C register is set to zero. The output of the adder is the sum of the logical complement of the number in ACS and the number in ACD.
Subtract: This is again a similar operation to add complement, but in this case the C register is set to 1 to create the two's complement of the number from ACS, now in M.

Notice the symmetry between the pairs-Complement and Negate, Move and Increment, and Add Complement and Subtract.
Add The number in the M register (ACS) is gated via the non-inverting gates to one adder input, and the number from ACD is gated to the other adder input.
AND: The number in the M register (ACS) is gated to one input of the logical AND gates, and the destination accumulator ACD is gated to the other input, thus forming the logical AND as, an input to the shift circuits.

The appropriate set of shift gates which gates the result of the arithmetic to the data bus is selected according to bits 8–9 in the arithmetic or logical instruction.

Skip tests are made on the final conditions of the C register and adder outputs as defined in the skip test condition defined by bits 13,

14, 15. If it is desired only to make the test and not transfer the result to any accumulator, as defined by the 'no load' bit 12, this is done by not enabling any input selection gates to the destination accumulator ACD.

In the store operation the output from an accumulator has to be transferred to the memory and this is done in a similar way to the Move instruction, but the output to the data bus is transferred to the memory buffer in this case.

Although our simple machine does not have the operations multiply and divide built into the arithmetic unit, these can be accommodated by a built-in microprogram of repeated additions and shifts.

So it can be seen that this simple basic arithmetic unit can provide all the arithmetic and logical functions required. Some more elaborate instructions exist on larger machines and these could be included by added features. The speed of the unit depends mainly on the speed of the adder, and of course high speed multiplication or division methods would require added complication in the shift circuits. In our case right or left shifts of more than 1 place and less than 8 have to be performed by repeated operations.

The most notable element in the arithmetic unit is the parallel adder (*see* Chapter 5). The speed of the arithmetic unit and to some extent the overall speed of the machine depends on the speed of the adder, and the speed of the adder in turn depends on the maximum time for carry propogation. It is therefore considered worth building the complete adder from sections of 4 bit lookahead adders which can be obtained as a single integrated circuit. The block diagram of the adder then appears as shown in Figure 9.8.

The decision as to whether to incorporate partial lookahead adders over a restricted number of bits, and the choice of the number of carry bits skipped, or just implementing a straightforward adder without lookahead is a direct compromise between speed and cost. The formulae for speeds of adders are discussed in Chapter 4.

To reduce the complication of the diagrams, only a single bit cell of the accumulator multiplexer (Figure 9.9) and the adder circuits (Figure 9.10) is shown This is denoted as the *i*th bit and the various accumulator outputs (AC_{0i}, AC_{1i}, AC_{2i}, AC_{3i}), merged accumulator outputs (ACB_i), adder inputs (X_i, Y_i) and the added result (Res_i) are given the subscript *i*.

The multiplexer for the accumulator output bus is very similar to the multiplexer for the data bus but only selecting one accumulator output from four and also with the provision for not selecting any accumulator and placing all zeros on the accumulator bus. A single bit cell of this is shown in Figure 9.9.

A single bit cell of the adder, and logical AND circuits with one cell

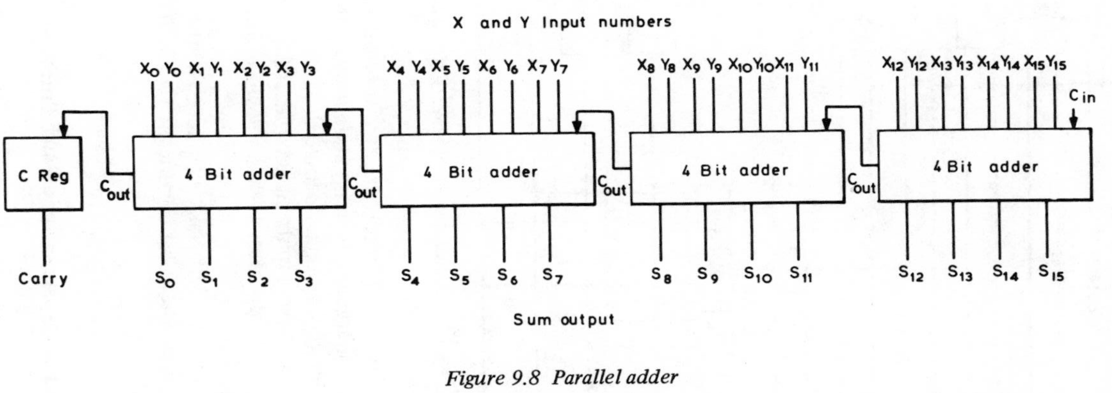

Figure 9.8 Parallel adder

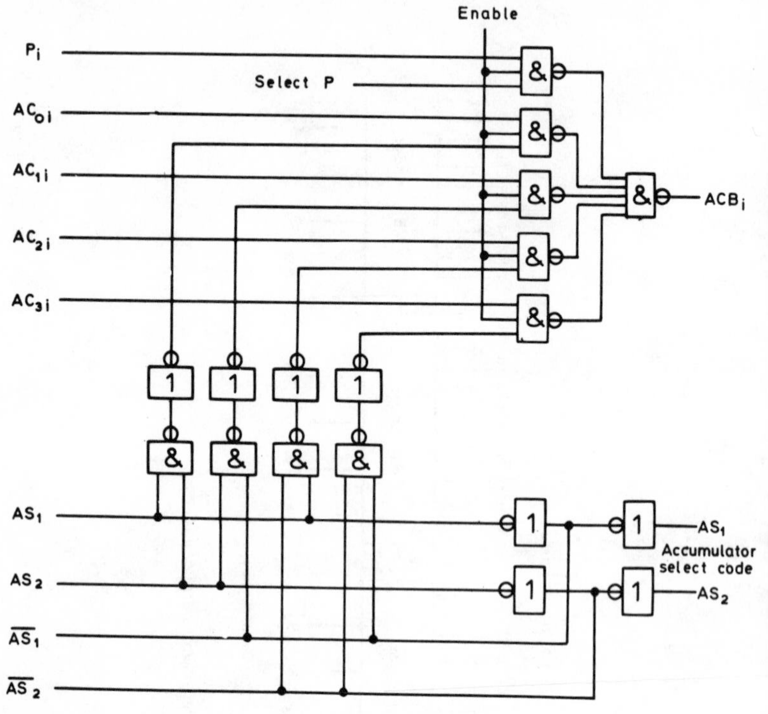

Figure 9.9 Accumulator multiplexer – single bit cell

of the adder is shown in Figure 9.10. It can be seen that several gating levels are used in merging adder inputs and outputs which lose some precious time in the adding operation. However, it is sometimes possible to select these inputs in advance of the actual operation.

A single bit cell of the shift logic is shown in Figure 9.11 for bit 8 on the data bus.

The least significant left shift cell receives the output of the C register, as also does the most significant right shift cell, as shown in Figure 9.12.

Alternative Data Flow Systems for a Small Processor

Having described one particular organisation for the data flow in a small processor, one may ask what alternative arrangement can be used.

The first determining factor is the type of memory that is used, and since in most contemporary machines this is a ferrite magnetic core

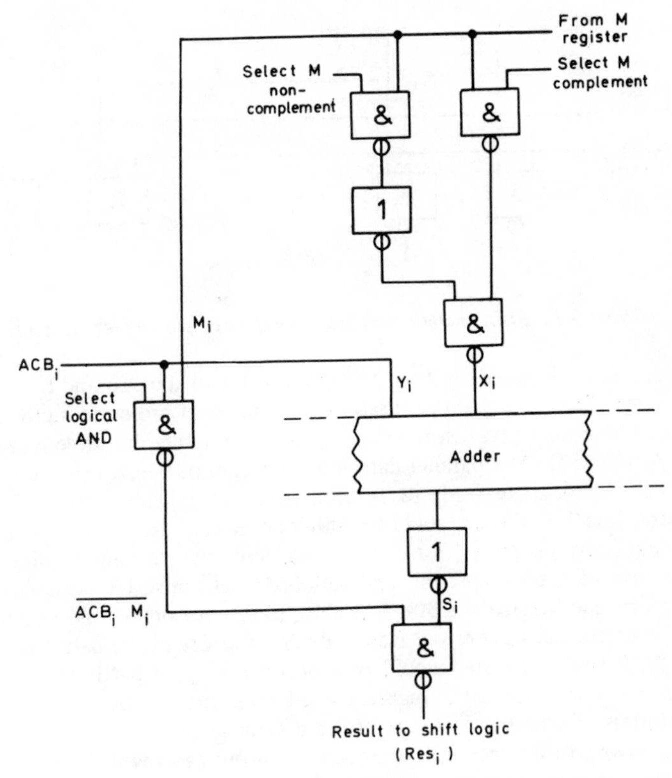

Figure 9.10 Adder selection logic – single bit cell

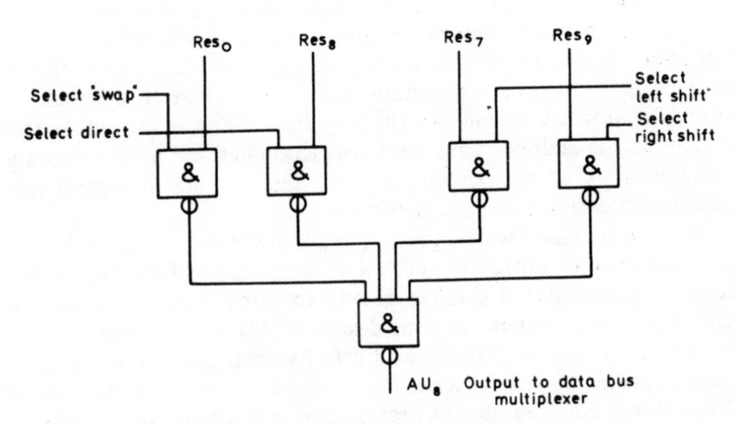

Figure 9.11 Shift logic – single bit cell

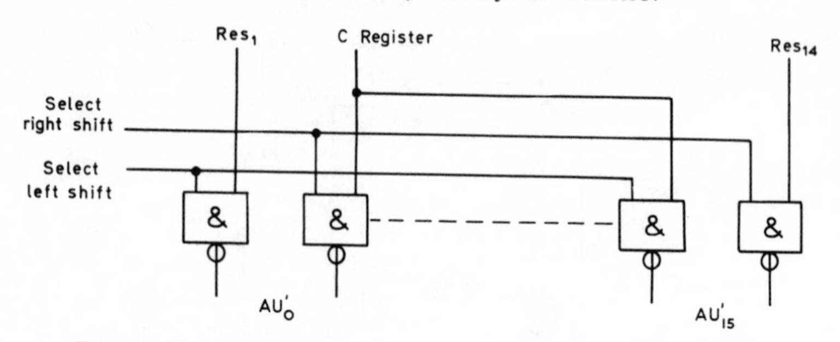

Figure 9.12 Right and left shift gates – extreme right and left bit cells

type, this leads naturally to a parallel transfer of data to and from the memory. The next question that arises is the most preferred method of transferring data between the memory and the non-addressable registers M, A, P and O. The parallel data bus chosen in our design provides the fastest transfer, but leads to an expensive multiplexer system. A less costly data bus system could be obtained at the sacrifice of speed by having fully or partly serial transfers, but this would require the insertion of a parallel-serial, and serial-parallel converter between the memory and serial data bus. The cost of this device would squander much of the savings derived from reducing the size of the data bus. The M, A, P and O register would now become fully or partly serial shift registers, and since these registers need the same number of flip-flops regardless of whether they operate in a serial or parallel mode, there is little saving to be obtained, although the input gates would be reduced to the same number as the number of lines in the data bus. When all things are considered the advantages of parallel operation would appear to outweigh any savings in hardware by serialising the data bus.

Can any of these registers be eliminated? The address register and operation register are essential, since the memory address must be held in a register and the instruction has to be stored throughout the operation. It is conceivable that the program counter could be eliminated by storing the address of the next instruction in some fixed location in the memory. The loss of time in doing this, and added control complications would not seem to justify this.

We now turn to the M register and arithmetic section. It can be seen that the parallel arithmetic unit is a complicated device for even a simple machine and it consists of cells repeated N times for an N bit unit. It is not infrequent in some designs in this section of the machine to reduce the number of repeated cells by using a partly serial organisation, at the expense of some loss in speed of arithmetic operations. When this is done we have an organisation with a separate data bus and arithmetic bus, the arithmetic section being partly serial in operation.

The M register now becomes important not only as a storage for intermediate data during arithmetic operations, but also as a mode converter receiving and transmitting data in both serial and parallel forms. A data flow system of this type is shown in Figure 9.13 for a system having a 16 bit data bus and 4 bit arithmetic bus and arithmetic unit.

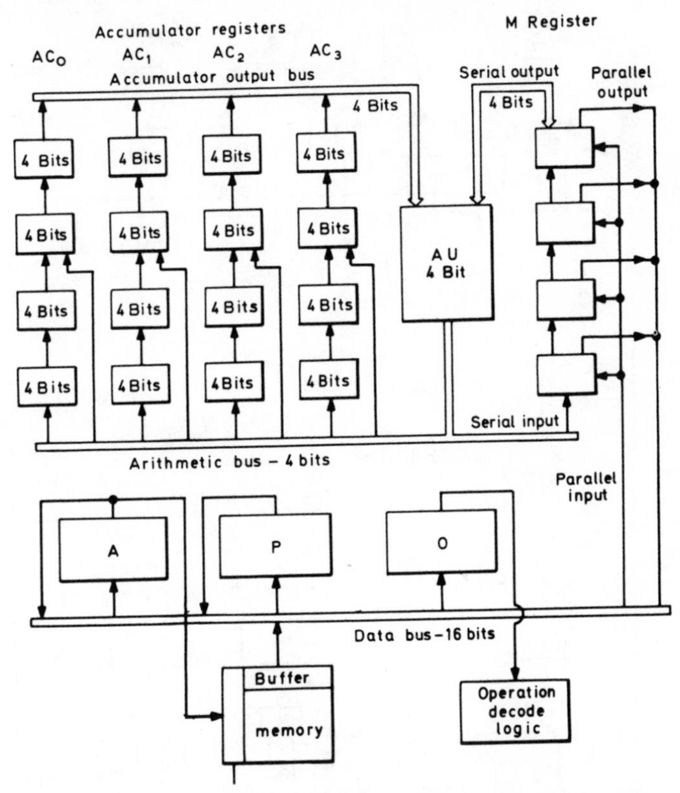

Figure 9.13 Data flow system diagram – four bit serial-parallel system

The separation of the data bus and arithmetic bus also brings some advantages since it is now possible to have an arithmetic transfer occurring simultaneously with transfer of data between the non-addressable registers A, P and O. The time saved by doing two operations can to some extent offset the loss in speed due to partly serial arithmetic. One can of course have a separate arithmetic and data bus with greater gain in speed by making both parallel buses, but with added cost.

The arrangement of the M register when used as a mode converter is shown in Figure 9.14. The M register now has both a 16 bit input and 4 bit serial parallel input as well as a 4 and 16 bit output. The mode of

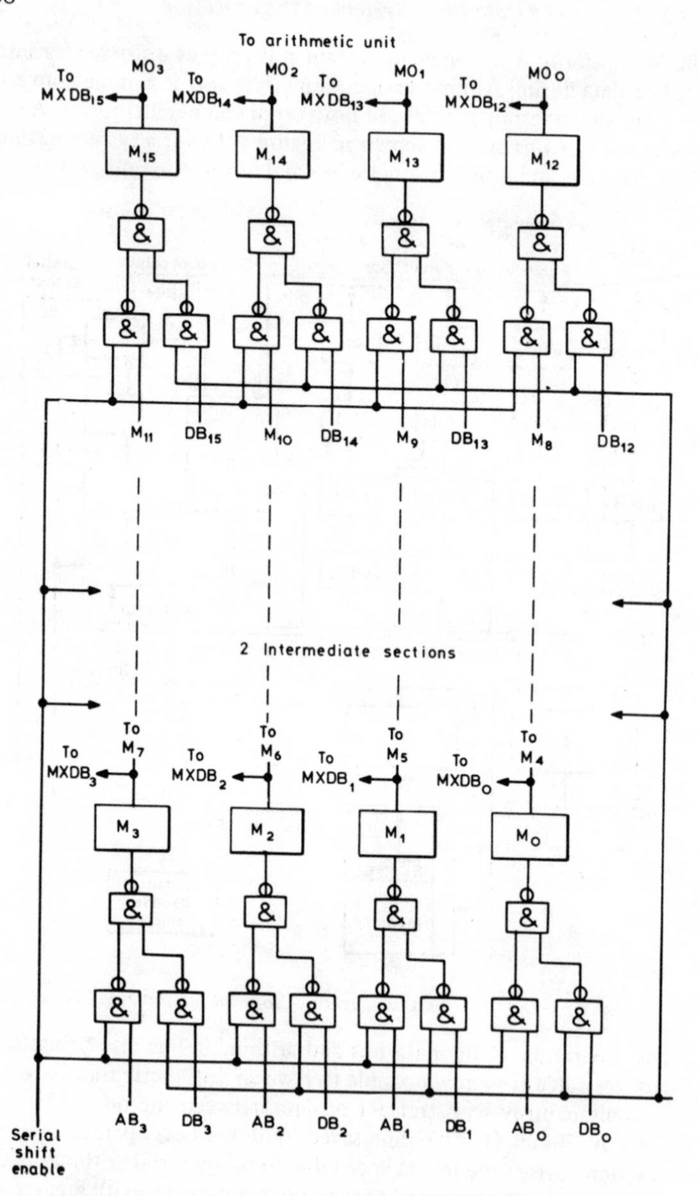

Figure 9.14 *M register – four bit serial-parallel system*
MXDB *Data bus multiplexer input*
MO *M register serial output*
AB *Arithmetic bus*
DB *Data bus*

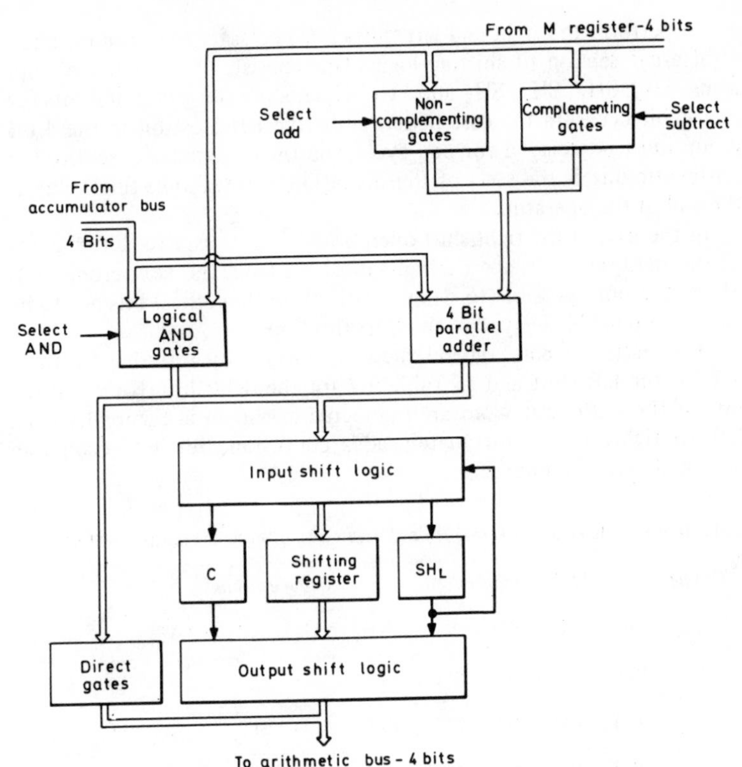

Figure 9.15 Block diagram of arithmetic unit – four bit serial-parallel system

operation is determined by control signals depending on the stage in the micro-program for the instruction being performed.

A block diagram of a 4 bit serial-parallel arithmetic unit is shown in Figure 9.15. It can be seen that it is in many ways similar to a quarter section of the parallel arithmetic unit of Figure 9.5. The significant difference lies in the carry system for the adder and the shifting logic.

Since the addition is now performed serially in 4 separate bytes, the C flip-flop acts as an intermediate carry storage for carries between bytes. Any final carry will of course remain in C at the end of an addition. The preliminary setting of C for the different arithmetic operations is exactly the same as for the parallel system.

Right and left shifting and swapping becomes considerably different in this system. Swapping is most conveniently handled by switching the gating to the accumulators which now have two inputs as shown in Figure 9.15. By reversing the order in which data is transferred from the arithmetic bus to the accumulators the data is swapped.

To perform the right and left shifts it is necessary to introduce quite a different section of shifting logic. This consists of a number of flip-flops, SH_0, SH_1, SH_2, SH_3 and SH_L which store the group of 4 bits for one 4 bit cycle. In the case of left shift, the left-most bit in the 4 bit group must be delayed for one cycle, and the contents of C sent to the arithmetic bus at the start of the operation. C is set to its final value at the end of the operatin.

In the case of the right shift operation it is necessary to shift the bits to the right, and advance the right most bit from the next group of 4. Since it is only possible to delay relatively in time, the 3 bits not to be advanced must be delayed in the shift flip-flops.

It is easier to comprehend these operations by referring to Table 9.1 for the left shift and to Table 9.2 for the right shift. Note that the bits of the arithmetic word are numbered as shown in Figure 8.1 from left to right. This unfortunately adds confusion, but has become an accepted way of numbering.

Table 9.1 THE POSITION OF EACH ARITHMETIC BIT DURING LEFT SHIFT OPERATION

Timing cycle	*Shift flip-flops*				*Arithmetic bus*				SH_L	C
	SH_3	SH_2	SH_1	SH_0	AB_3	AB_2	AB_1	AB_0		
0	BIT_{12}	BIT_{13}	BIT_{14}	BIT_{15}	—	—	—	—	—	C_{START}
1	BIT_8	BIT_9	BIT_{10}	BIT_{11}	BIT_{13}	BIT_{14}	BIT_{15}	C_{START}	BIT_{12}	C_{START}
2	BIT_4	BIT_5	BIT_6	BIT_7	BIT_9	BIT_{10}	BIT_{11}	BIT_{12}	BIT_8	C_{START}
3	BIT_0	BIT_1	BIT_2	BIT_3	BIT_5	BIT_6	BIT_7	BIT_8	BIT_4	C_{START}
4	—	—	—	—	BIT_1	BIT_2	BIT_3	BIT_4	—	BIT_0

Table 9.2 THE POSITION OF EACH ARITHMETIC BIT DURING THE RIGHT SHIFT OPERATION

Timing cycle	*Shift flip-flops*				*Arithmetic bus*				SH_L	C
	SH_3	SH_0	SH_1	SH_0	AB_3	AB_2	AB_1	AB_0		
0	BIT_{12}	BIT_{13}	BIT_{14}	BIT_{15}	—	—	—	—	—	C_{START}
1	BIT_8	BIT_9	BIT_{10}	BIT_{11}	BIT_{11}	BIT_{12}	BIT_{13}	BIT_{14}	BIT_{15}	C_{START}
2	BIT_4	BIT_5	BIT_6	BIT_7	BIT_7	BIT_8	BIT_9	BIT_{10}	BIT_{15}	C_{START}
3	BIT_0	BIT_1	BIT_2	BIT_3	BIT_3	BIT_4	BIT_5	BIT_6	BIT_{15}	C_{START}
4	—	—	—	—	C_{START}	BIT_0	BIT_1	BIT_2	—	BIT_{15}

These operations are realised in the flip-flops and gating logic shown in Figure 9.16. The group of 4 bits being emitted by the adding logic are gated into the shift flip-flops and from the shift flip-flops to the arithmetic bus according to the rules shown in the tables.

In order to simplify the diagram the gating for the direct unshifted output is not shown. In this case the output from the 4 bit adder RES_0, RES_1, RES_2, RES_3 is gated directly to the arithmetic bus AB_0, AB_1, AB_2, AB_3, during cycles 0, 1, 2, and 3.

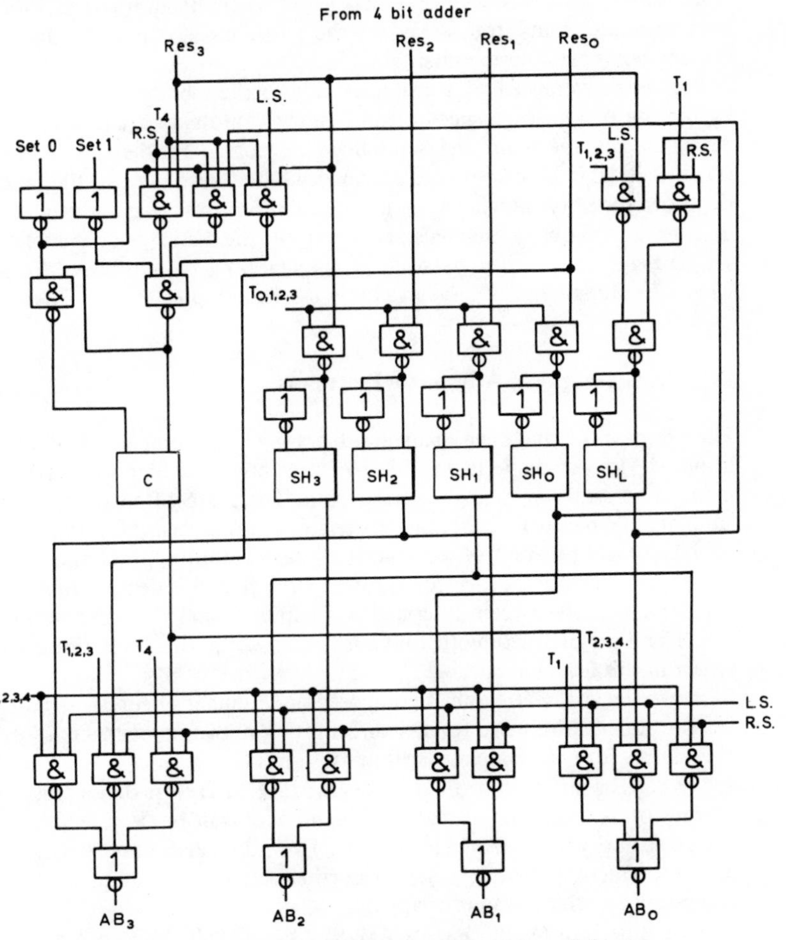

Figure 9.16 *Shifting logic for a four bit serial-parallel system*
$T_1, {}_2,$ Timing cycles
L.S. Left shift
R.S. Right shift

Larger and More Elaborate Processors

The data flow system for a very simple basic processor has been described, because to cover a larger system would soon become too much for a reasonably sized book, as anyone will agree who has studied the service manuals for these machines.

These larger machines usually have a much richer repertoire of instructions which leads to a more complicated arithmetic unit and input-output system. Commonly high speed mutliplication and division is incorporated, and the largest of the machines also have hardware floating point arithmetic units.

The effective speed of transfer of data to the memory is increased by the use of very high speed memories, with automatic transfer of the data between the main and scratchpad memories. Further automatic transfer of large blocks of data are incorporated between disc files and the main memory. Much of the information on these systems remains in internal company manuals. However, if the basic principle of a simple machine is well understood, a foundation is then provided from which the complexity of large machines can be explored.

Large Scale Integrated Arithmetic Processors

The progress that has been made in integrating large numbers of circuits in one device has made it possible to design complete high speed arithmetic processors on a single silicon chip. These are often used as an adjunct to the main processor to increase the speed of arithmetic operations and relieve it of work allowing time for other processing.

The bit-slice microprocessor is one approach to this design problem. Parallel adders have been described in Chapter 5, and the construction of a 16 bit parallel arithmetic unit based on these principles is discussed earlier in this Chapter.

A parallel arithmetic unit is composed of a number of similar circuits for the adder, arithmetic register and shifting networks connected side by side to form a complete arithmetic unit. This is shown in Figures 9.7, 9.8, 9.10 and 9.11 with the relevant text. It is clear that a section of one or several bits of the arithmetic unit can be separated as a complete entity by slicing between bits. This principle is used to make a bit slice microprocessor, which can then be stacked in parallel to compose an arithmetic unit of any desired size.

The American Micro Devices AM2901A is a typical bit slice microprocessor of this kind. This device is designed as a high speed element which can be cascaded to form a processing unit of the desired number of bits. A block diagram of this device is shown in Figure 9.17 which

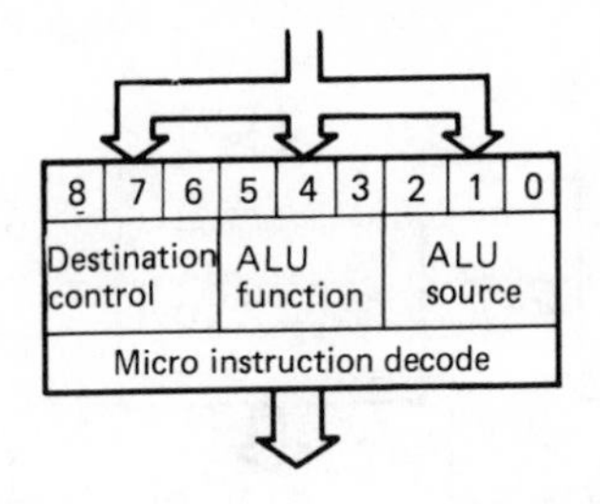
8
7
6
5
4
3
2
1
0
Destination control
ALU function
ALU source
Micro instruction decode

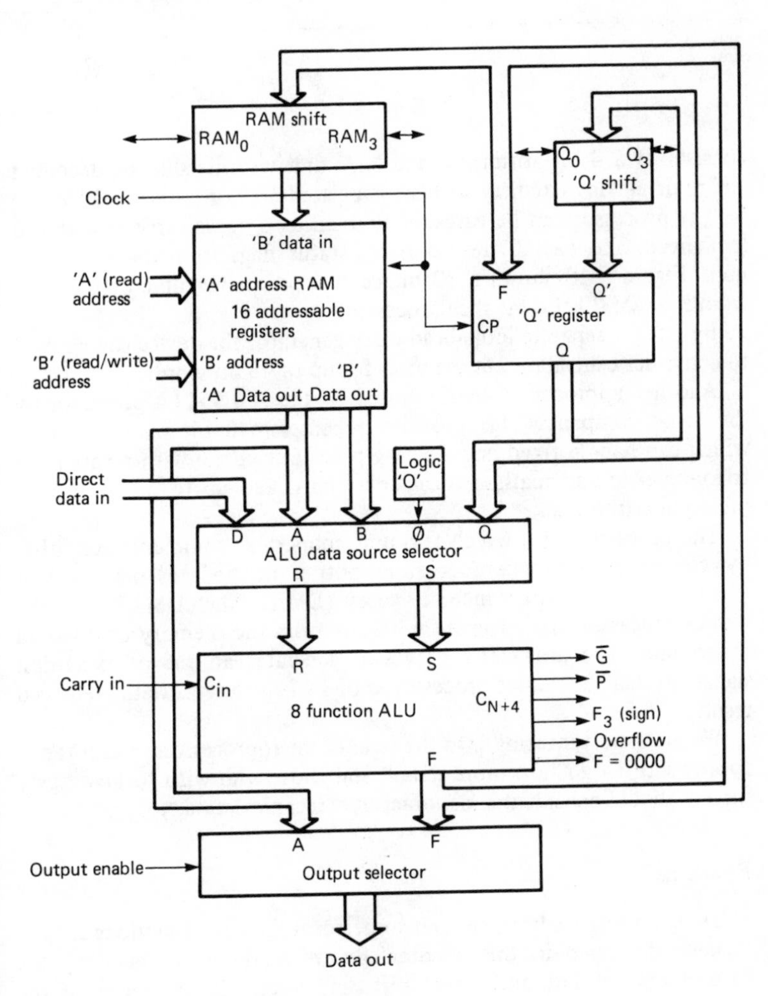
RAM shift
RAM0
RAM3
Q0
Q3
'Q' shift
Clock
'B' data in
'A' (read) address
'A' address RAM
16 addressable registers
'B' (read/write) address
'B' address
'A' Data out
'B' Data out
F
Q'
CP
'Q' register
Q
Logic 'O'
Direct data in
D
A
B
Ø
Q
ALU data source selector
R
S
R
S
Carry in
Cin
8 function ALU
CN+4
F
G
P
F3 (sign)
Overflow
F = 0000
A
F
Output enable
Output selector
Data out

Figure 9.17

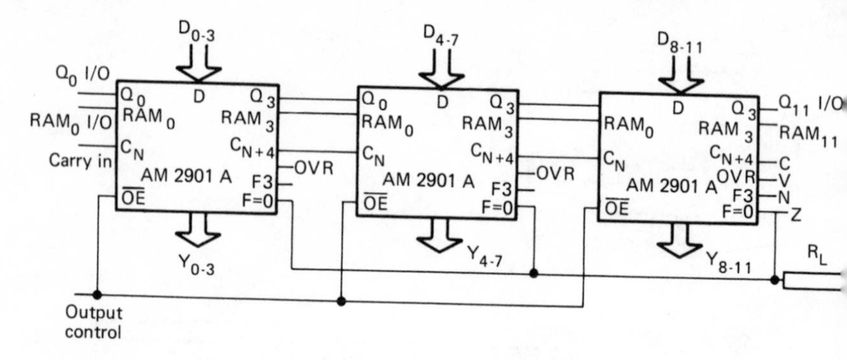

Figure 9.18

consists of a 4 bit arithmetic and logic unit with its shifting decoding and multiplexing circuitry with an associated 16 word – 4 bit RAM.

The processor can be cascaded with either a ripple carry or with full lookahead, and has all the necessary status flags from the arithmetic unit. Figure 9.18 shows a 12 bit central processing unit constructed from 3 – AM 2901A bit slice processors.

By using a separate lookahead carry generator the device can be used to construct central processing units for up to 48 bit words.

Another approach is demonstrated by the AM 9511A processor by the same company. This provides a complete 8 bit microprocessor which can handle fixed and floating point arithmetic with a variety of trigonometric and mathematical operations, and up to 32 bit double precision arithmetic.

The processor with which this unit cooperates communicates either by conventional programmed input-output methods as described in Chapter 11, or by direct memory access (DMA). When DMA is used the master processor can retrieve the results from the memory as it would other data. The arithmetic processor generates an end of execution signal, so that the master processor knows when to retrieve the required result.

We are here venturing into the field of microprocessors, and it is not appropriate to go into more detail, and those who wish to investigate further should consult the manufacturers technical data.

Problems

1. Design a serial arithmetic unit to perform the same functions as have been described in this chapter. Evolve methods for handling the problems of left and right shift, and swapping the halves of the number.

2. Consider the advantages of introducing two accumulator buses to the adder, one each for the source accumulator and the destination accumulator. This removes the need for transferring the source number to the memory register before adding or subtracting. Is the extra complication worth the increase in speed that is gained?
3. Suppose it is desired to design a machine with the absolute minimum number of registers, even though the speed is much reduced. Can any of the registers be eliminated and the data stored in the memory?

Chapter 10

The Processor Control System

The system for transferring data between different registers, the memory, and the arithmetic unit has been described. One can now proceed to investigate the control system which directs the flow of this data to achieve a meaningful result. An imperfect analogy between data and control signals might be to compare data to trains being moved around a railway system, and the control system to the signalling system and control of the railway points which causes the trains to be routed to their proper destinations.

During the design of the data flow system it has already been necessary to visualise the various operations, and to choose the best arrangement of register and data buses so that once this has been decided a clear picture emerges of the transfers of data from register to register, to the memory and to the arithmetic unit. Before proceeding the steps involved in every one of these transfers must now be clearly stated for every case, with the necessary control signals defined for each register concerned, the multiplexers, the arithmetic unit and so on.

As an example of these transfer operations we have:

Memory to A register
Memory to O register
A register to P register
P register to A register
Accumulator AC_N plus M register to accumulator AC_M
Accumulator AC_N minus M register to accumulator AC_M
Accumulator AC_N to memory

Each of these refers to the contents of registers, memory etc. but is often abbreviated to some form such as

$$\text{Mem} \rightarrow A$$
$$A \rightarrow P$$
$$AC_N + M \rightarrow AC_M$$

Many of these transfers are very simple, but stating them clearly in an orderly fashion avoids ambiguities, and prevents misunderstandings between the designers of different sections of the processor. Often this uncovers omissions and even fundamental problems at an early stage. Figure 10.1 shows one way of describing these transfers on a simple timing chart. The signals can be shown exactly as they are required, which helps to avoid confusion as to whether a control signal should be true or negated.

Instruction Flow Charts

A computer program consists of a series of instructions which accomplish the overall goal in a sequence of simple steps. In a similar way each

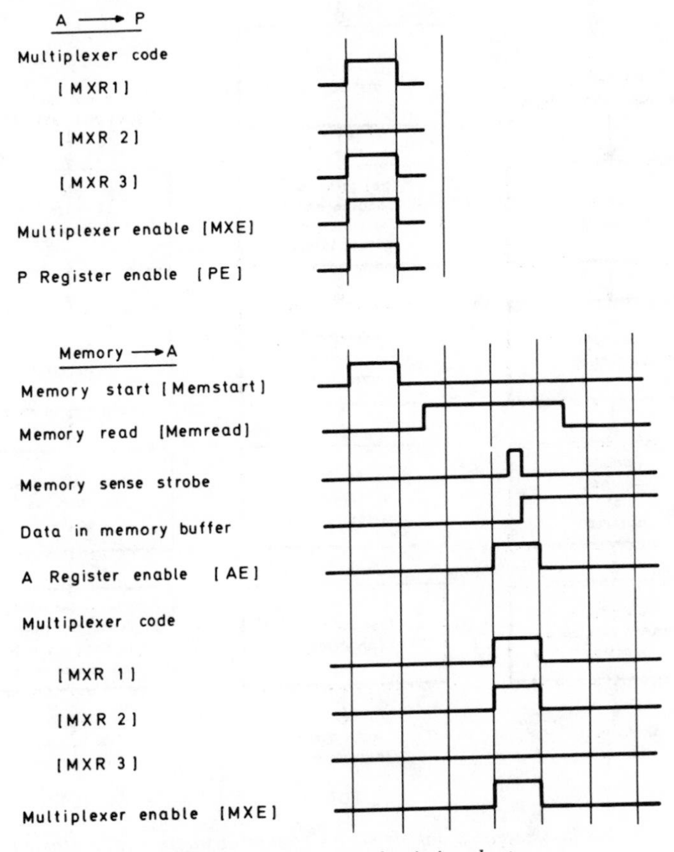

Figure 10.1 Data transfer timing charts

machine instruction consists of a sequence of micro-steps of very simple transfers or arithmetic operations which fulfil the specified instruction. This sequence of small steps is sometimes called the 'microprogram', but the terminology is inconsistent and the word is sometimes applied to a particular implementation of the step sub-sequence. The choice and implementation of these sub-sequences in the design of the processor is

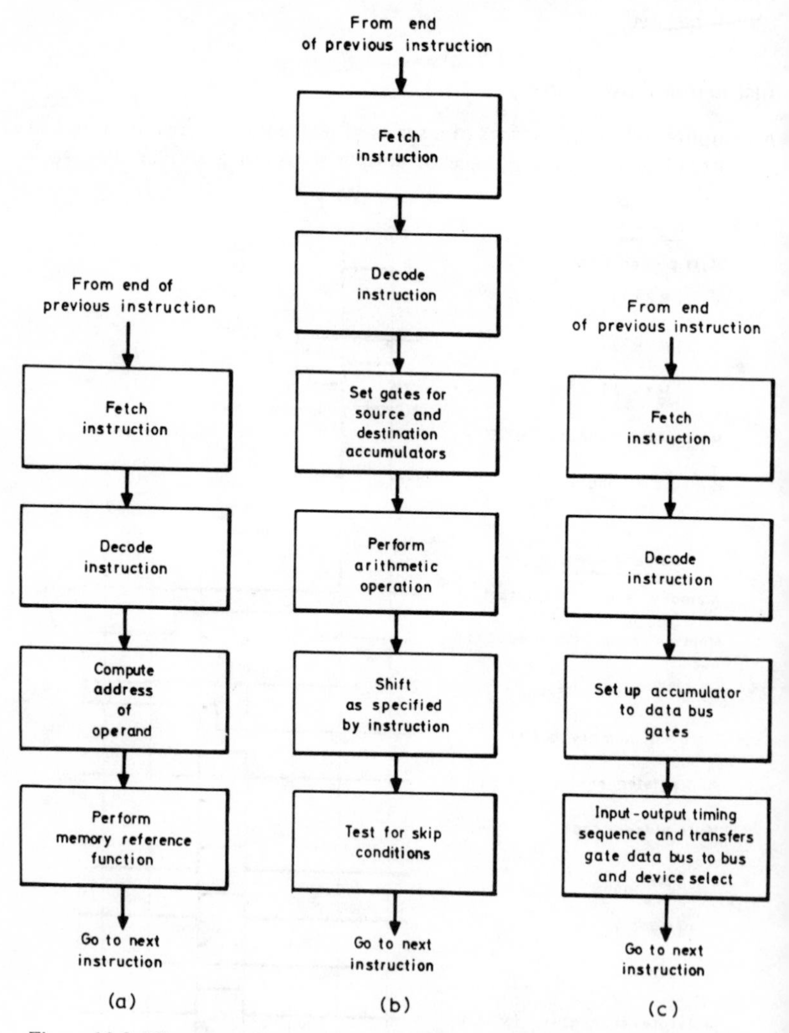

Figure 10.2 Flowcharts for: (a) Memory reference instruction (b) Arithmetic or logical instruction; (c) Input-output instruction

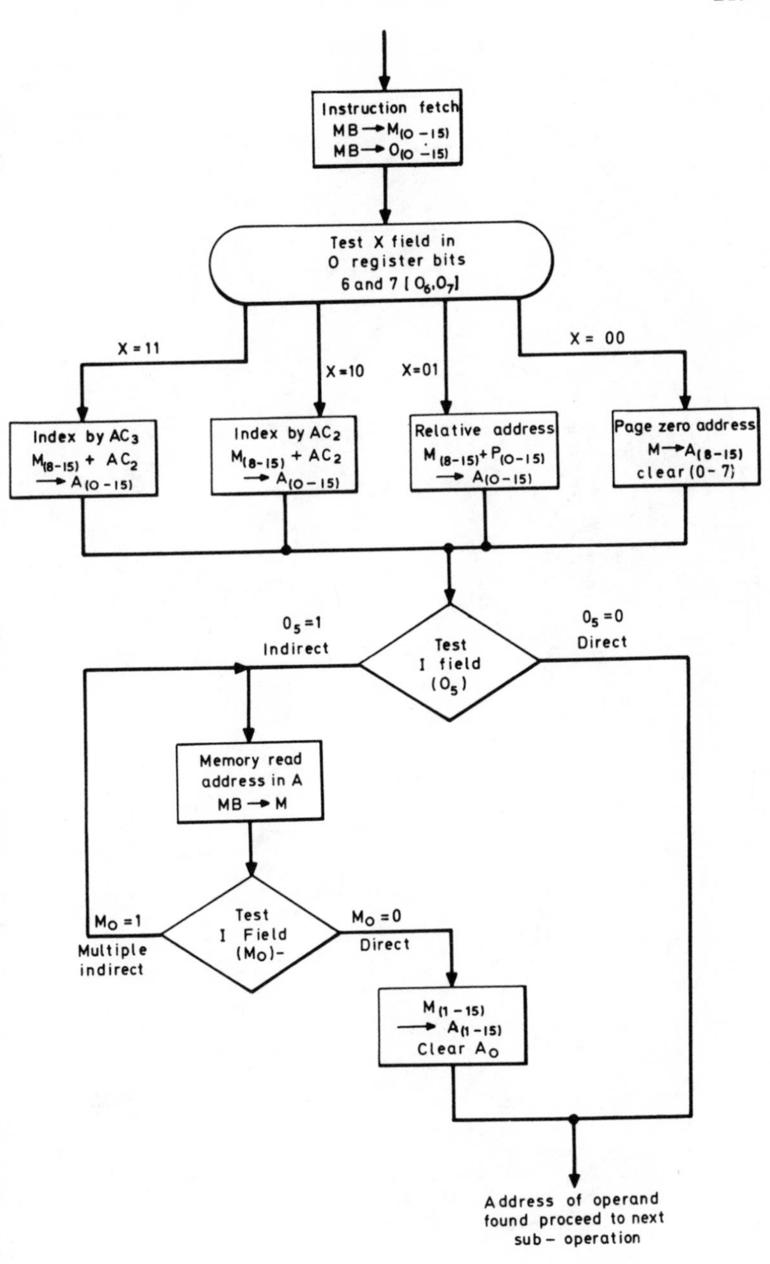

Figure 10.3 Flowchart for computing effective address

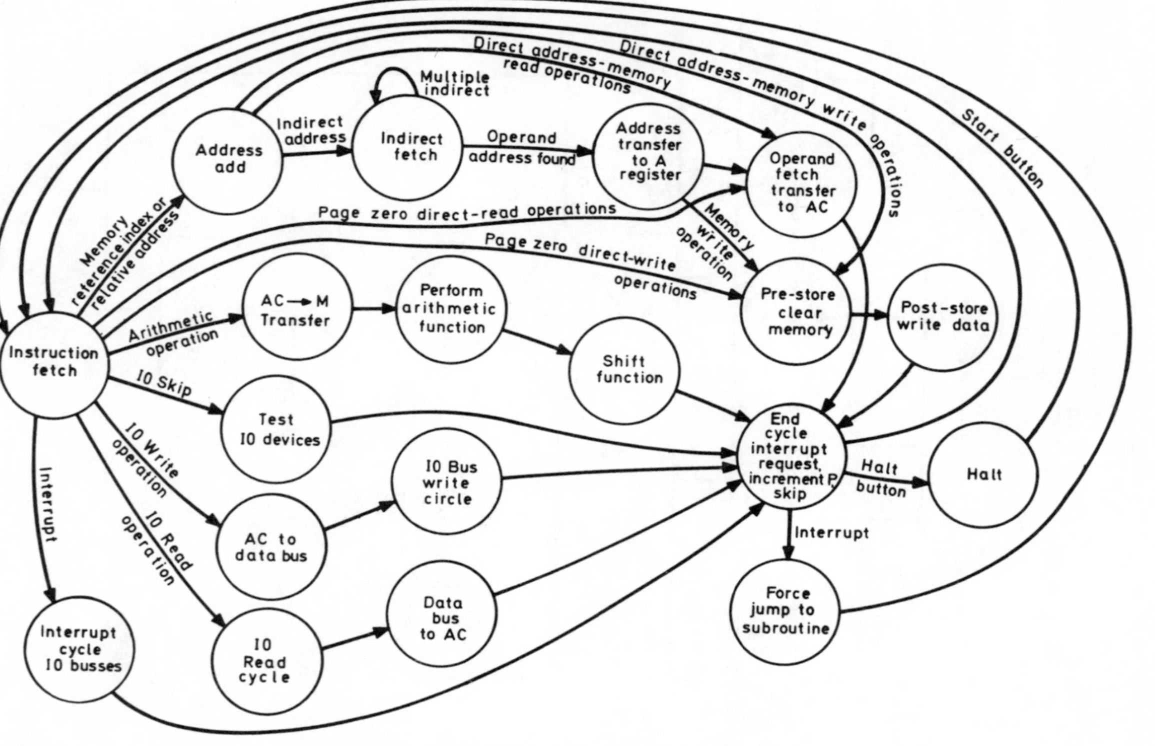

Figure 10.4 Microprogram of processor

still something of an art, in the same way that there is an art in designing a neat program in machine language.

One can commence by drawing flowcharts for each instruction, at first breaking up the instruction into rather broad sub-operations, as shown in Figure 10.2(a), (b) and (c). It is soon clear that certain groups of instructions have sections of microprogram that are either the same or very similar. For example the 'instruction fetch' sub-operation is usually similar for all instructions, because at this time the only thing to be done is to acquire the instruction in order to discover what next to do, so that all instructions must start in this way. As soon as the instruction word has been transferred to the O register, it is decoded and decisions can be made to branch into different sub-operations as specified in the instruction code. The broad sub-operations can be now dissected to explore their details.

As an example the computation of the effective memory address is shown in Figure 10.3. Having determined from the operation code that this is a memory reference instruction, the sequence commences with the examination of the X field to find if the instruction refers to a page zero address, a relative address or whether the address should be indexed by accumulator 2 or 3. The microprogram branches then at this point to one of four sub-sequences, and while these arithmetic and housekeeping operations are under way, the contents of the memory which have just been read can be restored (rewritten). Of course the contents of the A register cannot be changed until this is finished, or data would be written into the wrong memory location.

Having computed the addıess of the first location in the memory to be fetched, the I field in the instruction is tested to find if this is the direct address of the operand or an indirect address of another memory location. If it was a direct address the arithmetic or other function can proceed with the operand, and the microprogram jumps to another sub-operation. If it was an indirect address, the data from the new address is fetched and again the I field (now in bit 0 instead of bit 5) is tested to ascertain whether this is an operand or further indirect address. This continues until the operand is finally obtained, when the microprogram jumps to the next sub-operation to perform the operation defined by the instruction.

After analysis one can merge all the various sub-operations to form the complete microprogram. This can be shown on a larger flowchart, or it may be preferred to draw this in the form of a directed graph, which is shown in Figure 10.4, and which should be self-explanatory.

Control Timing Charts

So far the discussion of the microprogram has been in symbolic terms, and time has not been mentioned, as well as making only vague reference

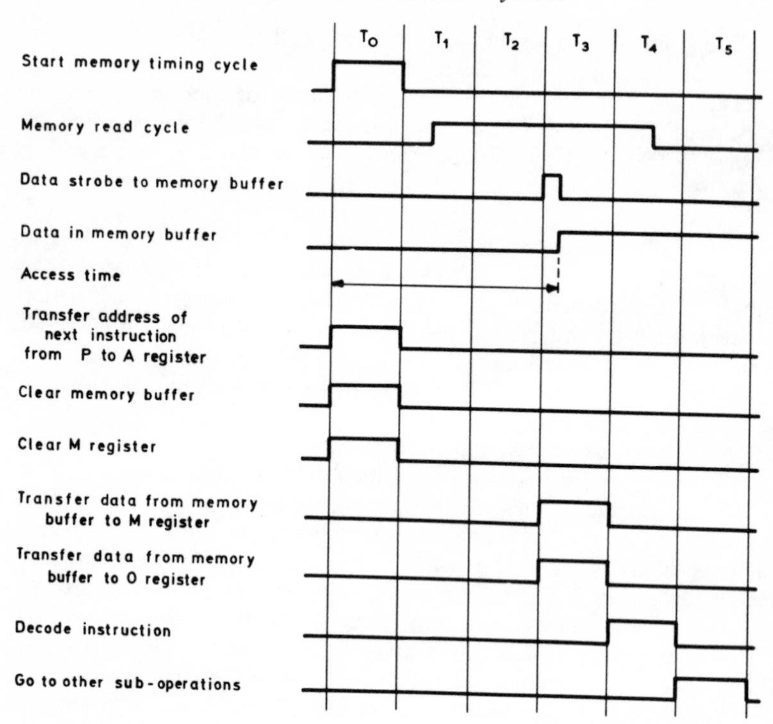

Figure 10.5 Timing chart for the 'instruction fetch' sub-operation

to physical actions within the processor. It is next necessary to reduce these various sub-operations, to a form from which it is possible to make an actual logical design. The way preferred by the author is to draw detailed timing diagrams for every sub-operation, which can be constructed from the original timing for the transfer operations as shown in Figure 10.1, and from the flow charts showing what is necessary to be done.

As examples of timing charts of sub-operations, those for 'instruction fetch', and for the arithmetic cycle are shown in Figures 10.5 and 10.6. The cycles for each sub-operation are divided into steps defined by the clock cycle of the processor and each of these is defined by a master timing counter from which the separated timing pulses are derived. Most of the logical operations in the machine start or finish at the division between one cycle and the next. Due to physical delays in the gating structures for the control signals, this obviously does not occur in practice. This must always be kept in mind, and for fast operations, it is essential that the control signal arrives on control gates, before the data which it must control. The double rank flip-flop system obviates most of the difficulties encountered due to timing skew between signals as described in Chapter 3. It is most important however, that the master clock signals to flip-flops in various parts of the mchine are as closely synchronised as possible.

In the 'instruction fetch' cycle, the timing of the memory is included, and since this operation is usually separately timed by the memory control system, and determined by the physical characteristics of the memory, it is not synchronous with the master clock. This timing discrepancy is accommodated during transfer from the memory buffer to the M and O registers.

The arithmetic cycle is shown for a parallel arithmetic unit. The first step is to transfer the contents of the source accumulator ACS to the M register preliminary to adding it to the contents of the destination accumulator ACD. Simultaneously the carry flip-flop is set to 1 or 0 as required. In the second step the contents of the destination accumulator

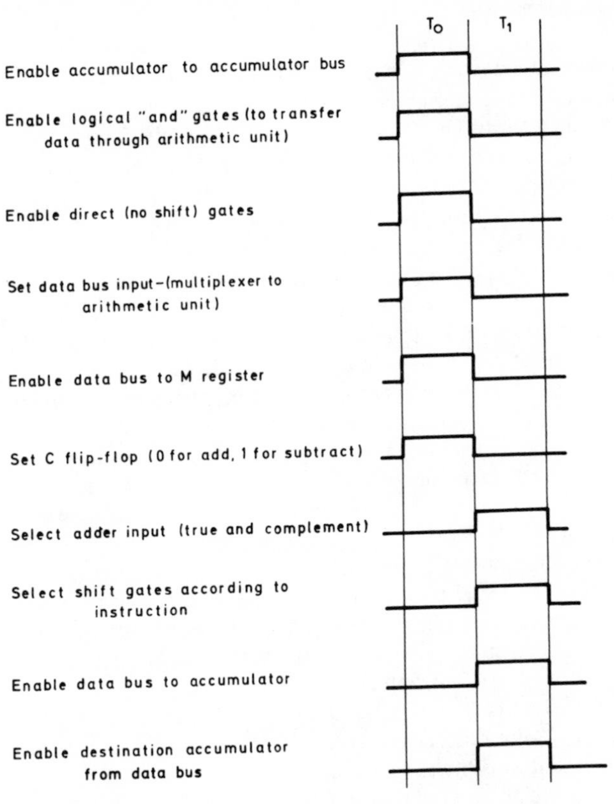

Figure 10.6 Timing chart for arithmetic cycle (parallel adder)

are gated on to the accumulator bus and to the arithmetic unit. The appropriate adder input gates are selected, and also the shift gates as indicated by the instruction. The output of the adder is transferred to the data bus, unless there is a 'no-load condition', and the destination accumulator input is selected.

There is obviously much detail which cannot be explored further, but once the complete set of timing charts has been produced it is possible to design the control logic of the processor. The inputs to this control logic are from the instruction decoding gates which indicate the instruction being performed and therefore the appropriate control gates to enable, the master timing counter and various control flip-flops, which it may be necessary to include, to define a sequence of operations.

Operation Decoding

The operation decoding logic is connected directly to the outputs of the operation (O) register in which the instruction is placed after it has been fetched from the memory. It is formed purely from combinational circuits and consists of a series of decoding AND functions from which are derived signals indicating the various types of instruction and the details of the functions within these groups.

The decoding and number of gates required in this section of the machine, are greatly reduced by the orderly design of the instruction formats, which are described in Chapter 8 for the memory reference and arithmetic and logical instructions, and Chapter 11 for the input-output instructions. This is the province of the computer architect, and demonstrates that the architecture of the instructions can have a serious effect on the complication of the hardware.

The way in which the instructions are decoded can be illustrated by the instruction decoding tree shown in Figure 10.7. Bit 0 determines whether it is a memory reference instruction (0) or arithmetic or logical instruction (1). If Bit 0 is 0, bits 1 and 2 are decoded to indicate (11) an IO instruction, (00) memory increment or decrement or jump instruction, (01) load accumulator, and (10) store accumulator.

In the next stage bits 3 and 4 define the accumulator for load and store, or determine the jump, jump to subroutine, increment or decrement memory and skip if zero instructions.

If bit 0 is a (1) then bits 1 and 2 decide the source accumulator, and bits 3 and 4, the destination accumulator. Bits 5, 6 and 7 then define eight different arithmetic functions.

And so the three fans out and the less significant bits define greater and greater detail in the functions. In the design of the logic one has the

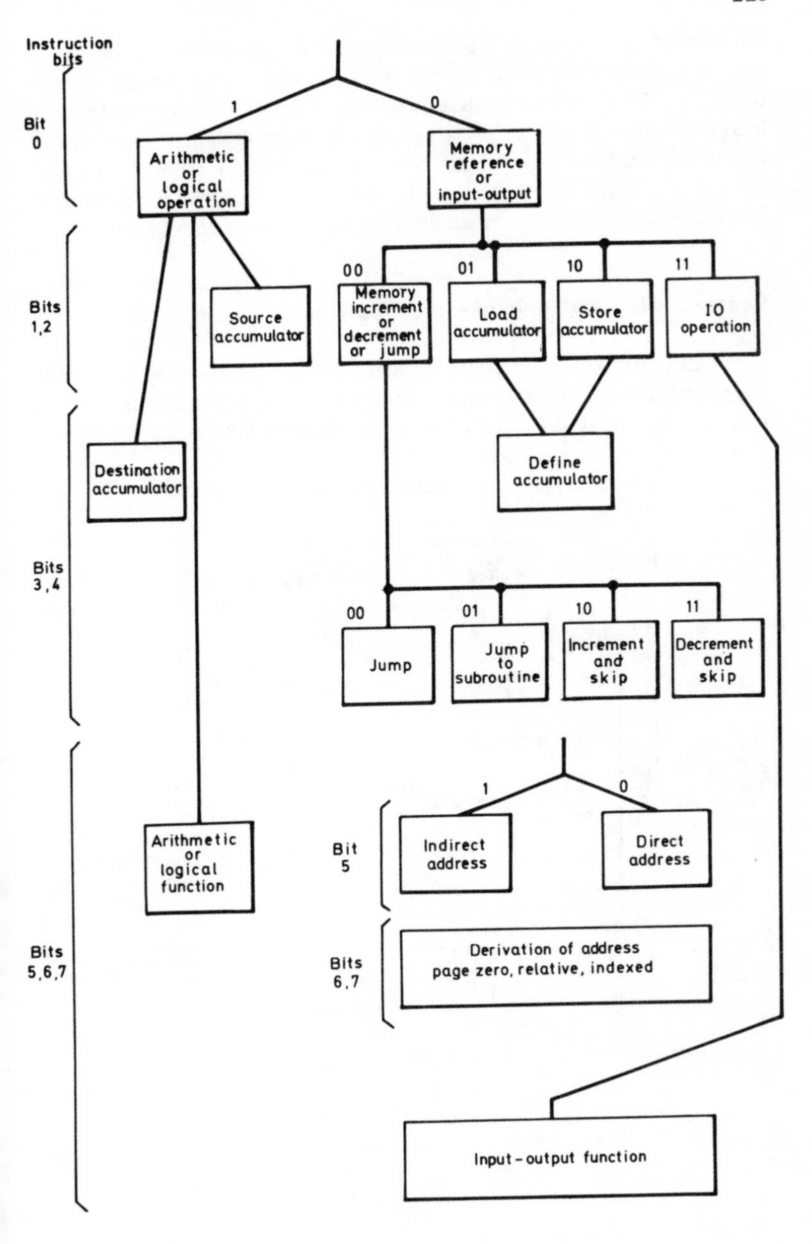

Figure 10.7 Instruction decoding tree

latitude of decoding by parallel input gates requiring few levels of decoding, or in a tree structure in a series of steps, reflecting the pattern of Figure 10.7, with a reduction of the number of gate inputs, but introducing more gating levels before the control signals are derived. Certain critical control signals may be decoded in parallel gates to obtain the signal at the earliest moment, other less critical signals can be obtained through a more economical but longer chain of gates.

Control System with Sub-operation Flip-Flops

In the discussion on the design of the microprogram it was seen that the microprogram can be segmented into a number of sub-operations which can be linked together. In one way of implementing the microprogram

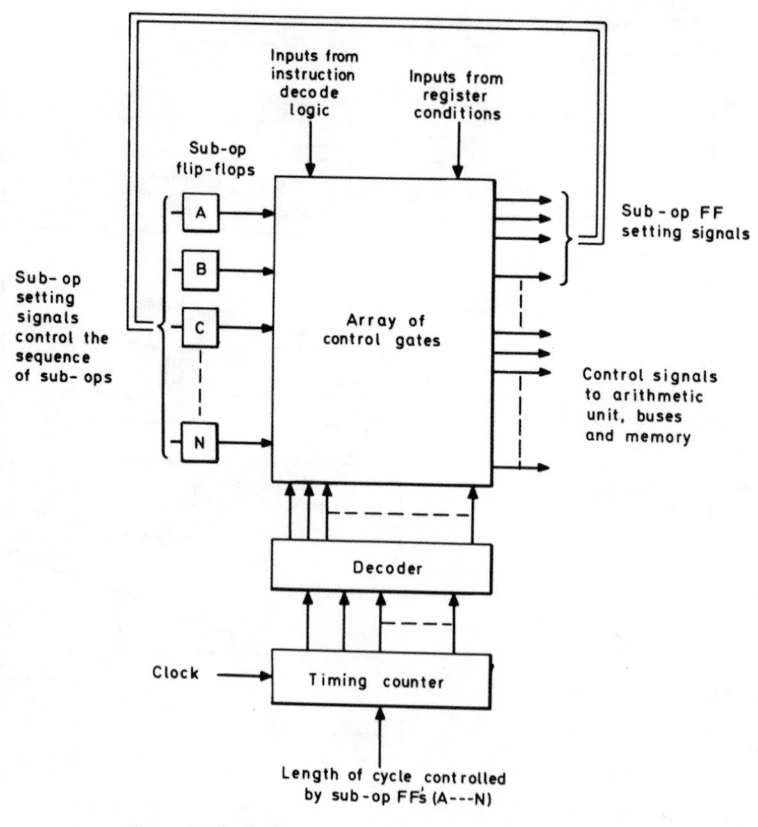

Figure 10.8 Control system with sub-operation flip-flops

in hardware, each of these sub-operations is represented by a flip-flop which defines the sub-operation in progress at the time, and only one of which is set at any one time. These sub-operation flip-flops, in conjunction with a timing counter driven by the master clock, control gates which produce the desired control signals at the instant they are needed. This form of organisation of the control system is shown as a block diagram in Figure 10.8.

The timing counter and the sub-operation flip-flops each provide one input at any particular time, to the array of gates which generate the various control signals. These define the sub-operation to be performed and the clock period within the sub-operation. The other important group of inputs to the control gates is from the operation decoding logic which indicates the instruction that is being performed. Combinations of these three sets of inputs are sufficient to generate the various necessary control signals when required, except for a few other inputs from registers, such as the C register which may determine skip conditions, or other inputs indicating indirect address conditions.

At the termination of each sub-operation it is necessary to go to the next one, which is done by resetting the sub-operation flip-flop, and simultaneously setting the next one. At the same time the timing is set back to its starting point to begin again at T_0. The set and reset signals to do this are also generated by gates in the array, having for input the operation decoding signals, the current sub-operation, and the timing step. The whole system forms a sequential system which steps continuously unless it is halted. The gates within the array are usually designed piecemeal and do not necessarily appear in any clear pattern. This type of control system has the disadvantage that it does not have any very systematic arrangement, but it does sometimes have the advantage that high speed portions can be specially designed.

Control System with Read-Only Memory Microprogram

An alternative and more modern approach to the design of the control system is to permanently store the microprogram within a read-only memory (ROM). Like many of the fundamental ideas in computers the concept is not new and was first formulated by Wilkes and Stringer in 1952. The method has become more attractive and widely used because of the availability of integrated circuit read-only memories, which are small and of reasonable cost. The various transfer operations described earlier can be designated as micro-operations, and these are strung together again to form sub-operations. The various sub-operations are then linked together by micro-jump operations.

A block diagram of this system is shown in Figure 10.9. The ROM

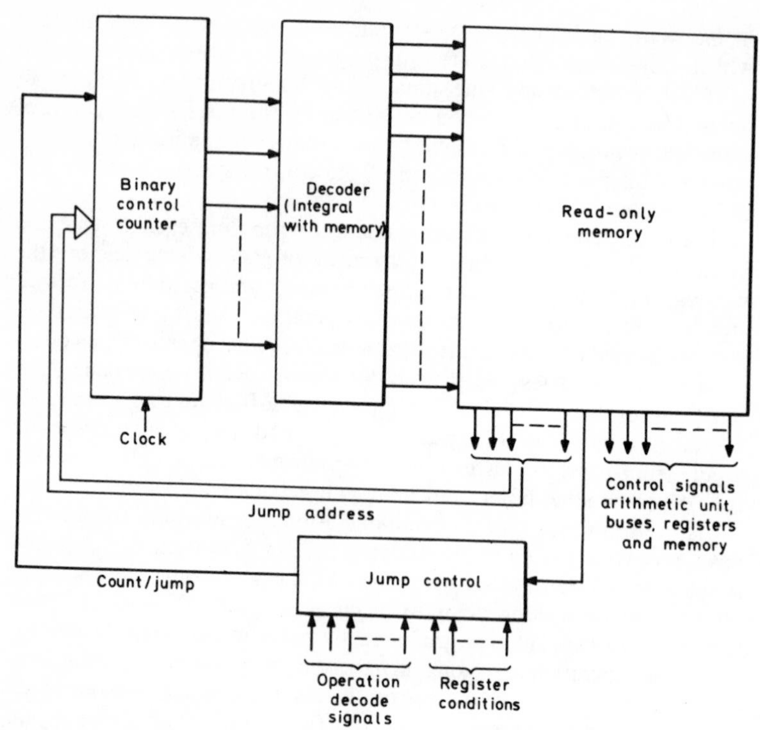

Figure 10.9 Control system with read-only memory microprogram

usually has its decoding logic designed integrally with the memory logic on the same chip. Since it is often necessary to have both more memory locations and more bits in a word than can be accommodated on a single chip, it is necessary to arrange that ROM chips can be assembled in arrays to increase the size in both dimensions.

The address input to the ROM is from a binary control counter which generates the input to the address selection. This counter will normally step from one micro-operation to the next at the clock rate, but need not necessarily do so. Pauses have to be instrumented by separate circuits which temporarily suspend the stepping from the clock. In order to jump from one sub-operation to another the control counter must be changed to the number representing the address of the beginning of the next sub-operation. This is done by inhibiting the count operation and forcing or entering the new address directly into the counter. The new address number is derived directly from the ROM, and another control signal causes the control count operation to be inhibited and the direct transfer to occur. Conditional jumps are implemented by allowing the control counter to either continue to count to the next micro-operation, or jump to a new address under control of operation decode signals derived from the main instruction. As before the system continues to step through a sequence of operations, and fetching new instructions from the main memory unless it is halted. It is interesting to notice how closely this resembles the idealised sequential circuit described in Chapter 3.

Since only two-way jump decisions are possible it is necessary to recast the microprogram in a way that is similar to writing an external program at the level of the machine language. This is less convenient where multi-way decisions occur which must be formed of a tree of two-way decisions. The attraction of the ROM is the systematic and orderly arrangement of the microprogram, and by the use of integrated circuit ROM's this can be constructed in a clean and straightforward manner.

A modern trend in larger processors is to design the basic machine with a nucleus of standard instructions, and the basic software is also written using these. But, in addition, a set of micro-operations are provided, which makes it possible to form extra instructions tailored to the particular application of the machine, so that in effect the basic machine can be metamorphosed into a variety of different machines. The read-only memory microprogram makes it possible to realise this in an orderly way, without drastic internal changes, and its flexibility in this respect makes it almost an essential method of design for this type of machine.

Problems

1. Complete the development of the operation decoding gates shown in this chapter.
2. Develop the operation decoding system needed for the rearranged instructions resulting from suggestions in the problems for Chapter 8.
3. Obtain the reference manual for any small computer and design a microprogram to perform the instructions there defined.

   Having designed the microprogram implement this in either a Read-Only Memory microprogram or with sub-operations.

REFERENCES

1. WILKES, M.V., and STRINGER, J.B., Microprogramming and the Design of the Control Circuits in an Electronic Digital Computer', *Proc. Cambridge Philos. Soc.*, **49**, 230–238 (1953)
2. 'Special Issue on Microprogramming', *IEEE Trans. Comp.*, **20**, 7 (1971)
3. 'Special Section on Microprogramming', *IEEE Trans. Comp.*, **23**, 8 (1974)

Chapter 11

The Input–Output System

Two basic methods of input-output control coexist in modern small computers. The first method is used for the majority of applications, in which the peripheral device operates relatively slowly in relation to the internal speed of the processor, and is known as Programmed Input-Output. This will apply to electromechanical devices such as teletype machines, printers, high speed paper tape readers, etc., and also to many transducers of physical, chemical and biological variables which are to be processed or monitored by computer. This system is very flexible and is under the control of the program, and it also requires the minimum of hardware in the interface logic and circuits.

The second type of system called variously, Direct Memory Access, Data Channel, or Data Break, is used in connection with peripheral devices which must send or receive data at high speed, such as Magnetic Disc Files, Magnetic Tape Machines, Magnetic Drums, and also certain scientific instruments from which data must be digested very rapidly. This system will be described later.

In the case of the NOVA, the maximum rate at which data transfers can be executed under program control is 80 000 words per second. The data channel allows rates of greater than 200 000 words per second.

Programmed Transfers

The program controlled system can operate in two ways. The programmer may elect to read or write information to or from a device or devices at specified time intervals. These might occur at convenient points in the program, or if the devices must be attended to at certain fixed time intervals, many computers are provided with an internal absolute timing device. If there are a number of input-output devices which have to be read in to the processor at regular intervals, such as in data logging, or in a time interval multiplexing application, the program will probably be designed to scan the devices at regular intervals. This operation is called 'polling'.

In the NOVA the control logic for each device contains two flip-flops, called the 'BUSY' and 'DONE' flags, which are used to signal its condition to the processor. When both flags are at '0', this indicates that the device is in the idle condition. It is ready to receive data, or could be set into action by a manual operator.

Once the device is launched into performing some operation, either by a signal from the processor or by external stimulus, the BUSY flag is set, indicating that the device cannot be interfered with until this is completed. When the operation is finished, the device may just return to the idle state, awaiting further commands. In other cases where a string of data is expected, as in a printer printing a line of characters, it may be desired to call the processor immediately to send further information. In this case the BUSY flag is reset, and the DONE flag is set. The Interrupt Request flip-flop INT REQ is set which interrupts the processor, which can then attend to the device. Having both BUSY and DONE flags set is a meaningless condition. The procedure is shown in Table 11.1.

Table 11.1 SEQUENCE FOR SETTING 'BUSY' AND 'DONE' FLAGS

	Busy	*Done*
Start—Idle state	0	0
Processor sets BUSY flag	1	0
Device completes operation—sets DONE flag	0	1
Processor again sets BUSY flag for next operation and resets DONE flag	1	0
OR		
Total operation is completed and processor sets device to the idle state	0	0

Returning to the description of the 'polling' method of operation, the program will call each device in turn, testing for the BUSY or DONE condition. This is done by first giving an IO skip instruction to test the state of the BUSY flag. If the device is ready, say, to receive data, the BUSY flag is at '0' and the DONE flag is '1'. Depending on the state of the BUSY flag the program will skip to the next device, or jump to the appropriate sub-routine to service the device.

Each device is selected by placing the device number code on the device selection lines DS (0–5). The 6 bit code makes it possible to select one out of 64 different devices, but it may sometimes be convenient to use more than one device number for a single complicated

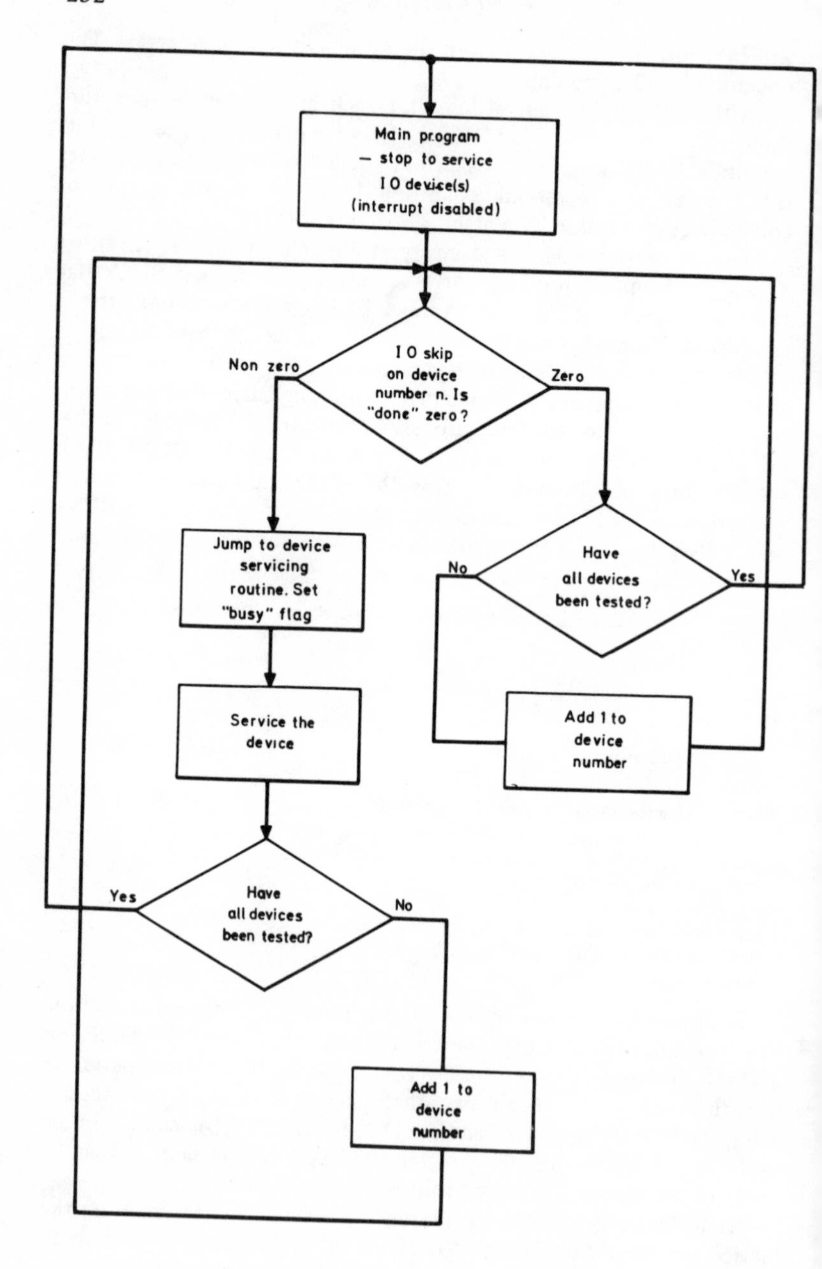

Figure 11.1 Flowchart for polling operation

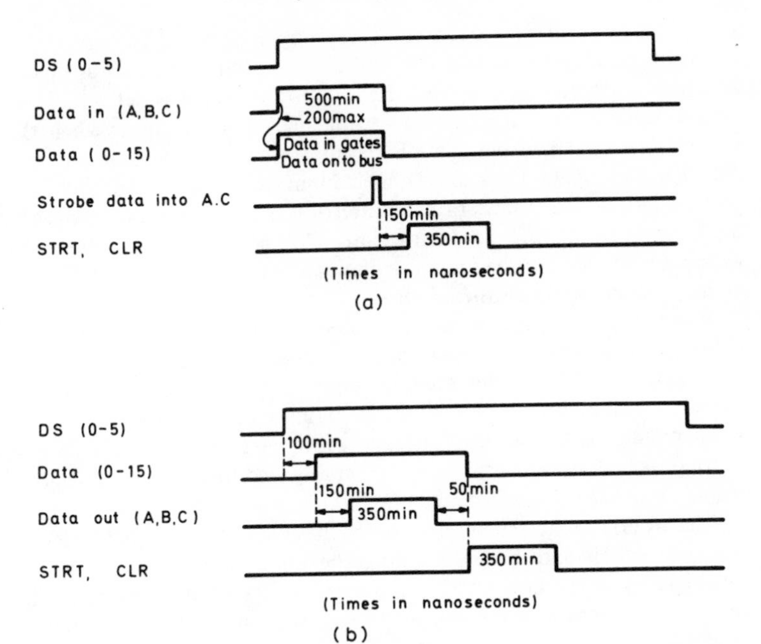

Figure 11.2 Timing diagram for the transfer of data (a) into the processor from a device and (b) out of the processor to a device

device. The data to be sent to the device is placed on the data lines (0–15). Or if a device is supplying input to the processor this will appear on the data lines (0–15). To actuate the transfer a signal Data Out (A, B or C) is placed on the appropriate line, or again in the case of input, Data In (A, B, or C) is supplied. These signals gate the appropriate registers of the selected device to or from the data lines. A description of the input-output buses is given which shows the function of the various signals.

A flowchart of this procedure is shown in Figure 11.1. Timing diagrams for programmed transfers in and out of the processor are shown in Figure 11.2.

Programmed Interrupt

In the programmed interrupt mode of operation, the processor continues operating on its main program until an input-output device requests attention. In distinction to the 'polling' method, the processor is allowed to proceed happily on its way getting on with some job, until some input-output operation is initiated by a device. The request for attention is done by setting the DONE flag. Each input-output device interface logic contains an INT REQ flip-flop which is set when the device needs attention either due to manual intervention or when the DONE flag is set and new data is required or is needed to be entered. All the INT REQ flags are connected in common to an interrupt request line to the processor. The interrupt input to the processor can be turned on or off by instruction. This is necessary because the processor cannot normally allow itself to be interrupted while it is already attending to another device.

When the interrupt input is enabled, it is sampled before each memory cycle (except for certain forbidden instructions), and if an interrupt condition is detected, a jump to subroutine instruction is forced, causing the address of the next instruction stored in P to be saved in address O, and the program continues to the interrupt service routine stored in address 1, or by indirect address if the routine is stored elsewhere. Simultaneously the interrupt input is disabled.

The interrupt service routine saves the contents of the addressable registers, which may be used during the input-output operation, and proceeds to determine which of many devices needs attention. The program then jumps to the appropriate service routine for that particular device.

Normally the interrupt is left 'off' during the service procedure, but the programmer may wish to interrupt the servicing of a low priority device, by a high priority one in which case the interrupt is turned 'on' again at the appropriate point.

At the termination of the device serving operation, the program jumps to another part of the interrupt service routine which replaces the contents of the addressable registers, and then jumps indirectly via address O back to the point where it left off when the interrupt occurred.

In the NOVA, as in many computers there is a single interrupt request line, and it is possible for more than one device to interrupt at one time, so that it is necesary to determine the device having the highest priority for attention. This can be done in several ways. In the simplest case the devices can be tested by IO skip instructions in order of their priority, so that the most urgent device is attended to first.

An ingenious method of determining priority is used in the NOVA in which a line is connected in 'daisy chain' fashion from one device to the next in order of priority, the highest priority device being nearest to the processor. An 'Interrupt-Acknowledge' instruction causes the device code of the first device on the bus requesting an interrupt, i.e. that nearest to the processor, to be placed in a specified accumulator, via the IO data lines, so that the highest priority device code is obtained immediately.

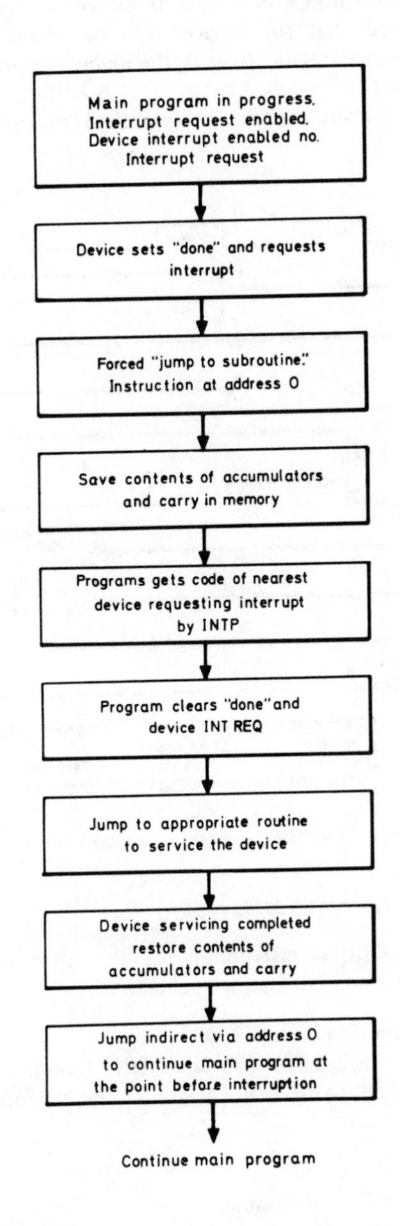

Figure 11.3 Flowchart of interrupt procedures

The sequence of operations that occur when an interrupt signal is received can be shown in a flowchart as shown in Figure 11.3. In this case it is assumed that the devices will be tested for the DONE condition in sequence starting from 0, the highest priority devices being the lowest numbers.

The timing diagram for the programmed interrupt operation is shown in Figure 11.4.

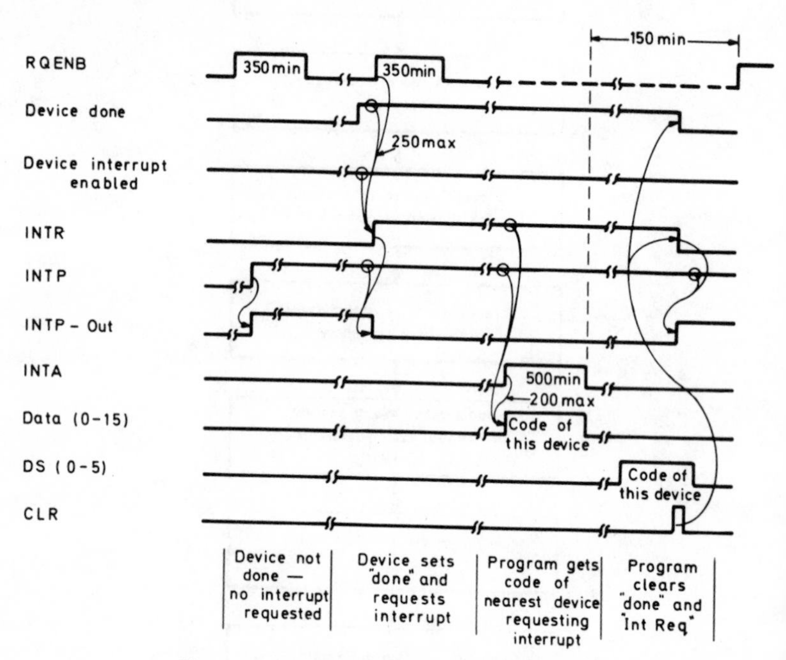

Figure 11.4 Timing chart for program interrupt

The Input-Output Instructions

The NOVA input-output instruction has the form shown in Figure 11.5. These instructions fall into several classes:

1. A control function in device D.
2. A skip on condition of BUSY and DONE flags in device D.
3. A data transfer to or from device D and performance of some defined function.
4. Special functions:

   Interrupt Enable and Disable
   Interrupt Acknowledge

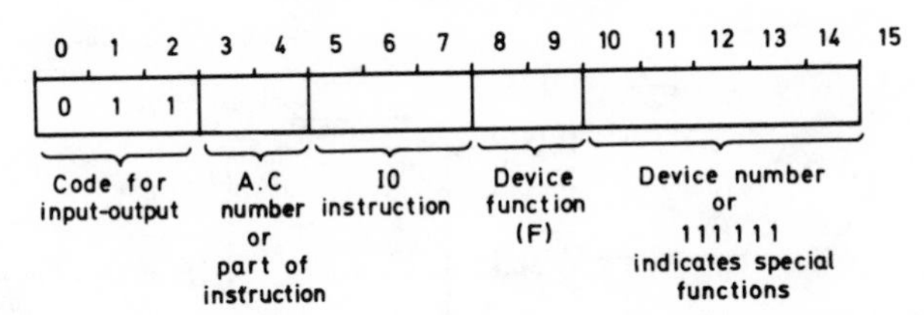

Figure 11.5 General form of input–output instruction

Read Console Switches
Halt
Clear control flip-flops in all devices
Power failure skips
etc.

It can be seen that the input-output instructions are very flexible, and are to some extent specified by the user in his particular application. It is not intended here to rewrite an application manual for a machine, since there is quite a wide difference between the provisions made in various processors for input-output instructions, the details of these can be extensive, and the manual for a particular processor must be studied.

The Input-Output Buses

The arrangement of the input-output bussing system is shown in Figure 11.6. The input-output data lines are for the transfer of data either to or from the device to the processor. These can be gated within the processor to either, place data from an accumulator on to the internal data bus and thence onto the data lines to a device, or to gate information from a device onto the data bus and thence to a specified accumulator.

The device selection number is obtained from the IO instruction in the O register ($O_{10}-O_{15}$) and is transmitted on the device selection lines on the appropriate instructions by the instruction decoding logic.

Data out and data in signals to the devices, either gate data, on the data bus onto a particular register in a device, or gate data in a device register onto the data lines to be sent to the processor.

STRT, sets the BUSY flag and clears the DONE flag and INT REQ flag in a selected device.

CLR clears the BUSY, DONE, and INT REQ flags in a selected device.

SELF, SELD – selected BUSY, and selected DONE, are signals to the processor indicating the state of the flags in a selected device and determine IO skip conditions.

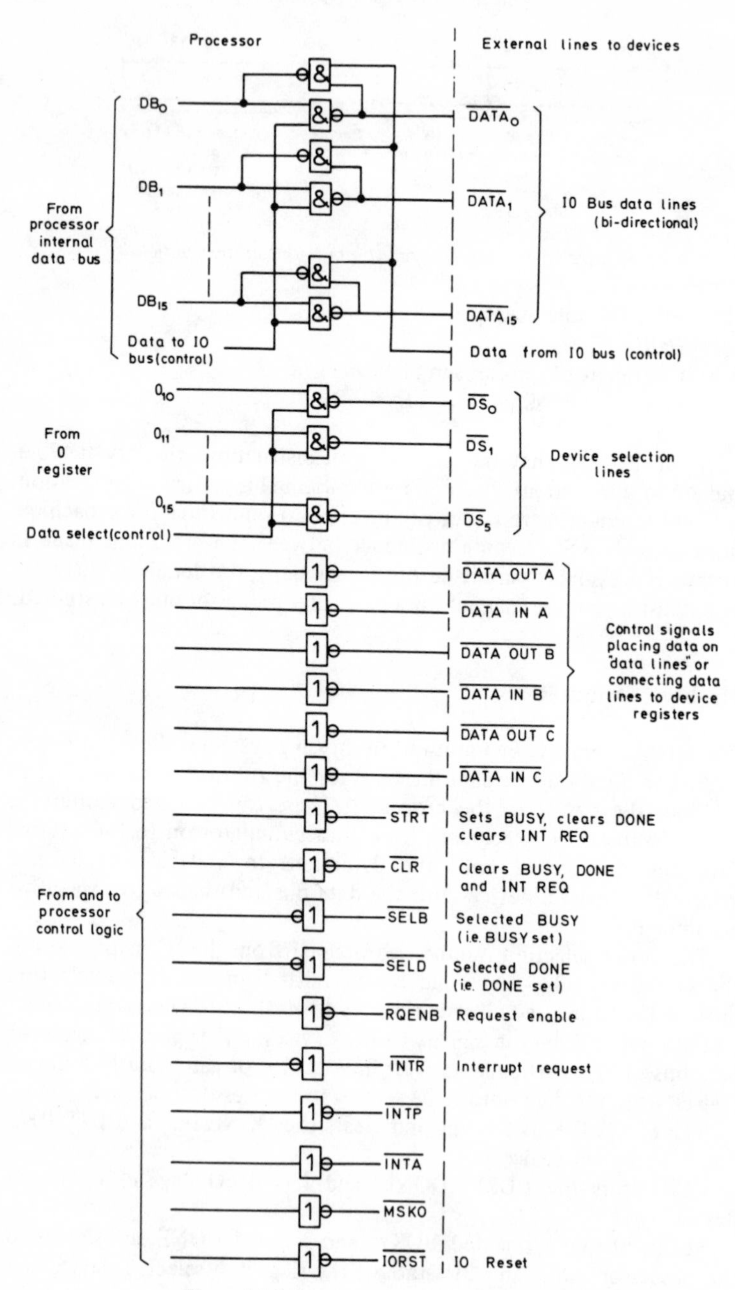

Figure 11.6 Input–output bussing system

RQENB – Request Enable is the sampling pulse generated at the beginning of every memory cycle to allow all devices on the bus to request program interrupts. RQENB also sets the INT REQ flag if DONE is set and Interrupt Disable is clear, otherwise it clears INT REQ.

INTR – Interrupt Request. This is generated by any device when its INT REQ flag is set. This informs the processor that the device is waiting for an interrupt.

INTP, INTA are signals to the device used in connection with the interrupt acknowledge instruction for placing the device number of the highest priority device which is interrupting on the data lines.

MSKO is a signal to the devices which sets Interrupt Disable flags in all devices according to a mask pattern which has been placed on the data lines. This allows the programmer to specify which device can interrupt a routine currently in progress at any given time.

Most of the lines to the IO devices must be used in common and this can be done by the wired OR connection using open collector gates as shown in Figure 11.7. Current drawn by any transistor grounds the line. Although gates are shown symbolically, they are of course incorporated in each open collector transistor gate. The potentiometer network at

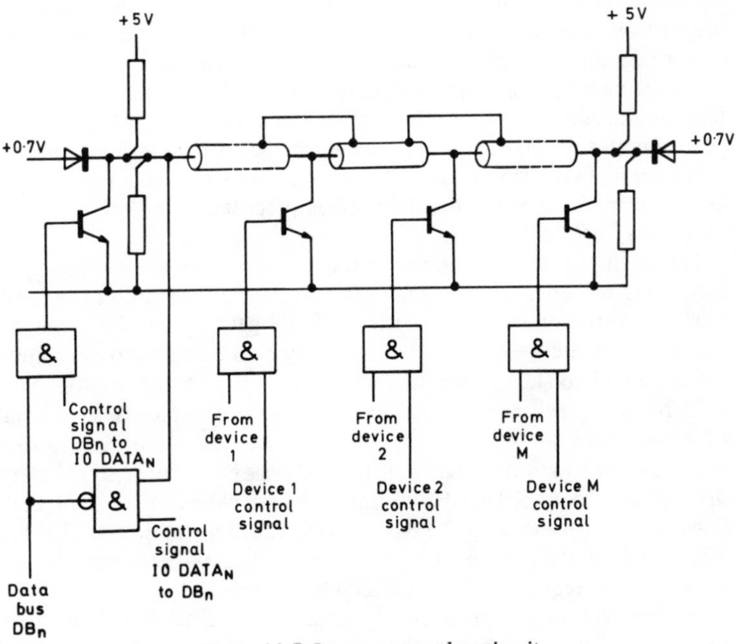

Figure 11.7 Input–output bus circuit

the far end of the line from the processor is a termination to match the line and reduce unnecessary reflections.

In Figure 11.6 and 11.7 the signals are all shown negated due to the wired OR connection, and it is necessary to invert signals in the interface logic to derive the true signal.

Examples of Interface Logic Circuit

An example of the interface logic needed for a device is shown in Figure 11.8. The standardisation of the input-output system has to end at this point, and each input-output device must have its own interface logic and circuits, designed especially to suit its requirements. The circuit shown is for a teletype input and output interface, but with many details omitted.

The teletype machine was originally intended solely to be used in telegraphic signalling systems, but it has been found to be a convenient means of input and output for computers. Therefore computer users are compelled to adapt the existing machine for their purpose. The machine is designed to send and receive a serial code with a start and stop pulse, so that it is necessary to convert incoming parallel data from the processor to serial form to be printed or punched, and the serial output from the keyboard and paper tape reader must be changed from serial to parallel form before transmitting to the processor.

It is assumed that it is not necessary to transmit and receive different data simultaneously so that one local register suffices for both purposes. For computer purposes an 8 bit character code is used and an example of the serial waveform to and from the teletype is shown in Figure 11.9 for the letter D, showing the data pulses preceded by a 'low' pulse for start and a 'high' pulse for stop.

During input to the processor the output from the keyboard or paper tape reader is taken from a distributor which generates the serial code and this is connected to the TYR IN gate on the shift register. Timing pulses are generated simultaneously by a commutator and these are converted to shift pulses to shift the data from the distributor into a 10 bit shift register, to accommodate 8 code bits plus the start and stop bits. When the start bit appears as a '1' at the end of the register, this indicates to control logic that the code has been fully entered. This then causes the TYR DONE flip-flop to be set. When the next RQENB signal is sent it causes the TYR INT REQ flip-flops to be set. The INT REQ flip-flop then causes a signal to be sent to the processor on the interrupt line, requesting that this data be accepted.

In due course, the processor generates a signal to test if the TYR DONE flip-flop (flag) is set, the device number having been decoded

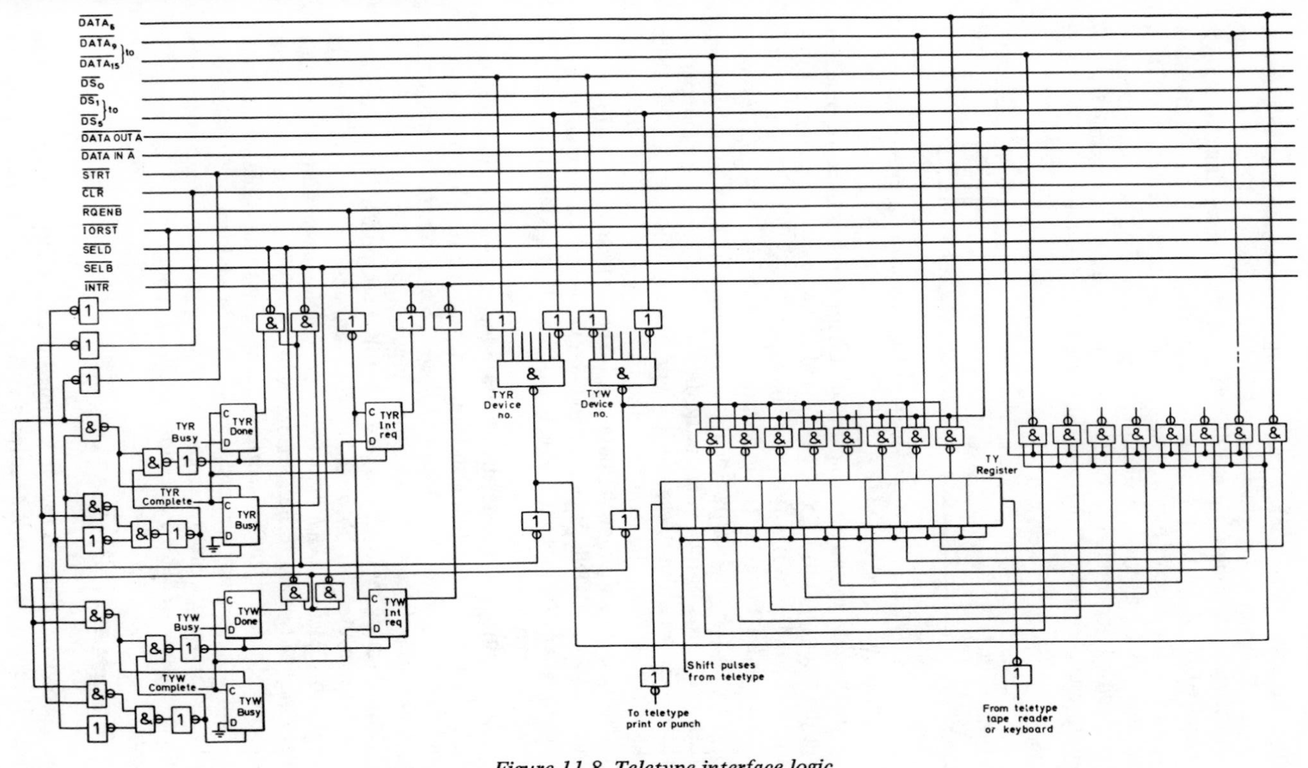

Figure 11.8 Teletype interface logic

by the local device selection decoding gate. Notice that two device numbers are used, one each for reading and writing. The processor can therefore determine from the device number that a reading operation is required. A data IN instruction is then given which causes the data stored in the register for the teletype to be gated to the data lines, from which it is transferred to the internal processor data bus, and thence to a specified accumulator, for subsequent processing. The same instruction resets the TYR DONE and the TYR REQ flip-flops.

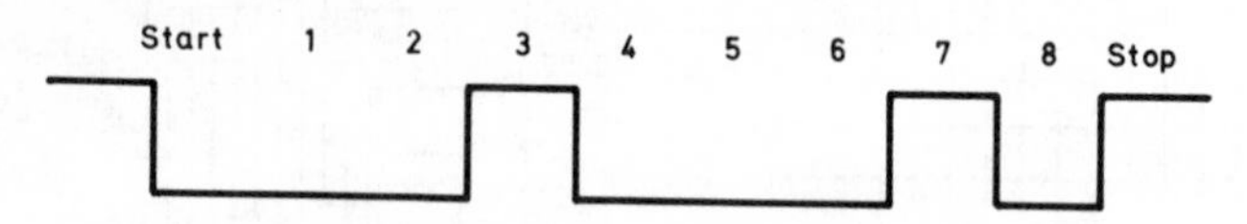

Figure 11.9 Serial waveform for teletype character D

In the case of output from the processor to be printed or punched on the teletype, both TYW, BUSY and DONE flags are assumed to be in the O conditions signifying the idle state.

To print a character the processor first tests the TYW BUSY flag to check that the teletype is ready to accept data. A data out instruction then places the output data on the data lines and the device number on the device selection lines, and the data out signal is sent. This enables the gates between the data lines and the TY register, so that the data is transferred into it from the data lines. The TYW BUSY flip-flop is set and the TYW DONE is cleared and simultaneously timing circuits are started which shift the data serially from the TY register to the teletype input to operate the printer.

The flip-flops shown in the interface logic are of the edge triggered type, in which a positive transition at C sets the flip-flop if D is high, and clears it if it is low. A ground level at S or R sets or clears the flip-flop respectively, and overrides the C input.

Although many details have necessarily been omitted this illustrates the method used for both reading data into and writing data from the processor. Many device interfaces are considerably simpler, because data may only have to be sent one way, as in the case of data logging, or input from a scientific instrument. In many applications an analogue output or input may be needed and digital to analogue and analogue to digital converters are required. Interface logic and programs can be designed to be suitable for a wide variety of applications.

Real Time Clock

It has been mentioned that it is sometimes necessary to read data from transducers at regular time intervals, as in the case of data logging. In other applications new data may have to be supplied to a device at regular intervals instead of allowing the device to interrupt the processor. Another use is in connection with very sensitive instruments, where ac power frequency noise can be superimposed on the analogue input to an analogue to digital converter before sending the data to the processor. Sampling the data at the same point in the power cycle allows the possibility for compensating for the ac noise component by program methods.

All these operations require that there must be some means by which the passage of real time, or the ac power frequency, can be sensed by the processor. This can be done by a real time clock which is treated as an input-output device, and is used mainly for low resolution timing in comparison with the speed of the processor.

A crystal controlled oscillator generates a series of accurately timed frequencies, which can interrupt the processor by the usual interrupt procedure. In the case of NOVA, these are at 10Hz, 100Hz, and 1000Hz, as well as the ac power frequency.

To use the real time clock, a Data Out Real Time Clock instruction sets the interrupt frequency required, determined by the F bits 8 and 9. Once the clock has been set to the required rate, the processor is interrupted at regular intervals at the given rate, and the program can read accordingly.

Power Failure

Power failure restart is a function which is very commonly built into processors, and which prevents the loss of any data if the power fails or the processor is accidentally turned off.

If the power fails at some random instant, the memory is very probably in the middle of a cycle, and data in the various stages of processing is in the accumulators. This data will be destroyed if power is turned off, but due to the capacity of the power supply, dc power does not immediately vanish, and the processor can continue operation for a few milliseconds. This gives sufficient time to store all important data in the memory and give a Halt instruction to stop in an orderly way.

Power failure is detected by a circuit in the power supply which senses that the dc power level has fallen below a safe level. When this occurs an interrupt signal is sent to the processor. When the processor responds to the interrupt, it treats power supply failure as the high priority interrupt, and skips to a program which stores the contents of accumulators and the carry flip-flop in the memory. By the usual interrupt procedure the address of the next instruction in the P register is stored by the jump to subroutine instruction, and the routine ends with a HALT instruction. When the power finally dies, all is safely battened down and nothing is lost. When power is switched on again the program goes through a start procedure which replaces the contents of the accumulators and returns to the instruction in the program where it was compelled to halt.

Data Channel

When a device delivers a program interrupt signal to the processor, it is, at the very least, necessary to store the address of the next instruction by the forced jump to subroutine procedure, the contents of the accumulators must be preserved in memory, and the interrupting device determined by program before data can be received or sent to the device. This may take 12.5 μsec in NOVA, and probably considerably more since this is an absolutely minimum program and highest priority device. This is inadequate for devices such as magnetic discs, and magnetic tape readers, with which the data transfer rate is very high once the instant to read or write arrives. So that the interrupt procedure cannot be used here.

Because it is wished to transfer data to or from memory in the processor, which is probably in action for some other purpose, and once the memory has commenced a cycle this cannot be stopped, since this is a circuit operation on the memory cores which would destroy data, the shortest waiting time is determined by the memory cycle.

The earliest instant at which the processor can break its operation is at the end of the current memory cycle, and it can pause in the middle of an instruction and service the high speed device. This is done in the fastest systems. With less complication the processor can be allowed to complete the current instruction before pausing and this is the method used in NOVA. The process occurs without any program intervention, and as far as the normal program is concerned, the only effect is the loss of a memory cycle, which increases the operating time of the program, and is called 'cycle stealing'. Notice that in memory reference instructions there are at least two memory cycles, for instruction fetch and operand read or write. If there is an indirect address, this may require several more memory references before the end of the instruction.

Since no time is available for shuffling data in this mode of operation, the action of the arithmetic unit, accumulators and control registers is suspended, and the memory is just preempted by the input-output device. If the break can be made at the end of the instruction, the address register can be freed, otherwise even this may not be used.

Only four input-output operations are possible on the data channel: Data In, Data Out, Increment Memory, and Add to Memory: because the program cannot effect the channel directly. Notice that each of these operations are performed in one memory cycle. The data channel transfers are conducted by way of the same data lines as are used for the programmed transfers, but extra control signals are necessary. In the case of Increment Memory and Add to Memory which involve simple arithmetic operations, the processor sends the result back to the device, and if the arithmetic operation causes an overflow to occur an overflow signal is sent to the device.

When a high speed device requires service a request is made for the memory via the data channel by a Data Channel Request Signal. At the beginning of every memory cycle, the data channel request signal is tested, and action is taken according to a two bit code on two data channel mode lines indicating which of the four operations are to be performed. Priority is determined by nearness to the processor on a data channel priority line as mentioned in the programmed interrupt procedure. As soon as an instruction is completed the processor takes care of requests in order of priority.

Problems

1. Obtain the reference manual for a small computer. Design the interface logic to couple some simple laboratory experiment to the computer. One example could be the monitoring of temperature or some other variable, which could be stored and printed at intervals.
2. Consider the problem of a colour film development process in which it is necessary to maintain the temperature of a number of different tanks accurately. The temperature must be monitored at intervals in each tank and heaters turned on or off as required. The computer is acting as a multiple thermostat. Design a system to do this.
3. In a large plant it is necessary to turn on lights in the evening, and turn them off when the employees have gone home. Certain lights must remain on for longer periods. The time to turn these lights on and off changes with the seasons. It must also be possible to overcome the computer control locally.

   Evolve a hypothetical plant and plan a system for performing the total light control of the plant.

Appendix

Graphic Symbols for Logic Diagrams

The logical and functional symbols used throughout this text are based on those adopted by the British Standards Institute, and the American National Standards Institute, following recommendations from the International Electrotechnical Commission. Since many readers may be more familiar with other existing, or superseded standards, different symbols for the principal logic functions used are shown in Figure 12.1.

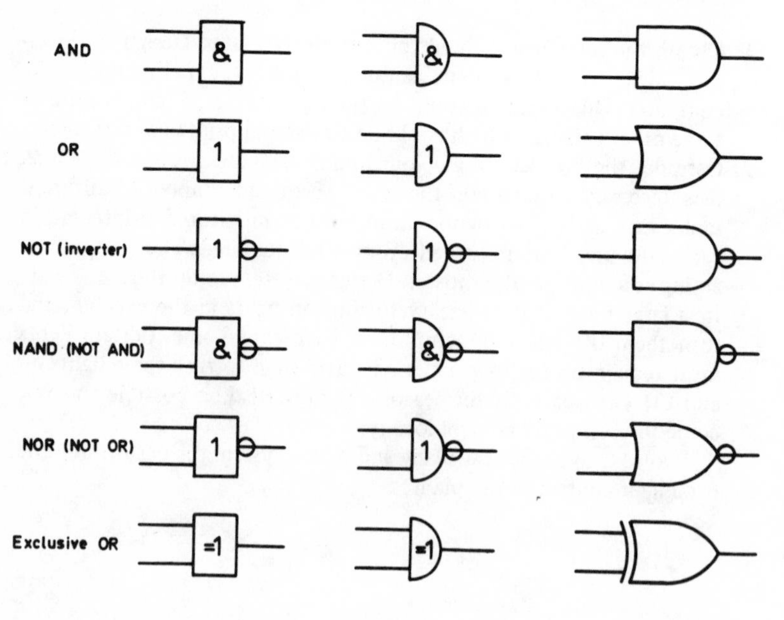

Figure 12.1

Index